LATIN MADE SIMPLE

LATIN
MADE SIMPLE

BY

RHODA A. HENDRICKS, M.A.

Formerly Head of Latin Department,
St. Timothy's School, Stevenson, Md.

MADE SIMPLE BOOKS

DOUBLEDAY & COMPANY, INC.

GARDEN CITY, NEW YORK

DESIGNED BY CAROL BASEN BAILYN

Library of Congress Catalog Card Number 62-12101
Copyright © 1962 by Doubleday & Company, Inc.
All Rights Reserved
Printed in the United States of America

ABOUT THIS BOOK

Although it is an ancient tongue, one of the "classical" languages, Latin is a vital and living language in every important sense—one of the pillars, part of the foundation, one of the main-streams of our language, of our culture, indeed of our civilization itself. It is the thread which connects us with our own history; and when such a thread snaps it severs our relationship to our own past.

Fortunately, more and more people are discovering the decisive importance of studying and learning Latin, so that we are at the present time witnessing what amounts to a major revival—which will, from all present signs, continue and grow. But obviously, since Latin is no longer a spoken language—with few special exceptions for ecclesiastical purposes—the interest of the present-day reader and student is primarily in the *reading* of Latin, so that he may read, for pleasure and profit, with reasonable facility and comprehension. It was with this objective in mind that LATIN MADE SIMPLE was conceived, organized and written.

The essentials of the grammatical foundations of Latin are presented in this book with remark-able economy and clarity—and this alone would make it valuable to the reader and student; but of even greater value is the book's steady concentration upon the practical *reading* requirements of the non-specialist, so that it will seem to you as though the author had at all points anticipated your interests, had guessed your needs with uncanny accuracy, had predicted the questions you would ask at the instant those questions were forming in your mind.

For LATIN MADE SIMPLE is for the modern reader and student who wants above all to be able to read in the original—for which there is *never* a really adequate substitute—a religious or secular text; who wants to understand the uses of Latin in the Church; who wants to be able to read the immense treasure-house of literature and other writings in the Latin language; who would like to increase his understanding of the innumerable ways in which Latin has nourished and enriched the English language itself; who wants to be able to cope with the countless ways in which Latin pervades all aspects of contemporary life: the coin in his pocket; the legend on his school diploma; the writing on a medical prescription; the scores of words and phrases he unconsciously uses every day—to cite only a few examples. It is for such a reader and student—in school or no longer in school—that LATIN MADE SIMPLE is intended; and that is to say it is intended for anyone with lively curiosity and active intelligence.

TABLE OF CONTENTS

CHAPTER 1

INFLECTION

In English, the use of a word is generally indicated by its position in the sentence, without any change in spelling. Sometimes, however, a word changes its form or spelling to show a corresponding change in its grammatical use and meaning.

singular: boy	subject: I	present: does
plural: boys	object: me	past: did

This process of change is called *Inflection*. You will notice that the change can take place either at the ending of the word or within the word.

In Latin, *Nouns, Pronouns, Adjectives,* and *Verbs* are inflected. This change in the form or ending of a Noun, Pronoun, or Adjective is called *Declension* and shows *Case, Number,* and *Gender.* As in English, Case indicates that a word is used as Subject, Object, Possessor, etc., and Number means that a word is either singular or plural. Gender can be Masculine, Feminine, or Neuter, but, unlike English, Gender in Latin can be natural (male or female) or grammatical (based not on sex, but the classification of the word or the spelling of the Nominative Case). The change in a *Verb* is called *Conjugation* and shows *Tense, Mood, Person, Voice,* and *Number.* Tense refers to time (present, past, or future); Mood to the manner in which a sentence is expressed (statement, question, command); Person to the speaker (I, you, he, etc.); Voice to whether the subject is acting or being acted upon (Active or Passive); and Number to one or more than one (Singular or Plural).

Because Latin is a highly inflected language, the ending of a Latin word is of primary importance and must be considered as carefully as the base of the word, which shows only the basic vocabulary meaning. Inflection will be clearly explained throughout this book and ample practice will be given.

PRONUNCIATION

Pronunciation, of course, is not necessary in the reading of Latin, but it is helpful in the comparison of Latin words with those of English and other languages. The consonants are pronounced as in English, except:

c and ch are always like k, as in coop.	t is always like t, as in tie, not like sh.
g is always hard, as in go.	v is always like w, as in woman.
i-consonant is like y, as in you.	x is like x, as in example.
s is always s, as in so, not like z.	gu, qu are like gw, qw, as in queen.

The vowels are either long or short. This means that a long vowel takes longer to pronounce than a short vowel does. There are no fixed rules for the length of vowels and the proper pronunciation can be learned best by paying close attention to the phonetic pronunciation given in the practice below and by hearing someone pronounce Latin correctly.

The diphthongs, two vowels pronounced as one, are pronounced:

ae like ai, as in aisle.   **oe** like oi, as in soil.
au like ou, as in ouch.   **ui** like we.
ei like ei, as in eight.

Syllables. A Latin word contains as many syllables as it has vowels and diphthongs. When dividing a word into syllables,

1. A single consonant is placed with the following vowel: **pa - ter.**
2. Double consonants are separated: **di - mit - te.**
3. If there are two or more consonants, the first is generally placed with the preceding vowel: **nos - trum.**

Accent. Latin words are accented as follows:

1. On the next to the last syllable, if it is long: **di - mit' - te.**
2. On the second to last syllable, if the next to last is short: **ad - ve' - ni - at.**
3. On the first syllable of a two syllable word: **nos' - ter.**

Practice reading aloud, following the English sound guide, until you can read this passage clearly and without hesitation. Remember that every consonant and vowel is pronounced in Latin.

Pater noster qui es in	Our father who art in
pah-*tehr* naws-*tehr qwee ehs in*	
caelis, sanctificetur	heaven, hallowed
kai-*lees* sahnk-*tih-fih-*kay-*toor*	
nomen tuum. Adveniat	be thy name. Thy
noh-*mehn* too-*uhm.* ahd-weh-*nee-aht*	
regnum tuum. Fiat	kingdom come. Thy will
reg-*nuhm* too-*uhm.* fee-*aht*	
voluntas tua sicut in	be done on earth as it is
woh-**luhn**-*tahs* too-*ah* seek-*uht in*	
caelo et in terra. Panem	in heaven. Give us this day
kai-*loh eht in* tehr-*rah.* pah-*nehm*	
nostrum cotidianum da	our daily bread.
nohs-*truhm* koh-*tee-dee-*ah-*nuhm dah*	
nobis hodie. Et dimitte	And forgive us our debts
noh-*bees* hoh-*dee-ay. eht* dee-**miht**-*eh*	
nobis debita nostra sicut	as we forgive our debtors.
noh-*bees* deh-*biht-ah* naws-*trah* seek-*uht*	
et nos dimittimus	And lead us not
eht nohs dee-**miht**-*tih-muhs*	
debitoribus nostris. Et	into temptation,
deh-*bih-***taw**-*rih-buhs* naws-*trees. eht*	
ne nos inducas in tentationem	but deliver us
nay nohs in-**doo**-*kahs in* ten-*tah-tee-oh-*nehm*	
sed libera nos a malo.	from evil.
sehd lee-*beh-rah nohs ah* mah-*loh.*	
Amen.	Amen.
ah-*mehn.*	

The Lord's Prayer. Matthew VI, 9–13

THE PARTS OF SPEECH

The parts of speech are the same in Latin and English, but Latin has no article (the, a, an). The article must, therefore, be supplied in English.

Noun—the name of a person, place, or thing. e.g., *Caesar, Rome, town*
Pronoun—a word used instead of a noun. e.g., *he*
Adjective—a word that describes a noun or pronoun. e.g., *good*
Verb—a word that shows action or state of being. e.g., *run, is*
Adverb—a word that modifies a verb, adjective, or adverb. e.g., *quickly, very*
Preposition—a word that shows relationship between a noun or pronoun and another word or words. e.g., *in, by, with*
Conjunction—a word that joins words, phrases, clauses, or sentences. e.g., *and*
Interjection—an exclamation showing emotion. e.g, *oh*

CHAPTER 2

WORD DERIVATION

1. Many of our English words have been inherited directly from Latin, with little or no change in spelling.

animal	labor	captivus	fortuna	multitudo	natio
animal	labor	captive	fortune	multitude	nation

2. Other English words have come to us indirectly through the Romance (Roman) Languages.

LATIN	ITALIAN	FRENCH	SPANISH	PORTUGUESE	ENGLISH
filia	la figlia	la fille	la hija	a filha	daughter
vos	voi	vous	vosotros	vos	you
bonus	buono	bon	bueno	bom	good
terra	la terra	la terre	la tierra	a terra	earth

3. A third group of English words comes from Latin in the form of Derivatives.

LATIN	ENGLISH	ENGLISH DERIVATIVE
agricola	farmer	agriculture
stella	star	constellation
terra	earth	terrace
filia	daughter	filial

You will find that you are familiar with more Latin than you realized. Watch for Latin words that have come directly or indirectly into English, for English Derivatives, and for Latin phrases and expressions in everyday use. These will be brought to your attention throughout the book.

SOME GIRLS' NAMES OF LATIN ORIGIN AND THEIR MEANINGS

Rosa, rose	**Regina**, queen	**Flora**, flowers
Victoria, victory	**Gloria**, glory	**Augusta**, majestic
Beatrice, making happiness	**Celestine**, heavenly	**Letitia**, happiness
Barbara, foreign	**Viola, Violet**, violet	**Alma**, cherishing
Amabel, lovable	**Clara**, bright	**Miranda**, worthy of admiration
Amy, beloved	**Laura**, laurel	**Sylvia**, of the forest
Amanda, worthy of love	**Stella, Estelle**, star	**Gratia, Grace**, grace, gratitude

As you study the Reading Grammar in this section, you will see that most of these names end in -a because they are feminine and come from the **a-declension**.

READING VOCABULARY

Nouns

stella (steh-*lah*), **stellae** (steh-*lai*), **f.**, star (stellar, constellation)

puella (*poo*-eh-*lah*), **puellae** (*poo*-eh-*lai*), **f.**, girl

casa (kah-*sah*), **casae** (kah-*sai*), **f.**, cottage, house

femina (fay-*mih-nah*), **feminae** (fay-*mih-nai*), **f.**, woman (feminine)

aqua (ah-*kwah*), **aquae** (ah-*kwai*), **f.**, water (aquarium)

terra (tehr-*rah*), **terrae** (tehr-*rai*), **f.**, land, earth (terrace, territory)

agricola (*ah*-grih-*koh-lah*), **agricolae** (*ah*-grih-*koh-lai*), **m.**, farmer (agriculture)

In giving the vocabulary, the first two forms of a Noun are given, as above, as well as its gender. The first form is the case of the subject. The second form is the case of possession and furnishes the base to which the rest of the case endings are added. Base: **stell-, puell-, cas-, femin-, aqu-, terr-, agricol-.**

Verbs

amo (ah-*moh*), **amare** (*ah*-mah-*reh*), like, love (amateur)

porto (por-*toh*), **portare** (*por*-tah-*reh*), carry (portage, deportment)

laudo (lou-*doh*), **laudare** *lou*-dah-*reh*), praise (laudable)

laboro (lah-bor-*oh*), **laborare** (*lah*-bor-ah-*reh*), work (laboratory)

voco (woh-*koh*), **vocare** (*woh*-kah-*reh*), call (vocation, vocative)

The first form of each Verb given here is the first person singular of the present tense. For example, **amo**, I like, I am liking, I do like. The second form is the present infinitive. For example, **amare**, to like. The infinitive furnishes the base on which the present tenses are formed. Base: **ama-, porta-, lauda-, labora-, voca-.**

Conjunction   et (eht), and

READING GRAMMAR

A. Nouns.

1. The change in the ending of a Noun to show its use in the sentence is called declension. Note that the endings are added to the second or base form.

2. Nouns that have **-ae** as the ending of the second form are **a-declension.**

3. **a-declension** Nouns have **-a-** in most of the case endings.

4. **a-declension** Nouns are all feminine, unless the word indicates a male.

SINGULAR		USE	PLURAL	
stella	the star	subject	stellae	the stars
stellae	of the star	possession	stellarum	of the stars
stellae	to, for the star	indirect object	stellis	to, for the stars
stellam	the star	direct object	stellas	the stars
stella	from, with, by, in the star	prepositional phrases	stellis	from, with, by, in the stars

Grammar Practice No. 1

Decline **puella, casa femina, aqua, terra,** and **agricola** in the same way, giving the Latin form and its English meaning, and then check your answers below. Do this until you can give all the forms easily and quickly.

Example: puella, the girl; **puellae,** of the girl; **puellae,** to, for the girl; **puellam,** the girl; etc.

Check on Grammar Practice No. 1

puella, the girl
puellae, of the girl
puellae, to, for the girl
puellam, the girl
puella, from, with, by, in the girl
puellae, the girls
puellarum, of the girls
puellis, to, for the girls
puellas, the girls
puellis, from, with, by, in the girls

casa, the cottage
casae, of the cottage
casae, to, for the cottage
casam, the cottage
casa, from, with, by, in the cottage
casae, the cottages
casarum, of the cottages
casis, to, for the cottages
casas, the cottages
casis, from, with, by, in the cottages

terra, the land
terrae, of the land
terrae, to, for the land
terram, the land
terra, from, with, by, in the land
terrae, the lands
terrarum, of the lands

terris, to, for the lands
terras, the lands
terris, from, with, by, in the lands

femina, the woman
feminae, of the woman
feminae, to, for the woman
feminam, the woman
femina, from, with, by, in the woman
feminae, the women
feminarum, of the women
feminis, to, for the women
feminas, the women
feminis, from, with, by, in the women

aqua, the water
aquae, of the water
aquae, to, for the water
aquam, the water
aqua, from, with, by, in the water
aquae, the waters
aquarum, of the waters
aquis, to, for the waters
aquas, the waters
aquis, from, with, by, in the waters

agricola, the farmer
agricolae, of the farmer
agricolae, to, for the farmer

agricolam, the farmer

agricola, from, with, by, in the farmer

agricolae, the farmers

agricolarum, of the farmers

agricolis, to, for the farmers

agricolas, the farmers

agricolis, from, with, by, in the farmers

B. Verbs.

1. The change in the ending of a Verb to show tense (time) and person (the subject of the verb) and number (singular or plural) is called conjugation. Note that the endings are added to the second or infinitive form.

2. Verbs that have -a- in the infinitive are **a-conjugation**. Note that the endings are added to the second or base form.

3. **a-conjugation** Verbs have -a- in most of the forms.

4. A Verb must be in the same person and number as its subject. For example,

agricola laborat, the farmer works (third person singular)

agricolae laborant, the farmers work (third person plural)

C. Present Tense of **a-conjugation** Verbs.

SINGULAR		PLURAL	
amo	I like; am liking; do like	amamus	we like; are liking; do like
amas	you like; are liking; do like	amatis	you like; are liking; do like
amat	he, she, it likes; is liking; does like	amant	they like; are liking; do like

Grammar Practice No. 2

Conjugate the Present Tense of **porto, laudo, laboro,** and **voco** in the same way, giving the Latin form and its English meaning, and then check your answers below. Do this until you can give all the forms easily and quickly. The ability to read Latin depends on the rapid recognition of the meanings of the endings and of the vocabulary and so it is essential that these should be mastered.

Example: porto, I carry, I do carry, I am carrying; portas, you carry, you do carry, you are carrying; portat, he, she, it carries, he, she, it does carry, he, she, it is carrying; etc.

Check on Grammar Practice No. 2

porto, I carry, do carry, am carrying

portas, you carry, do carry, are carrying

portat, he, she, it carries, does carry, is carrying

portamus, we carry, do carry, are carrying

portatis, you carry, do carry, are carrying

portant, they carry, do carry, are carrying

laboro, I work, do work, am working

laboras, you work, do work, are working

laborat, he, she, it works, does work, is working

laboramus, we work, do work, are working

laboratis, you work, do work, are working

laborant, they work, do work, are working

laudo, I praise, do praise, am praising

laudas, you praise, do praise, are praising

laudat, he, she, it praises, does praise, is praising

laudamus, we praise, do praise, are praising

laudatis, you praise, do praise, are praising

laudant, they praise, do praise, are praising

voco, I call, am calling, do call

vocas, you call, are calling, do call

vocat, he, she, it calls, is calling, does call

vocamus, we call, are calling, do call

vocatis, you call, are calling, do call

vocant, they call, are calling, do call

PRACTICE EXERCISES

No. 1. For each of these singular forms give the corresponding plural.

Example: **stellam,** the star   **stellas,** the stars
vocas, you call   **vocatis,** you call

1. **aquam,** the water
2. **puellae,** of the girl
3. **terra,** the land
4. **agricolae,** for the farmer
5. **stella,** by the star

6. **vocat,** he calls
7. **laboras,** you work
8. **porto,** I carry
9. **laudo,** I praise
10. **amat,** he likes

No. 2. Supply the English to complete the translation.

Example: **puellarum,** _____the girls   of the girls

1. **agricolarum,** _____ the farmers
2. **puellam,** _____ girl
3. **casae,** _____ cottages
4. **feminae,** for the _____
5. **terris,** by the _____

6. **laudat,** _____ is praising
7. **vocatis,** _____ call
8. **laborant,** _____ are working
9. **amamus,** _____ like
10. **portas,** you _____ carry

No. 3. What is the English pronoun shown by each of the following?

1. -mus   2. -t   3. -o   4. -tis   5. -nt   6. -s

No. 4. What use in the sentence would each of these pairs of Noun endings have?

1. am, as   2. a, is   3. a, ae   4. ae, is   5. ae, arum

No. 5. Change the following to the singular or plural.

Example: **portat**   **portant**

1. **porto**   3. **portamus**   5. **vocat**   7. **portant**   9. **amo**
2. **amant**   4. **laudo**   6. **laboras**   8. **vocatis**   10. **laudas**

CHAPTER 3

THE SIGNS OF THE ZODIAC

The Signs of the Zodiac are all Latin words and are easily remembered by associating their meanings with the way in which they are depicted.

Aries, the Ram
Taurus, the Bull
Gemini, the Twins
Cancer, the Crab

Leo, the Lion
Virgo, the Maiden
Libra, the Scales
Scorpio, the Scorpion

Sagittarius, the Archer
Capricorn, the Goat
Aquarius, the Water Bearer
Pisces, the Fishes

Many of the Planets are named for Roman deities, as:

Jupiter, King of the gods	**Mars,** god of War
Saturn, god of Sowing	**Neptune,** god of the Sea
Mercury, the Messenger god	**Pluto,** god of the Lower World
Venus, goddess of Love	

READING VOCABULARY

Nouns

nauta (nou-*tah*), **nautae** (nou-*tai*), **m.**, sailor (nautical)

filia (fee-*lee-ah*), **filiae** (fee-*lee-ai*), **f.**, daughter (filial)

Adjectives

magna (mahg-*nah*), large, great
parva (pahr-*wah*), small
bona (boh-*nah*), good (bonanza)
mala (mah-*lah*), bad, evil (malice)
mea (may-*ah*), my, mine
tua (too-*ah*), your, yours
Romana (*roh*-mah-*nah*), Roman (romance)
pulchra (puhl-*krah*), pretty, beautiful

Verbs

sum (*suhm*), **esse** (ehs-*seh*), be
nato (nah-*toh*), **natare** (*nah*-tah-*reh*), swim (natatorium)

Adverbs

non (*nohn*), not (non-stop)
bene (beh-*neh*), well (benefactor)
male (mah-*leh*), badly (malformed)

Sign of a question

-ne (*neh*)

READING GRAMMAR

A. Adjectives.

1. An Adjective describes, or tells something about, a Noun.

filia	**filia pulchra**	**filia bona**
daughter	pretty daughter	good daughter

2. An Adjective must be in the same gender (masculine, feminine, or neuter), number (singular or plural), and have the same use in the sentence, as the Noun it modifies.

SINGULAR		USE	PLURAL	
casa magna	large cottage	subject	casae magnae	large cottages
casae magnae	of the large cottage	possession	casarum magnarum	of the large cottages
casae magnae	to, for the large cottage	indirect object	casis magnis	to, for the large cottages
casam magnam	large cottage	direct object	casas magnas	large cottages
casa magna	from, with, by, in the large cottage	prepositional phrase	casis magnis	from, with, by, in the large cottages

B. Adverbs.

An Adverb that tells something about the Verb, such as a negative, stands in front of the Verb.

Agricola non natat.　　The farmer does not swim.

C. Questions.

-ne on the end of the first word of a sentence indicates a question.

Natatne agricola?　　Does the farmer swim?

D. Present Tense of **sum**, to be.

SINGULAR		PLURAL	
sum	I am	sumus	we are
es	you are	estis	you are
est	he, she, it is; there is	sunt	they are; there are

FAMILIAR PHRASES

Many Latin Phrases are in everyday use and can be recognized and used easily with a little practice.

1. **nota bene**, note well, is used in writing and speaking to draw attention to something that should be noticed especially. It is often abbreviated: **N.B.**
2. **bona fide**, with good faith or honesty. Example: It is a **bona fide** certificate. Thus, a genuine certificate. The opposite is **mala fide**, in bad faith.
3. **adsum**, I am present, is used often in roll call answering.
4. **meum et tuum**, mine and thine, is used frequently in place of the English phrase.
5. **terra firma**, firm land. Example: They were glad to step on **terra firma**.
6. **aqua** occurs frequently in English: **aqua pura**, pure water. **aqua vitae**, water of life, meaning brandy or alcohol. **aqua fortis**, literally, strong water, is nitric acid. **aqueous humor**, a watery fluid between the cornea and lens of the eye.

FAMILIAR QUOTATIONS

Many quotations from Latin authors are in use today, either in their Latin form or in translation. If you become so familiar with these quotations and their meanings that you know them by memory, you will have acquired some of the real flavor of the Latin language and thought.

Roma aeterna, Eternal Rome. Tibullus

Laborare est orare, To labor is to pray. motto of the Benedictine Monks

Errare humanum est, To err is human. Seneca

Dira necessitas, Dire necessity. Horace

Aurea mediocritas, The golden mean. Horace

Rara avis, A rare bird. Horace

Ars longa, vita brevis, Art is long, life is short. Seneca

Fortuna caeca est, Fortune is blind. Cicero

PRACTICE EXERCISES

No. 6. Supply the correct ending for each adjective.

Example: aquam mal_____, bad water   aquam malam

1. casam parv_____, small cottage
2. me_____ filiarum, of my daughters
3. pulchr_____ stellas, pretty stars
4. tu_____ terra, your land
5. filiae mal_____, to the bad girl
6. casis Roman_____, for Roman cottages
7. puellas parv_____, small girls
8. aquam bon_____, good water
9. feminae parv_____, to the small woman
10. casarum pulchr_____, of small cottages

No. 7. What is the English for each of the following?

1. estis   2. est   3. sunt   4. sum   5. es   6. sumus

No. 8. Make questions of the following and then translate the questions.

Example: natat   natatne? Does he (she, it) swim?

1. natant
2. portas
3. amamus
4. laborat
5. vocatis
6. sunt
7. natamus
8. portat
9. estis
10. laudas
11. laudat
12. vocant
13. est
14. natas
15. amant

No. 9. Give three translations for each of the following.

1. amas
2. laudamus
3. vocas
4. laboro
5. amant
6. vocatis
7. natat
8. portamus
9. laboras
10. laudat

CHAPTER 4

ROMAN NUMERALS

The basic Roman numerals, and the corresponding Arabic numerals, are:

I	1	**X**	10	**C**	100	**M**	1000
V	5	**L**	50	**D**	500		

These Roman numerals are used in various combinations to form any desired numeral:

1. A smaller numeral placed in front subtracts from the larger. For example, IV, 4; IX, 9; **XC**, 90; **CM**, 900.

2. A smaller numeral placed after adds to the larger. For example, **VI**, 6; **XI**, 11; **CX**, 110; **MC**, 1100.

3. Repeated numerals double, triple, and so on. For example, **XX**, 20; **XXX**, 30; **CC**, 200; **CCC**, 300.

4. When a line is drawn over a numeral, it multiplies that numeral by 1000. For example, $\overline{V}$, 5000; $\overline{X}$, 10,000; $\overline{C}$, 100,000; $\overline{D}$, 500,000.

A GUIDE TO ROMAN NUMERALS

I	1	XV	15	LXI	61	CDI	401
II	2	XVI	16	LXX	70	D	500
III	3	XVII	17	LXXI	71	DI	501
IV or IIII	4	XVIII	18	LXXX or XXC	80	DC	600
V	5	XIX	19	LXXXI or XXCI	81	DCI	601
VI	6	XX	20	XC	90	DCC	700
VII	7	XXI	21	XCI	91	DCCI	701
VIII	8	XXX	30	C	100	DCCC or CCM	800
IX or VIIII	9	XXXI	31	CI	101	DCCCI or CCMI	801
X	10	XL or XXXX	40	CC	200	CM	900
XI	11	XLI	41	CCI	201	CMI	901
XII	12	L	50	CCC	300	M	1000
XIII	13	LI	51	CCCI	301	MI	1001
XIV	14	LX	60	CD	400	MM	2000
						MMI	2001

Roman Numeral Practice No. 1

Give the corresponding Arabic numerals for the following.

XIII	MC	XLIII	DII	CXX
CCC	XXV	DCX	CDXX	$\overline{X}$CCC
IX	CM	XXXVI	XCV	LXXIV

Check on Roman Numeral Practice No. 1

13	1100	43	502	120
300	25	610	420	10,300
9	900	36	95	74

Roman Numeral Practice No. 2

Give the corresponding Roman numeral for the following.

59	42	65	2222	818
304	5040	1066	26	271
85	1492	753	960	101

Check on Roman Numeral Practice No. 2

LIX	MCDXCII	XXVI
CCCIV	LXV	CMLX
LXXXV or XXCV	MLXVI	DCCCXVIII or CCMXVIII
XLII	DCCLIII	CCLXXI
$\overline{V}$XL	MMCCXXII	CI

READING VOCABULARY

Nouns

insula (**een**-*soo-lah*), **insulae** (**een**-*soo-lai*), **f.,** island (insular, insulate)

patria (**pah**-*tree-ah*), **patriae** (**pah**-*tree-ai*), **f.,** native country (patriot)

paeninsula (*pai*-**neen**-*soo-lah*), **paeninsulae** (*pai*-**neen**-*soo-lai*), **f.,** peninsula (peninsular)

copia (**koh**-*pee-ah*), **copiae** (**koh**-*pee-ai*), **f.,** supply, abundance (copious, cornucopia). In the plural, **copiae** means forces, troops

silva (**sihl**-*wah*), **silvae** (**sihl**-*wai*), **f.,** forest, woods (sylvan)

Germania (**gehr**-mah-*nee-ah*), **Germaniae** (**gehr**-mah-*nee-ai*), **f.,** Germany

Britannia (*brih*-tah-*nee-ah*), **Britanniae** (*brih*-tah-*nee-ai*), **f.,** Britain

Italia (*ih*-**tah**-*lee-ah*), **Italiae** (*ih*-**tah**-*lee-ai*), **f.,** Italy (Italian)

Iulia (**yoo**-*lee-ah*), **Iuliae** (**yoo**-*lee-ai*), **f.,** Julia

Adjectives

multa (**muhl**-*tah*), much. In the plural, **multae** means many (multicolored)

clara (**klah**-*rah*), clear, famous, bright (clarity)

antiqua (**ahn**-tee-*kwah*), ancient, old (antique)

Verbs

pugno (**puhg**-*noh*), **pugnare** (*puhg*-**nah**-*reh*), fight (pugnacious)

oppugno (**ohp**-**puhg**-*noh*), **oppugnare** (*ohp*-*puhg*-**nah**-*reh*), attack (oppugnance)

iuvo (**yoo**-*woh*), **iuvare** (*yoo*-**wah**-*reh*), help, aid

Adverbs

cur (*kuhr*), why

Conjunction

quod (*kwohd*), because

READING GRAMMAR

A. The Nominative Case shows:
1. the Subject of the Verb.

Nauta pugnat.	The sailor fights.
Nautae pugnant.	The sailors fight.

    nauta is the Subject of **pugnat**; **nautae** is the Subject of **pugnant**; both are in the Nominative Case.

2. the Predicate Noun. **Britannia est insula.** Britain is an island. **insula** is a Noun in the Predicate and tells something about the subject (**Britannia**).
3. the Predicate Adjective. **Britannia est pulchra.** Britain is pretty. **pulchra** is an Adjective in the Predicate and describes the Subject (**Britannia**).

The **a-declension** Nouns and Adjectives end in **-a** in the Nominative Singular and **-ae** in the Nominative Plural.

B. The Genitive Case shows Possession and tells something about the Noun next to it, almost the way an Adjective does.

> **terra agricolae,** the land of the farmer—the farmer's land
> **terra agricolarum,** the land of the farmers—the farmers' land

agricolae (of the farmer) and **agricolarum** (of the farmers) tell something about **terra.** Compare this to the use of an Adjective: **terra pulchra,** the pretty land—**pulchra** (pretty) tells something about **terra.** The **a-declension** Nouns and Adjectives end in **-ae** in the Genitive Singular and **-arum** in the Genitive Plural.

PRACTICE EXERCISES

No. 10. Give the English for each of the following.

Example: filiae nautarum, the daughters of the sailors

1. casa puellae
2. copia aquae
3. terra agricolarum
4. casae feminarum
5. patria nautae
6. insula nautae
7. filia agricolae
8. casae nautarum
9. copia stellarum
10. patria feminae

No. 11. Pick out and translate the Subjects.

Example: Femina laborat. Femina, the woman

1. Feminae laborant.
2. Puella portat.
3. Agricolae amant.
4. Copiae pugnant.
5. Nauta oppugnat.
6. Agricola amat.
7. Filiae laudant.
8. Patria est.
9. Insulae sunt.
10. Filia laborat.

No. 12. Pick out and translate the Predicate Adjectives.

Example: Insula est pulchra. pulchra, pretty

1. Insula est magna.
2. Silvae sunt pulchrae.
3. Filiae sunt bonae.
4. Casa est mea.
5. Copiae sunt Romanae.
6. Terra est mala.
7. Paeninsula est tua.
8. Casae sunt parvae.
9. Silva est pulchra.
10. Femina est bona.

No. 13. Pick out and translate the Predicate Nouns.

Example: Sunt agricolae. agricolae, farmers

1. Est agricola.
2. Sunt nautae.
3. Germania est patria mea.
4. Estne insula?
5. Sunt casae.
6. Sum nauta.
7. Estis feminae.
8. Es puella.
9. Sumus agricolae.
10. Non est silva.

CHAPTER 5

READING

Italia	Italy
1. Italia est paeninsula in Europa.	1. Italy is a peninsula in Europe.
2. Paeninsula longa est et non lata.	2. The peninsula is long and not wide.
3. Incolae multae sunt agricolae et nautae.	3. Many inhabitants are farmers and sailors.
4. Italia est clara et antiqua.	4. Italy is famous and old.
5. Magna est fama Italiae.	5. The fame of Italy is great.
6. In Italia sunt viae multae et pulchrae et longae.	6. In Italy there are many beautiful and long roads.
7. Sicilia et Sardinia et Corsica sunt magnae et pulchrae insulae.	7. Sicily and Sardinia and Corsica are large and pretty islands.
8. Incolae patriam amant et bene laborant.	8. The inhabitants love their country and work hard.

READING VOCABULARY

Nouns

fabula (fah-*buh*-lah), fabulae (fah-*buh*-lai), f., story (fable, fabulous)

via (wee-*ah*), viae (wee-*ai*), f., road, way, street (via, viaduct)

incola (ihn-*koh*-lah), incolae (ihn-*koh*-lai), m. or f., inhabitant

fama (fah-*mah*), famae (fah-*mai*), f., rumor, renown, report (fame)

Europa (*yoo*-roh-*pah*), Europae (*yoo*-roh-*pai*), f., Europe

Verbs

do (*doh*), dare (dah-*reh*), give (dative)

ambulo (ahm-*buh*-loh), ambulare (*ahm*-buh-lah-*reh*), walk (ambulance, perambulator)

narro (nah-*roh*), narrare (*nah*-rah-*reh*), tell, relate (narrate)

monstro (mawn-*stroh*), monstrare (*mawn*-strah-*reh*), point out, show (monstrance)

habito (hah-*bih*-toh), habitare (*hah*-bih-tah-*reh*), dwell, live (habitat)

navigo (nah-*wih*-goh), navigare (*nah*-wih-gah-*reh*), sail, cruise (navigate)

Adjectives

longa (lawn-*gah*), long (longitude)

lata (lah-*tah*), wide (latitude)

Prepositions

ad (*ahd*), to, toward (administer)

a (*ah*) or ab (*ahb*), from, away from (abdicate)

e (*ay*) or ex (*ehks*), from, out from (emit, exceed)

cum (*kuhm*), with

in (*ihn*), in, on, into, onto (inhabit, induce)

READING GRAMMAR

A. The Dative Case shows the Indirect Object of the Verb.
  1. The Indirect Object shows to whom or what something is given, said, or directed.

Puellae aquam do.	I give the water *to the girl*.
Puellis aquam do.	I give the water *to the girls*.

Puella (to the girl) and **Puellis** (to the girls) are the Indirect Objects of **do** (I give). Both are in the Dative Case.

  2. The **a-declension** Nouns and Adjectives end in -ae (*ai*) in the Dative Singular and -is (*ees*) in the Dative Plural.

B. The Accusative Case shows the Direct Object of the Verb.
  1. The Direct Object shows the person or thing that receives the action of the Verb.

Fabulam narro.	I tell *a story*.
Fabulas narro.	I tell *stories*.

Fabulam (story) and **Fabulas** (stories) are the Direct Objects of **narro** (I tell). Both are in the Accusative Case.

  2. The **a-declension** Nouns and Adjectives end in -am (*ahm*) in the Accusative Singular and -as (*ahss*) in the Accusative Plural.

C. Prepositional Phrases in Latin are in either the Accusative or Ablative Case.

1. Accusative Prepositional Phrases are used with these Prepositions:

ad, to, toward	**Ad casam ambulo.**	I walk *toward the cottage.*
	Ad casas ambulo.	I walk *toward the cottages.*
in, into	**In casam ambulo.**	I walk *into the cottage.*
	In casas ambulo.	I walk *into the cottages.*

2. Ablative Prepositional Phrases are used with these Prepositions:

| **cum**, with | **Cum puella ambulo.** | I walk *with the girl.* |
| | **Cum puellis ambulo.** | I walk *with the girls.* |

Cum is used only with Nouns or Pronouns indicating people.

in, in, on	**In casa sum.**	I am *in the cottage.*
	In casis sunt.	They are *in the cottages.*
	In terra sum.	I am *on land.*
	In viis sunt.	They are *on the streets.*
e or **ex**, from, out from	**ex via**	*out of the street*
	ex viis	*out of the streets*
a or **ab**, from, away from	**a silva**	*away from* the forest
	a silvis	*away from* the forests

a or **e** is not used before a vowel or **h**.

WORD DERIVATION

Derivatives are words that come from the same origin or source. Thus, many English words have the same basic meaning as their Latin sources, even though there may have been some changes in spelling and general meaning during the course of time. For example, **terra**, *earth, land.* From this Latin word are derived: 1) *terrestrial*, having to do with the earth or land; 2) *territory*, a tract of land or earth; 3) *terrace*, a flat raised area of earth or land. Therefore, these three English words are derived from the Latin word **terra** and contain the same basic meaning.

Remember that similarity of sound and appearance alone are not enough, but must be combined with similarity of meaning to make a derivative. Continue to notice the English derivatives given in the Reading Vocabularies and see if you can add to them.

PRACTICE EXERCISES

No. 14. Give the English for the following.

Example: in vias, into the roads

1. ad viam	6. ab terra	11. in silvas	16. ad insulam
2. in casa	7. a casis	12. cum puella	17. ex terra
3. cum femina	8. e silvis	13. in aqua	18. cum agricola
4. in silvam	9. in insulas	14. ad aquam	19. in patria
5. ex casis	10. ad vias	15. ab puellis	20. cum puellis

No. 15. Pick out and translate the Direct Objects in the following.

Example: Puellam amat.   Puellam, the girl

1. Puellis aquam do.	6. Nautis fabulam narrat.
2. Puellae fabulam narro.	7. Nautae viam monstras.
3. Puellae aquam do.	8. Terram amant.
4. Nautam monstro.	9. Nautae terram amant.
5. Agricolas iuvat.	10. Insulas amo.

No. 16. Pick out and translate the Indirect Objects in the following.

Example: Nautis aquam do.   Nautis, to the sailors

1. Feminae silvas monstramus.	6. Feminis casas monstratis.
2. Nautae aquam dat.	7. Agricolis terram dant.
3. Nautis fabulas narrant.	8. Feminae casam das.
4. Puellae viam monstrat.	9. Puellis silvas monstrat.
5. Puellis fabulam narrat.	10. Agricolae fabulas narratis.

No. 17. Give three English meanings for each of the following, except 13 and 14, which have one English meaning each.

1. ambulatis	6. das	11. laudatis	16. natas
2. narrat	7. dat	12. amant	17. pugnat
3. ambulant	8. vocant	13. estis	18. pugnamus
4. habito	9. laboras	14. sumus	19. oppugno
5. navigamus	10. portamus	15. natant	20. oppugnant

FIRST REVIEW SECTION (CHAPTERS 1–5)

VOCABULARY REVIEW

NOUNS

1. agricola	9. fama	17. nauta	1. farmer	9. rumor, renown, report	17. sailor
2. aqua	10. femina	18. paeninsula	2. water	10. woman	18. peninsula
3. Britannia	11. filia	19. patria	3. Britain	11. daughter	19. native country
4. casa	12. Germania	20. puella	4. cottage	12. Germany	20. girl
5. copia	13. incola	21. silva	5. supply, abundance	13. inhabitant	21. forest, woods
6. copiae	14. insula	22. stella	6. troops	14. island	22. star
7. Europa	15. Italia	23. terra	7. Europe	15. Italy	23. land, earth
8. fabula	16. Iulia	24. via	8. story	16. Julia	24. road, way, street

ADJECTIVES

1. antiqua	6. magna	11. parva	1. ancient, old	6. large, great	11. small
2. bona	7. mala	12. pulchra	2. good	7. bad, evil	12. pretty, beautiful
3. clara	8. mea	13. Romana	3. clear, bright, famous	8. my, mine	13. Roman
4. lata	9. multa	14. tua	4. wide	9. much	14. your, yours
5. longa	10. multae		5. long	10. many	

VERBS

1. ambulo	6. laboro	11. navigo	1. walk	6. work	11. sail, cruise
2. amo	7. laudo	12. oppugno	2. love, like	7. praise	12. attack
3. do	8. monstro	13. porto	3. give	8. point out, show	13. carry
4. habito	9. narro	14. pugno	4. dwell, live	9. tell, relate	14. fight
5. iuvo	10. nato	15. sum	5. help, aid	10. swim	15. be
		16. voco			16. call

ADVERBS

1. bene	2. cur	3. male	4. non	1. well	2. why	3. badly	4. not

PREPOSITIONS

1. a, ab	3. cum	5. in
2. ad	4. e, ex	

1. from, away from	3. with	5. in, on; into
2. to, toward	4. from, out from	

CONJUNCTIONS

1. et   2. quod   1. and   2. because

PRACTICE EXERCISES

No. 18. Give the correct form of these Adjectives with their Nouns.

Example: aquam (pulchra), aquam pulchram

1. Europam (antiqua)	5. insularum (multa)	8. famam (mala)
2. aquae (pulchra)	6. terra (Romana)	9. puellarum (pulchra)
3. silvis (parva)	7. filias (bona)	10. incolis (multa)
4. stellas (clara)		

No. 19. Give the Genitive and Gender of these Nouns.

Example: casa, casae, f.

1. casa	6. insula	11. terra	16. patria
2. femina	7. puella	12. Britannia	17. incola
3. stella	8. copia	13. fama	18. Europa
4. aqua	9. filia	14. Italia	19. agricola
5. fabula	10. nauta	15. silva	20. via

No. 20. Give the Infinitive for each of these Verbs.

Example: amo, amare

1. amo	4. sum	7. monstro	10. porto	13. nato
2. laudo	5. voco	8. do	11. narro	14. pugno
3. navigo	6. oppugno	9. habito	12. laboro	15. ambulo

No. 21.

1. Make a list of the Latin cases and give the use of each.
2. Give the complete declension of these phrases, with the English meaning of each form.

> **insula lata,** the wide island   **via longa,** long road
> **insulae latae,** of the wide island   **viae longae,** of the long road

3. Give the complete Present Tense of these Verbs, with the English meaning of each form.

> **laboro,** I work; I am working; I do work
> **laudo,** I praise; I am praising; I do praise
> **sum,** I am

The author of this hymn is unknown, but it was composed in the seventeenth century and translated by Frederick Oakley in the nineteenth century.

Adeste, Fideles	Oh Come All Ye Faithful
Adeste, fideles, laeti triumphantes,	Oh come, all ye faithful, joyful and triumphant,
Venite, venite in Bethlehem;	Oh come ye, oh come ye to Bethlehem;
Natum videte regem Angelorum;	Come and behold him, born the King of Angels;
Venite adoremus Dominum.	Oh come, let us adore him, Christ the Lord.

Adeste, Fideles

Deum de Deo, Lumen de Lumine,
Gestant puellae viscera;
Deum verum, genitum non factum;
Venite adoremus Dominum.

Cantet nunc hymnos, Chorus Angelorum;
Cantet nunc aula caelestium,
Gloria in excelsis Deo!
Venite adoremus Dominum.

Ergo Qui natus die hodierna,
Iesu, tibi sit gloria;
Patris aeterni verbum caro factum;
Venite adoremus Dominum.

Oh Come All Ye Faithful

God of God, Light of Light,
Lo! he abhors not the Virgin's womb;
Very God, begotten, not created;
Oh come, let us adore him, Christ the Lord.

Sing, choirs of angels, sing in exultation,
Sing, all ye citizens of heaven above:
"Glory to God in the highest!"
Oh come, let us adore him, Christ the Lord.

Yea, Lord, we greet thee, born this happy morning,
Jesu, to thee be glory given,
Word of the Father, now in flesh appearing;
Oh come, let us adore him, Christ the Lord.

CHAPTER 6

READING

Proserpina

1. Dea agricolarum est Ceres.
2. Filia est Proserpina et Ceres filiam pulchram amat.
3. Ceres et Proserpina terram et silvas amant et agricolas iuvant.
4. Proserpina est clara et incolae terrarum multarum Proserpinam bene amant et laudant.
5. Pluto Proserpinam ad terram infernam[1] portat quod puellam amat.
6. Dea Ceres filiam vocat quod misera est et agricolae non laborant et terra non bona est.
7. Pluto agricolis Proserpinam dat et terra est pulchra et bona quod bene laborant.
8. Aestate[2] Proserpina est hic cum agricolis et hieme[3] est ibi in terra inferna et non cum agricolis.

Proserpina

1. The goddess of the farmers is Ceres.
2. Her daughter is Proserpina and Ceres loves her beautiful daughter.
3. Ceres and Proserpina love the land and woods and help the farmers.
4. Proserpina is famous and the inhabitants of many lands love Proserpina well and praise her.
5. Pluto carries Proserpina to the lower world because he loves the girl.
6. The goddess, Ceres, calls her daughter because she is unhappy and the farmers do not work and the land is not good.
7. Pluto gives Proserpina to the farmers and the earth is pretty and good because they work hard.
8. In summer Proserpina is here with the farmers and in winter she is there in the lower world and not with the farmers.

NOTES: 1. inferna, lower.　　2. aestate, in summer.　　3. hieme, in winter.

READING VOCABULARY

Nouns

provincia, provinciae, f., province (provincial)
gloria, gloriae, f., glory (glorious)
praeda, praedae, f., booty, plunder (predatory)
victoria, victoriae, f., victory (victorious)
Graecia, Graeciae, f., Greece
Hispania, Hispaniae, f., Spain
fossa, fossae, f., ditch (foss)

Adjective

alta, high, deep (alto, altitude)

Verbs

supero, superare, surpass, overcome, conquer (superable)

aedifico, aedificare, build (edify)
sto, stare, stand (station)
exspecto, exspectare, to await, expect, wait for (expectant)

Adverbs

saepe, often
ubi, where, when (ubiquitous)
ibi, there, in that place
hic, here, in this place

Prepositions

ante, before, in front of   With the Accusative Case (antedate, antecedent)
post, behind, in back of   With the Accusative Case (postdate, postpone)

READING GRAMMAR

A. Latin Sentence Construction.

Because the meaning of an English sentence is shown by the position of the words, any change in the position of the words changes the meaning of the sentence. For example, The farmer calls the girl. -or- The girl calls the farmer.

Since the inflection or form of the endings of Latin words shows their use in the sentence, a change in the position of the words in a Latin sentence does not change the actual meaning of the sentence. For example, **Agricola puellam vocat.** -or- **Puellam agricola vocat.** Both sentences have the same meaning.

B. Latin Word Order.

1. There is a normal order of words in a Latin sentence.

   a. The Subject or question word stands first.

Puella fabulas narrat.	The girl (subject) tells stories.
Narratne puella fabulas?	Does (question) the girl tell stories?

   b. Adjectives and Genitives stand next to their nouns.

filia pulchra -or- **pulchra filia**	pretty daughter
filia agricolae -or- **agricolae filia**	the farmer's daughter

   c. Adverbs precede the word they modify.

non narrat	she does not tell
non multae puellae	not many girls
non saepe	not often

   d. An Indirect Object usually precedes the Direct Object.

Puella agricolae fabulas narrat.	The girl tells stories to the farmer.

e. Verbs stand at the end of their clauses. The Verb "to be", however, usually has the same position as in English.

Puella fabulas narrat.   The girl tells stories.
Puella est pulchra.   The girl is pretty.

2. Any change in the normal word order of a Latin sentence is usually for emphasis or a special effect.

Puellam femina amat quod bona est.   The woman likes the girl because she is good.

C. The word "there".
Be careful to distinguish between the two uses of the word "there".
1. With the third person of the Verb "to be", *there is* or *there are*.

Est femina in casa.   There is a woman in the cottage.
Sunt feminae in casa.   There are women in the cottage.

2. The Adverb **ibi**, *there* or *in that place*.

Ibi pugnant.   They are fighting there.
Ibi sunt feminae.   There are the women.

FAMILIAR QUOTATIONS

Many of the words in these quotations belong to the **a-declension** or to the **a-conjugation**.

Sed non culpa mea est. But the blame is not mine. Ovid.
Licentia poetica. Poetic license. Seneca
Summa summarum. The total of totals. Plautus
Periculum in mora. Peril in delay. Livy

Si qua via est. If there is any way. Virgil
Tanta potentia formae est. So great is the power of beauty. Ovid
Sollicitae tu causa, pecunia, vitae. You, money, are the cause of an anxious life. Propertius

PRACTICE EXERCISES

No. 22. Give the English meanings for these forms.

1. sumus	4. est	7. sunt	10. navigant	13. aedificamus
2. superant	5. exspectatis	8. natamus	11. datis	14. ambulant
3. stat	6. aedificat	9. superat	12. vocas	15. statis

No. 23. Translate these Prepositional Phrases.

1. in Italia	5. in provincia	9. post casas	13. ad insulam
2. ad Britanniam	6. cum copiis	10. cum puella	14. in casas
3. cum feminis	7. in paeninsula	11. in silvis	15. ante fossam
4. ad Italiam	8. ante casas	12. ad viam	

No. 24. Give the English translations for the following.

1. incolae
2. Cur laborant?
3. Patriam tuam iuvas.
4. Praedam portat.
5. Bene pugnat.
6. Sunt pulchrae.
7. multarum victoriarum
8. patria clara
9. fabulam longam
10. ex casa
11. ab via
12. Ubi est?
13. Hic sum.
14. ante insulam
15. post victoriam
16. cum copiis
17. ex provinciis
18. Sunt copiae hic.
19. ad vias
20. Ibi est provincia.
21. Ibi sunt feminae.
22. Est gloria.
23. Sunt multae puellae.
24. Ubi sunt?
25. Hic sunt.

CHAPTER 7

SOME BOYS' NAMES OF LATIN ORIGIN AND THEIR MEANINGS

Rex, king, ruler
Sylvester, of the woods
Victor, conqueror
Claude, lame
Augustus, majestic, august
Lucius, light
Constant, firm, true
Valentine, healthy, strong
Felix, happy, lucky
Patrick, patrician
Dominic, of the Lord
Septimus, the seventh child

Octavius, the eighth child
Martin, of Mars
Aurelius, golden
Dexter, on the right, fortunate
Vincent, conquering
Benedict, blessed
Pius, devoted, faithful
Rufus, red
Clement, kind, mild
Leo, Leon, lion
Clarence, Clare, bright
Paul, small

READING VOCABULARY

Nouns

amicus, amici, m., friend (amicable)
inimicus, inimici, m., (personal) enemy (inimical)
puer, pueri, m., boy (puerile)
vir, viri, m., man (virile)
ager, agri, m., field (agriculture)
bellum, belli, n., war (bellicose)
oppidum, oppidi, n., town (oppidan)

arma, armorum, n. pl., arms, weapons (armory)
castra, castrorum, n. pl., camp (castle)
periculum, periculi, n., danger (peril)
socius, socii or soci, m., ally, comrade (social)
gladius, gladii or gladi, m., sword (gladiatorial)
nuntius, nuntii or nunti, m., messenger, message (nuncio)
proelium, proelii or proeli, n., battle
auxilium, auxilii or auxili, n., help, aid (auxiliary)

Adjective

angusta, narrow (anguish)

Verbs

aro, arare, plow (arable)
occupo, occupare, seize, take possession of (occupy)
armo, armare, arm (army)
neco, necare, kill
nuntio, nuntiare, announce, report (pronounce)

Prepositions

per, through   With the Accusative Case (persevere, permeate)
de, about, concerning, down from   With the Ablative Case (descend)

Adverb

etiam, even, also

Conjunction

sed, but

READING GRAMMAR

A. 1. Nouns that have **-i** as the ending of the second or Genitive form are **o-declension.**
   2. **o-declension** Nouns that end in **-us** or **-er** or **-ir** in the Nominative Case, or first form, are masculine.
   3. **o-declension** Nouns that end in **-um** in the Nominative Case, or first form, are neuter.
B. **o-declension** Nouns fall into two main groups—the masculine and the neuter.
   1. masculine **o-declension** Nouns.

SINGULAR		USE	PLURAL	
amicus	the friend	subject	**amici**	the friends
amici	of the friend	possession	**amicorum**	of the friends
amico	to, for the friend	indirect object	**amicis**	to, for the friends
amicum	the friend	direct object	**amicos**	the friends
amico	from, with, by, in the friend	prepositional phrases	**amicis**	from, with, by, in the friends

Other masculine **o-declension** Nouns are spelled with an **-i-** in the stem. Compare **socius** with **amicus:**

SINGULAR		PLURAL	
socius	the ally	**socii**	the allies
socii or soci	of the ally	**sociorum**	of the allies
socio	to, for the ally	**sociis**	to, for the allies
socium	the ally	**socios**	the allies
socio	from, with, by, in the ally	**sociis**	from, with, by, in the allies

Some masculine **o-declension** Nouns end in **-er.** Of these, some keep the **-e-** in all forms and others drop the **-e-** after the Nominative. Notice these Nouns and compare them with **amicus** and **socius** above:

SINGULAR		PLURAL	
puer	the boy	**pueri**	the boys
pueri	of the boy	**puerorum**	of the boys
puero	to, for the boy	**pueris**	to, for the boys
puerum	the boy	**pueros**	the boys
puero	from, with, by, in the boy	**pueris**	from, with, by, in the boys

SINGULAR		PLURAL	
ager	the field	**agri**	the fields
agri	of the field	**agrorum**	of the fields
agro	to, for the field	**agris**	to, for the fields
agrum	the field	**agros**	the fields
agro	from, with, by, in the field	**agris**	from, with, by, in the fields

2. neuter **o-declension** Nouns.

SINGULAR		PLURAL	
bellum	the war	**bella**	the wars
belli	of the war	**bellorum**	of the wars
bello	to, for the war	**bellis**	to, for the wars
bellum	the war	**bella**	the wars
bello	from, with, by, in the war	**bellis**	from, with, by, in the wars

Some neuter **o-declension** Nouns are spelled with an **-i-** in the stem. Compare **proelium** with **bellum:**

SINGULAR		PLURAL	
proelium	the battle	**proelia**	the battles
proelii or **proeli**	of the battle	**proeliorum**	of the battles
proelio	to, for the battle	**proeliis**	to, for the battles
proelium	the battle	**proelia**	the battles
proelio	from, with, by, in the battle	**proeliis**	from, with, by, in the battles

PREFIXES

In both Latin and English, prefixes are used to modify the basic meaning of a word. These prefixes are usually Latin Prepositions. An understanding of the meaning of the prefix makes the meaning of the Latin or English compound word clearer. Prefixes occur most frequently in Verb forms. These are some of the most common Latin Prepositions and their meanings as prefixes:

a, ab, abs, away	**absum,** be away, be absent
ad, to, toward	**advoco,** call to
ante, before, in front	**antecedo,** go before
post, after, behind	**postpono,** put after, put behind
de, down, from, away	**depono,** put down, put away

PRACTICE EXERCISES

No. 25. Give the English for these forms.

1. **agro**	4. **pueri**	7. **castra**	10. **nuntio**	13. **oppidi**
2. **bellis**	5. **socium**	8. **gladios**	11. **pericula**	14. **virum**
3. **proeliorum**	6. **amicos**	9. **auxilium**	12. **armorum**	15. **inimicos**

No. 26. Change each of these forms to the plural, and give the English.

1. amicus	4. belli	7. periculum	10. auxilio	13. periculo
2. pueri	5. oppidum	8. gladi	11. nuntio	14. ager
3. agro	6. vir	9. nuntium	12. viro	15. bellum

No. 27. Fill in the blanks with the correct English.

1. castrorum, _____ the camp
2. socius, _____ ally
3. gladium, _____ sword
4. de bello, _____ the war
5. per periculum, _____ the danger
6. oppidi, _____ the town
7. viri, _____ the man
8. inimici, _____ enemies
9. agros, _____ fields
10. pueri, _____ the boy

No. 28. Give the English translation for the following.

1. ex agro
2. Armantne?
3. angusta via
4. amicos
5. cum puero
6. Ibi arat.
7. post castra
8. amicorum
9. cum viro
10. Bellum pugnant.
11. Oppida monstrant.
12. Viro arma dant.
13. Fabulas de bello narramus.
14. Pericula amat.
15. **Castra sunt in agro.**
16. **Per agros ambulatis.**
17. **Sunt oppida.**
18. **Auxilium das.**
19. **Gladii necant.**
20. **In castris habitant.**

CHAPTER 8

THE HISTORICAL PRESENT

Latin sometimes uses the Present Tense in narrative where English would use the Past Tense. This use in Latin is called the Historical Present.

READING

Servi	Slaves
1. **Romani servos multos in bello occupant.**	1. The Romans seized many slaves in war.
2. **Ex oppidis Graeciae ad Italiam servos portant.**	2. They carried the slaves to Italy from the towns of Greece.
3. **Servi erant boni, sed in Italia saepe non erant laeti.**	3. The slaves were good, but in Italy they were often not happy.
4. **Servi erant praeda belli et multi servos bene curant, sed multi servos male curant.**	4. Slaves were the booty of war and many people cared for their slaves well, but many cared for them badly.

5. Servi in agris et in casis et in viis laborant.

5. The slaves worked in the fields and in the houses and on the roads.

6. Saepe aegri erant, sed multi servos aegros bene curant.

6. They were often sick, but many people took good care of the sick slaves.

7. Romani servis multa dant et curam bonam dant.

7. The Romans gave many things to the slaves and gave them good care.

8. Servi dominos bonos et dominas bonas amant.

8. The slaves liked good masters and good mistresses.

9. Multi servi erant clari et filios dominorum bene iuvant.

9. Many slaves were famous and aided the sons of their masters very much.

10. Multi domini servos liberant et multi servi liberi erant viri clari.

10. Many masters freed their slaves and many free slaves were famous men.

READING VOCABULARY

Nouns

filius, filii or fili, m., son (filial)
cura, curae, f., care (curate)
equus, equi, m., horse (equestrian)
frumentum, frumenti, n., grain (frumentaceous)
servus, servi, m., slave, servant (servitude)
dominus, domini, m., master (dominion)
domina, dominae, f., mistress

Adjectives

miser, misera, miserum, wretched, unhappy (miser)

laetus, laeta, laetum, happy
liber, libera, liberum, free (liberal)
aeger, aegra, aegrum, sick, ill

Verbs

libero, liberare, free, set free (liberate)
curo, curare, care for, cure (curator)
erat, he, she, it was; there was
erant, they were; there were

Adverb

hodie, today

READING GRAMMAR

A. **a-declension** and **o-declension** Adjectives.
You have already had **a-declension** Adjectives. These Adjectives also belong to the **o-declension**. **a-declension** and **o-declension** Adjectives have the same endings as the Nouns of these declensions.

a-declension—fem.	o-declension—masc.		
bona	bonus	miser	pulcher
bonae	boni	miseri	pulchri
bonae, etc.	bono, etc.	misero, etc.	pulchro, etc.

o-declension—neuter		
bonum	miserum	pulchrum
boni	miseri	pulchri
bono, etc.	misero, etc.	pulchro, etc.

B. Agreement of Adjectives.

Adjectives must agree with the Nouns they modify in Gender, Number, and Case. Note that they do not necessarily agree in declension or spelling.

cura bona, good care (fem.)   **equus pulcher,** pretty horse (masc.)
nauta bonus, good sailor (masc.)   **frumentum bonum,** good grain (neut.)
equus bonus, good horse (masc.)   **bellum miserum,** wretched war (neut.)
puer bonus, good boy (masc.)   **oppidum pulchrum,** pretty town (neut.)
servus miser, wretched slave (masc.)

C. Omission of the Noun with the Adjective.

The masculine and neuter Nominative and Accusative plural of Adjectives are commonly used to mean men (or persons) or things. Because the gender makes it clear, the Noun may be omitted.

boni, good people (subject)   **multi,** many people (subject)
bonos, good people (direct object)   **multos,** many people (direct object)
bona, good things or goods (subject, direct object)

Sometimes the Noun is omitted with other cases in the plural.

multorum, of many people (possession)
multis, to, for many people (indirect object)

FAMILIAR PHRASES

ante bellum, before the war.

post bellum, after the war. These two phrases usually apply to the Civil War.

ad nauseam, to the point of nausea, or disgust. She talked about it **ad nauseam.**

summum bonum, the greatest good, and source of all other benefits. It was the **summum bonum** for all.

ut supra, as above.

ut infra, as below. These phrases are used to refer to something mentioned in writing, either above or below. **ut supra,** see above. **ut infra,** see below.

PRACTICE EXERCISES

No. 29. Give the English for the following.

1. Amicus meus ibi est.   5. cum viris claris   8. de aqua bona
2. ad casas tuas   6. ante castra Romana   9. per silvam magnam
3. ex fossis altis   7. post agros meos   10. mali amici
4. in via longa

No. 30. Complete the correct ending of the Adjectives.

1. virorum mult_____   5. me_____ filiis   8. soci liber_____
2. filiae me_____   6. pueros aegr_____   9. feminam miser_____
3. frumento bon_____   7. puellae miser_____   10. agris pulchr_____
4. equis tu_____

No. 31. Match the Latin Adjective in Column II with the English Adjective in Column I.

Column I	Column II	Column I	Column II
1. many **viros**	1. **pulchrum**	6. good **fili**	6. **boni**
2. sick **pueri**	2. **multorum**	7. bad **famam**	7. **laetus**
3. pretty **oppidum**	3. **multos**	8. wretched **equis**	8. **malam**
4. many **servorum**	4. **laetam**	9. Roman **terrae**	9. **miseris**
5. happy **puellam**	5. **aegri**	10. happy **agricola**	10. **Romanae**

No. 32. Complete the Verbs with the correct endings.

1. cura_____ (we)
2. libera_____ (you s.)
3. labora_____ (you pl.)
4. lauda_____ (they)
5. porta_____ (he)
6. ar_____ (I)
7. neca_____ (they)
8. nuntia_____ (she)
9. occupa_____ (we)
10. sta_____ (you pl.)

No. 33. Give the English for the following.

1. Sunt liberi.
2. dominarum laetarum
3. in aquam altam
4. de curis magnis
5. in agris latis
6. de dominis bonis
7. Cur estis laeti?
8. Sunt multi.
9. Sumus aegri.
10. cum amicis bonis
11. in terris liberis
12. Est pulchra.
13. Suntne pulchrae?
14. Est miser.
15. multa

CHAPTER 9

READING

Dei Antiqui	The Ancient Gods
1. Romani deos multos et deas multas adorant et fabulas antiquas de deis suis narrant.	1. The Romans worshiped many gods and many goddesses and told old stories about their gods.
2. Iuppiter in caelo habitat et erat bonus et magnus.	2. Jupiter lived in the sky and was good and great.
3. Mercurius erat nuntius deorum et trans terram et aquam viris et deis famas portat.	3. Mercury was the messenger of the gods and carried reports to men and gods across land and water.
4. Nautae Neptunum adorant quod deus oceani erat.	4. The sailors worshiped Neptune because he was the god of the ocean.
5. In aqua habitat et amicus nautarum erat.	5. He lived in the water and was the sailors' friend.
6. Mars viros in proeliis et in bellis curat.	6. Mars took care of men in battles and in wars.
7. Vulcanus erat deus et deis arma dat.	7. Vulcan was a god and he gave weapons to the gods.
8. In patria nostra et in vestra deas et deos non adoramus, sed in Italia antiqua deae et dei erant amici virorum et feminarum.	8. In our native country and in yours we do not worship goddesses and gods, but in ancient Italy goddesses and gods were the friends of the men and women.
9. Hodie in Italia deos multos non adorant.	9. Today in Italy they do not worship many gods.

Deae Antiquae

1. Multas fabulas de deabus Romanis narrant.

2. Feminae Romanae deas in templis et in casis suis saepe adorant.

3. Iuno regina dearum erat.

4. Clara et bona erat et deas regnat.

5. Vesta curam casarum habet.

6. Diana puellas curat et nautae non timent quod nautis in oceano fortunam bonam et auxilium dat.

7. Dea lunae etiam erat et silvas bene amat.

8. Venus pulchra erat et erant feminae multae in templo.

9. Agricolae bene arant quod Ceres agricolas iuvat et frumentum curat.

10. Etiam hodie magna est fama dearum Romanarum.

The Ancient Goddesses

1. They tell many stories about the Roman goddesses.

2. Roman women often worshiped the goddesses in the temples and in their homes.

3. Juno was the queen of the goddesses.

4. She was famous and good and she ruled the goddesses.

5. Vesta had the care of houses.

6. Diana cared for girls and sailors were not afraid because she gave good fortune and help to sailors on the ocean.

7. She was also the goddess of the moon and liked the forests very much.

8. Venus was beautiful and there were many women in her temple.

9. Farmers plowed well because Ceres helped farmers and cared for the grain.

10. Even today the fame of the Roman goddesses is great.

READING VOCABULARY

Nouns

deus, dei, m., god (deity)
dea, deae, f., goddess
oceanus, oceani, m., ocean (oceanic)
caelum, caeli, n., sky, heaven (celestial)
regina, reginae, f., queen
sapientia, sapientiae, f., wisdom (sapience)
templum, templi, n., temple (templar)
luna, lunae, f., moon (lunar)
fortuna, fortunae, f., fortune, fate, luck (fortunate)

Adjectives

suus, sua, suum, his, her, its, their (own)
noster, nostra, nostrum, our, ours (nostrum)
vester, vestra, vestrum, your, yours

Verbs

adoro, adorare, worship, adore (adorable)
habeo, habere, have, hold (habit)
timeo, timere, fear, be afraid of (timid)
video, videre, see (vision, video)
regno, regnare, rule (regnant)

Preposition

trans, across With the Accusative Case (trans-Atlantic)

READING GRAMMAR

A. Note the spelling of **deabus** in the Reading above. The Dative and Ablative Plural of **dea** is **deabus,** to distinguish it from **deis.**

B. Possessive Adjectives are used when the Subject of the Verb is the possessor. Thus, the word "own" may always be added for clarity.

SINGULAR	1st person	**meus, mea, meum,**	my (own), mine
	2nd person	**tuus, tua, tuum,**	your (own), yours
	3rd person	**suus, sua, suum,**	his (own), her (own), its (own)
PLURAL	1st person	**noster, nostra, nostrum,**	our (own), ours
	2nd person	**vester, vestra, vestrum,**	your (own), yours
	3rd person	**suus, sua, suum,**	their (own), theirs

C. **e-conjugation** Verbs have an **-e-** in the Present Infinitive.

hab-e-re, to have   **tim-e-re,** to fear   **vid-e-re,** to see

e-conjugation Verbs form the Present Tense in the same way as the **a-conjugation** Verbs, but there is an **-e-** in each form.

SINGULAR	**habeo**	I have, do have, am having	PLURAL **habemus**	we have
	habes	you have	**habetis**	you have
	habet	he, she, it has	**habent**	they have

LATIN ON TOMBSTONES AND MONUMENTS

Latin often appears on tombstones and monuments. The following are some of the abbreviations and phrases frequently used.

c., standing for **circa** or **circum,** meaning about, used with dates.
in aeternum, forever
in perpetuum, forever
ae.; aet.; aetat., standing for **aetatis,** of age
anno aetatis suae, in the year of his (her) age.
ob., standing for **obiit,** meaning he (she) died

hic iacet, here lies
R.I.P., standing for **requiescat in pace,** meaning may he (she) rest in peace.
in memoriam, in memory, to the memory of
A.D., standing for **Anno Domini,** meaning In the year of (our) Lord.

PRACTICE EXERCISES

No. 34. Fill in the correct Possessive Adjective.

1. *our* **reginam**
2. *your (sing.)* **deas**
3. *his own* **fortuna**
4. *my own* **deis**
5. *their own* **templa**
6. *your (pl.)* **reginae**
7. *our own* **patriam**
8. *its own* **oceani**
9. *their own* **filiarum**
10. *my* **sapientiam**

No. 35. Give the English for the following.

1. timeo
2. videt
3. timetis
4. adorat
5. regnant
6. vides
7. timent
8. habemus
9. regnamus
10. habent
11. timet
12. videtis
13. habeo
14. regnas
15. adoratis

No. 36. Give the English for the following.

1. antiquos deos
2. deae Romanae
3. meorum amicorum
4. vestri nautae
5. tuam praedam
6. filias nostras
7. suus dominus
8. suum filium
9. sua sapientia
10. gloriam nostram

No. 37. Translate the following sentences into English.

1. Gloria vestra non est magna.
2. Cur inimicum tuum necas?
3. Nuntiusne multa narrat?
4. Viri trans agros suos ambulant.
5. Feminae in casis suis sunt.
6. Filiae tuae hodie sunt aegrae.
7. Multi trans oceanum navigant.
8. Sunt deae nostrae.
9. Sunt dei nostri.
10. Femina suas filias curat.
11. Ante casas sto.
12. Non multa habet.
13. De luna narramus.
14. Fortuna vestra est bona.
15. Servi dominos timent.
16. Cur non timetis?
17. Templa pulchra videmus.
18. Castra ibi habet.
19. Pueros post fossam videmus.
20. Sapientiam magnam habetis.

SECOND REVIEW SECTION (CHAPTERS 6–9)

VOCABULARY REVIEW

NOUNS

1. ager	14. filius	27. periculum	1. field	14. son	27. danger
2. amicus	15. fortuna	28. praeda	2. friend	15. fortune, fate, luck	28. booty, plunder
3. arma	16. fossa	29. proelium	3. arms, weapons	16. ditch	29. battle
4. auxilium	17. frumentum	30. provincia	4. aid, help	17. grain	30. province
5. bellum	18. gladius	31. puer	5. war	18. sword	31. boy
6. caelum	19. gloria	32. regina	6. sky, heaven	19. glory	32. queen
7. castra	20. Graecia	33. sapientia	7. camp	20. Greece	33. wisdom
8. cura	21. Hispania	34. servus	8. care	21. Spain	34. slave, servant
9. dea	22. inimicus	35. socius	9. goddess	22. (personal) enemy	35. comrade, ally
10. deus	23. luna	36. templum	10. god	23. moon	36. temple
11. domina	24. nuntius	37. victoria	11. mistress	24. messenger, message	37. victory
12. dominus	25. oceanus	38. vir	12. master	25. ocean	38. man
13. equus	26. oppidum		13. horse	26. town	

ADJECTIVES

1. aeger	4. laetus	7. noster	1. sick, ill	4. happy	7. our, ours
2. altus	5. liber	8. suus	2. high, deep	5. free	8. his, her, its, their
3. angustus	6. miser	9. vester	3. narrow	6. wretched, unhappy	9. your, yours

VERBS

1. adoro	9. neco	1. worship, adore	9. kill
2. aedifico	10. nuntio	2. build	10. announce, report
3. armo	11. occupo	3. arm	11. seize, take possession of
4. aro	12. regno	4. plow	12. rule
5. curo	13. sto	5. care for, cure	13. stand
6. exspecto	14. supero	6. await, expect, wait for	14. surpass, overcome
7. habeo	15. timeo	7. have, hold	15. fear, be afraid of
8. libero	16. video	8. free, set free	16. see

ADVERBS

1. etiam	3. hodie	5. saepe	1. even, also	3. today	5. often
2. hic	4. ibi	6. ubi	2. here, in this place	4. there, in that place	6. where, when

PREPOSITIONS

1. ante	3. per	5. trans	1. before, in front of	3. through	5. across
2. de	4. post		2. about, concerning, down from	4. behind, in back of	

CONJUNCTION

1. sed		1. but

PRACTICE EXERCISES

No. 38. Give the Infinitive of each of these Verbs.

1. aedifico	4. supero	7. regno	10. curo	13. timeo
2. nuntio	5. video	8. aro	11. neco	14. habeo
3. exspecto	6. libero	9. sto	12. adoro	15. occupo

No. 39. Give the Genitive and Gender of these Nouns.

1. dea	5. oceanus	9. inimicus	13. castra	17. gladius
2. proelium	6. socius	10. regina	14. periculum	18. cura
3. provincia	7. fortuna	11. puer	15. victoria	19. praeda
4. bellum	8. amicus	12. ager	16. vir	20. equus

No. 40.

1. Rearrange these sentences in the correct Latin order:

> a. **Frumentum cur datis non viris?**
> b. **Curam dat insularum bonamne incolis?**

2. Give the Present Tense with English meanings of **sto** and **timeo**.

No. 41. Put into English:

1. agricolas nostros	6. suos filios	11. multi
2. filiarum laetarum	7. miseros	12. parvus puer
3. caelum altum	8. vias angustas	13. agrorum latorum
4. patriae liberae	9. tuus nuntius	14. cura bona
5. vester servus	10. fortuna mea	15. gladi longi

GAIUS VALERIUS CATULLUS

Catullus was born about 84 B.C. at Verona, in northeastern Italy, but spent most of his life in Rome. He was a master of lyric poetry, especially love poems, and made use of many of the best features of Greek verse. Catullus died in 54 B.C.

Da mi basia mille, deinde centum,
dein mille altera, dein secunda centum,
deinde usque altera mille, deinde centum.
Dein, cum milia multa fecerimus,
conturbabimus illa, ne sciamus,
aut ne quis malus invidere possit,
cum tantum sciat esse basiorum.

Catullus V

Give me a thousand kisses, then a hundred,
then another thousand, then a second hundred,
then up to a thousand more, then a hundred.
At the last, when we have given many thousands,
we shall mix their count, lest we know,
or lest any wicked person might envy us,
when he learns our kisses are so many.

Catullus 5

Odi et amo. Quare id faciam, fortasse requiris.
Nescio, sed fieri sentio et excrucior.

Catullus LXXXV

I hate and I love. Why I do this, perhaps you ask.
I do not know, but I feel it happen and I am
    tortured.

Catullus 85

Toward the end of the fourth century, the Bible was translated into Latin by Saint Jerome and others, and this Latin version is called the Vulgate, or commonly accepted, Bible.

In principio erat Verbum et
Verbum erat apud Deum, et Deus erat
Verbum. Hoc erat in principio
apud Deum. Omnia, per ipsum facta
sunt, et sine ipso factum est nihil,
quod factum est; in ipso vita erat,
et vita erat lux hominum; et lux in
tenebris lucet, et tenebrae eam non
comprehenderunt. Fuit homo missus
a Deo, cui nomen erat Ioannes. Hic
venit in testimonium, ut
testimonium perhiberet de lumine,
ut omnes crederent per illum. Non
erat ille lux, sed ut testimonium
perhiberet de lumine. Erat lux
vera, quae illuminat omnem hominem
venientem in hunc mundum: in mundo
erat, et mundus per ipsum factus
est et mundus eum non cognovit.

Evangelium Secundum Ioannem, I, i–x

In the beginning was the Word, and the Word was with God, and the Word was God. The same was in the beginning with God. All things were made by him; and without him was not any thing made that was made; in him was life, and the life was the light of men. And the light shineth in darkness; and the darkness comprehended it not. There was a man sent from God, whose name was John. The same came for a witness, to bear witness of the Light, that all men through him might believe. He was not that Light, but was sent to bear witness of that Light. That was the true Light, which lighteth every man that cometh into the world. He was in the world, and the world was made by him, and the world knew him not.

St. John, 1, 1–10

CHAPTER 10

READING

Populus Romanus	The Roman People
1. Populus Romanus certe clarus erat.	1. The Roman people were indeed famous.
2. Nonne populum Romanum amas? Ita.	2. You like the Roman people, don't you? Yes.
3. Populos terrarum multarum superant et viri Romani in provinciis Romanis habitant.	3. They conquered the peoples of many lands and the Roman men lived in the Roman provinces.
4. Multae copiae in provinciis manent et incolas bene regnant.	4. Many troops stayed in the provinces and ruled the inhabitants well.
5. Vias bonas et aedificia magna et templa pulchra ibi aedificant.	5. They built good roads and large buildings and beautiful temples there.
6. Incolis fortunam bonam portant.	6. They brought good fortune to the inhabitants.
7. Incolae provinciarum saepe erant socii et populus Romanus erat dominus bonus.	7. The inhabitants of the provinces often were allies and the Roman people were good masters.
8. Socii populo Romano auxilium vero dant.	8. The allies truly gave aid to the Roman people.

Alba Longa

1. Alba Longa erat oppidum in Italia antiqua.
2. In Latio erat et agros latos et bonos habet.
3. Vergilius de Alba Longa in fabula sua narrat.
4. Quod populus Graeciae Troiam superat, multi viri erant clari.
5. Aeneas est vero clarus.
6. In Troia non manet, sed ad Latium navigat.
7. Latinus in Latio regnat.
8. Aeneas Latinum oppugnare parat et castra ibi aedificat.
9. Castra erant Alba Longa.
10. Aeneas Latinum superat et Latium occupat.
11. Populus Lati erat Latinus et lingua erat Latina.

Alba Longa

1. Alba Longa was a town in ancient Italy.
2. It was in Latium and had wide and good fields.
3. Vergil told about Alba Longa in his story.
4. Because the people of Greece conquered Troy, many men were famous.
5. Aeneas is truly famous.
6. He did not stay in Troy, but sailed to Latium.
7. Latinus ruled in Latium.
8. Aeneas prepared to attack Latinus and built a camp there.
9. The camp was Alba Longa.
10. Aeneas conquered Latinus and seized Latium.
11. The people of Latium were Latin and the language was Latin.

READING VOCABULARY

Nouns

populus, populi, m., people (popular)
aedificium, aedificii or aedifici, n., building (edifice)
lingua, linguae, f., language (linguist)
Latinus, Latini, m., Latinus
Troia, Troiae, f., Troy
Latium, Latii or Lati, n., Latium

Adjective

latinus, latina, latinum, Latin

Verbs

paro, parare, prepare, get ready (preparation)
maneo, manere, remain, stay (manor, mansion)
debeo, debere, owe, ought (debit)
propero, properare, hurry, hasten

Adverbs

nonne, expects the answer "yes"
num, expects the answer "no"
ita, yes; thus, so
minime, by no means, not at all (minimum)
vero, truly, in truth (verity)
certe, certainly, surely, indeed (certes, certo)

When **populus** is a collective Noun (represents a group), it is in the singular and its Verb is also singular. In the plural, it means peoples.

populus est, the people are   **populi terrae sunt,** the peoples of the earth are

READING GRAMMAR

A. Questions and Answers.
    1. Questions. Latin had no question mark and so a question had to be shown by a word in the sentence.
        a. A question word like **cur**, why?, asks a direct question.

> **Cur manes,**   Why do you stay?

        b. A simple question is indicated by **-ne** on the end of the first word.

> **Suntne boni,**   Are they good?

        c. **Nonne** at the beginning of a sentence asks a question expecting the answer "yes".

> **Nonne sunt boni,**   They are good, aren't they?

        d. **Num** at the beginning of a sentence asks a question expecting the answer "no".

> **Num sunt boni,**   They are not good, are they?

    2. Answers to questions may be stated in various ways.
        a. By a statement, either positive or negative.

> **Sunt boni,**   They are good.
> **Non sunt boni,**   They are not good.

        b. By a positive or affirmative word.

> **Ita,** Yes.   **Vero,** Yes, truly.   **Certe,** Certainly.

        c. By a negative word.

> **Non,** No.   **Minime,** By no means or Not at all.

B. Completing Infinitives.
Some Verbs, such as **paro** (prepare), **debeo** (ought), or **propero** (hasten), are not complete unless another Verb is used with them to complete their meaning. The completing Verb is always an Infinitive.

> **Manere debeo,**   I ought to stay.   **Manere parat,**   He prepares to stay.
> **Navigare properas,**   You hasten to sail.

FAMILIAR PHRASES

persona grata, an acceptable (or welcome) person.

persona non grata, an unacceptable (or unwelcome) person.

verbatim ac litteratim, word for word and letter for letter.

pro bono publico, for the public good.

ad infinitum, to infinity; with no limit.

sine dubio, without doubt.

vice versa, changed and turned; turned about.

addenda et corrigenda, things added and corrected; a supplement, especially to a book.

PRACTICE EXERCISES

No. 42. Give the English for these questions and answers.

1. Nonne amicos habetis? Certe.
2. Aedificantne casas? Ita. Casas aedificant.
3. Nonne vero times? Vero timeo.
4. Num populus pugnat? Populus non pugnat.
5. Num viae sunt longae? Viae minime sunt longae.
6. Cur ad oppidum ambulant?
7. Manetne vir in aedificio? Vir in aedificio manet.
8. Estne provinca libera? Provincia vero est libera.
9. Num in oceano navigat? In oceano non navigat.
10. Estne regina tua magna? Regina mea certe magna est.

No. 43. Complete these Verbs by filling in the correct vowel.

1. vid_____tis	6. iuv_____t	11. par_____nt
2. oppugn_____t	7. hab_____o	12. deb_____mus
3. hab_____s	8. man_____nt	13. proper_____t
4. ador_____s	9. tim_____t	14. aedific_____s
5. vid_____o	10. st_____tis	15. ambul_____tis

No. 44. Fill in the correct completing Infinitive.

1. (To walk) debeo.	6. (To swim) non parant.
2. (To fight) parat.	7. (To help) properatis.
3. (To kill) non debent.	8. (To work) non debetis.
4. (To conquer) paratis.	9. (To attack) parat.
5. (To call) debemus.	10. (To stay) debes.

No. 45. Translate these sentences into English.

1. Cur frumentum ibi parat?
2. Nonne linguam latinam amatis?
3. Ubi aedificia vestra stant?
4. Pueris gladios dare non debetis.
5. Dei arma sua etiam habent.
6. De bello longo Troiae fabulam narrant.
7. Aeneas cum viris suis ad Italiam navigat.
8. Deus populum Graeciae iuvat.
9. Cur Romani socios suos timent?
10. In caelo lunam claram videt.

CHAPTER 11

READING

Romulus et Remus

1. Quod Romulus et Remus filii erant dei armorum et belli, populus Romanus proelia amabat.
2. Erant etiam filii Rheae Silviae.
3. Amulius erat avunculus Rheae Silviae et Albam Longam regnabat, sed pueros non amabat.
4. Pueros amare debebat.
5. Amulius filios Rheae Silviae necare parabat, sed servus in aqua in arca pueros locabat et vitas puerorum servabat.
6. Mars filios suos ad ripam Tiberis portabat.
7. Lupa pueros ibi curabat et agricola bonus ad casam suam Romulum et Remum portabat.

Romulus and Remus

1. Because Romulus and Remus were the sons of the god of weapons and of war, the Roman people liked battles.
2. They were also the sons of Rhea Silvia.
3. Amulius was the uncle of Rhea Silvia and ruled Alba Longa, but he did not love the boys.
4. He ought to have loved the boys.
5. Amulius prepared to kill the sons of Rhea Silvia, but a slave placed the boys in the water in a chest and saved the lives of the boys.
6. Mars carried his sons to the bank of the Tiber.
7. A wolf took care of the boys there and a good farmer carried Romulus and Remus to his cottage.

Sabini

1. Romulus et Remus cum amicis suis Romam aedificabant, sed oppidum erat parvum et viri erant miseri quod sine feminis tum ibi erant.
2. Romulus ad ludos magnos Sabinos vocat et Sabini ad ludos feminas et filias suas portant.
3. Viri Romani ad casas suas puellas portant et Sabini pugnare properant.
4. In Foro Romano tum pugnabant, sed feminae erant miserae quod Sabini multos necabant.
5. Sabini vitas virorum suorum servabant, sed Romani praemium victoriae habebant.
6. Feminae et filiae Sabinorum cum Romanis nunc habitabant.

The Sabines

1. Romulus and Remus were building Rome with their friends, but the town was small and the men were unhappy because then they were there without women.
2. Romulus calls the Sabines to great games and the Sabines bring their women and daughters to the games.
3. The Roman men carry the girls to their cottages and the Sabines hasten to fight.
4. They fought then in the Roman Forum, but the women were unhappy because the Sabines were killing many people.
5. The Sabines saved the lives of their men, but the Romans had the reward of victory.
6. The women and daughters of the Sabines now lived with the Romans.

READING VOCABULARY

Nouns	Verbs

Nouns

avunculus, avunculi, m., uncle (avuncular)
arca, arcae, f., chest, box (ark)
vita, vitae, f., life (vital)
ripa, ripae, f., bank (of a river) (riparious)
lupa, lupae, f., wolf (lupine)
praemium, praemii or praemi, n., reward (premium)
ludus, ludi, m., game (ludicrous)
forum, fori, n., forum, market place (forensic)
Roma, Romae, f., Rome
Sabini, Sabinorum, m., the Sabines
Romanus, Romani, m., a Roman

Verbs

servo, servare, save, preserve (preservation)
loco, locare, place, put

Adverbs

nunc, now
tum, then

Preposition

sine, without   With the Ablative Case (sinecure)

READING GRAMMAR

A. 1. The Imperfect Tense is used to show action going on in the past over a period of time. The -ba- in the Latin Verb may be translated "was", "used to", or "did".

2. Imperfect Tense of **a-conjugation** Verbs.

SINGULAR		PLURAL	
amabam	I was loving; I loved	amabamus	we were loving; we loved
amabas	you were loving; you loved	amabatis	you were loving; you loved
amabat	he, she, it was loving; he, she, it loved	amabant	they were loving; they loved

3. Imperfect Tense of **e-conjugation** Verbs.

SINGULAR		PLURAL	
habebam	I was having; I had	habebamus	we were having; we had
habebas	you were having; you had	habebatis	you were having; you had
habebat	he, she, it was having; he, she, it had	habebant	they were having; they had

4. The Imperfect Tense of **sum** is irregular, but may be recognized easily by the Stem, **era-**.

SINGULAR		PLURAL	
eram	I was	eramus	we were
eras	you were	eratis	you were
erat	he, she, it was	erant	they were

B. **Cum** is used as both a Conjunction and a Preposition.

1. **Cum**, as a Conjunction, means "when" or "while" and introduces a clause showing time.

Cum puerum videbat, ambulabat.	When he saw the boy, he was walking.
Cum ambulabat, puerum videbat.	While he was walking, he saw the boy.

2. **Cum**, as a Preposition, means "with" and is used with the Ablative Case.

Cum puero ambulabat.	He was walking with the boy.
Cum pueris ambulabat.	He was walking with the boys.

STATE MOTTOES

Ditat Deus, God enriches. Arizona
Regnant populi, The people rule. Arkansas
Esto perpetua, May it be everlasting. Idaho
Ad astra per aspera, To the stars through hardships. Kansas
Dirigo, I direct. Maine
Virtute et armis, By courage and weapons. Mississippi

Excelsior, Loftier. New York
Imperium in imperio, An empire in an empire. Ohio
Montani semper liberi, Mountaineers are always free. West Virginia
Cedant arma togae, Let weapons yield to the toga. Wyoming

PRACTICE EXERCISES

No. 46. Fill in the blanks with the correct forms of the Imperfect Tense.

1. deb_____mus
2. par____m
3. proper_____nt
4. man____nt
5. tim____t
6. vid____s
7. cur____m
8. ador_____mus
9. loc____s
10. d____tis
11. hab_____tis
12. st____t
13. laud_____m
14. man____s
15. vid_____mus
16. hab_____s
17. port_____tis
18. iuv____t
19. voc____t
20. tim_____mus

No. 47. Give the English for the following.

1. monstrabat
2. voco
3. paramus
4. regnabatis
5. debebas
6. timetis
7. erat
8. pugnatis
9. properabam
10. videbant
11. laudabatis
12. portatis
13. superabatis
14. narrant
15. manemus
16. servabat
17. locabam
18. oppugnabas
19. habebatis
20. eratis

No. 48. Translate these phrases and clauses.

1. cum stabat
2. cum filia
3. cum laboramus
4. cum exspecto
5. cum amicis
6. cum superat
7. cum lupa
8. cum videtis
9. cum erat
10. cum pugnabatis
11. cum puella
12. cum erant
13. cum avunculo meo
14. cum Romanis
15. cum feminis multis

No. 49. Translate the following into English.

1. Num viros in castris habet?
2. Ibi esse hodie parabamus.
3. Amicus tuus in oppido nostro famam bonam habet.
4. Cum puellis manere parabam.
5. Nonne in silvis multas lupas saepe necat?
6. Romani gladios Sabinorum timere non debent.
7. Cum oppidum aedificant, templa et aedificia ibi locant.
8. Cur servis suis praemia dant?
9. Agricola cum amico suo in agro erat.
10. Nonne sine aqua estis?

CHAPTER 12

READING

Graecia

1. Gloria Graeciae et fama incolarum suarum sunt clarae.
2. Graecia est paeninsula et agri et silvae populo bonam fortunam et vitam laetam dabant.
3. Nautae trans oceanum ad terras multas navigabant et multa ad fora oppidorum Graeciae portabant.
4. Graecia est propinqua Italiae, sed non est finitima.
5. Proelia et bella non erant grata incolis, sed cum populis finitimis pugnare saepe parabant.
6. Populus multis amicus erat et bellum populo non idoneum erat.
7. Italia erat inimica Graeciae et terram occupabat.
8. Tum populus Graeciae erat socius populi Italiae, sed populus Romanus linguam et templa et aedificia Graeciae laudabat.

Greece

1. The glory of Greece and the fame of her inhabitants are well-known.
2. Greece is a peninsula and the fields and forests gave good fortune and a happy life to the people.
3. The sailors sailed across the ocean to many lands and brought many things to the market places of the towns of Greece.
4. Greece is near to Italy, but it is not neighboring.
5. Battles and wars were not pleasing to the inhabitants, but they often got ready to fight with the neighboring peoples.
6. The people were friendly to many and war was not suitable to the people.
7. Italy was unfriendly to Greece and seized the land.
8. Then the people of Greece were allies of the people of Italy, but the Roman people praised the language and temples and buildings of Greece.

Barbari

1. Romani multos finitimos barbaros habebant.
2. Barbari ob praedam bella et proelia saepe incitabant.
3. Nonne nuntii de periculo monebant?
4. Cum nuntium portabant, socii auxilium portare atque copias suas armare debebant.
5. Romani non timebant, sed in terris barbaris pugnabant.
6. Oppida multa ibi oppugnabant et superabant.
7. Populus Germanus non erat amicus Romanis.
8. Erat barbarus et patriae Romanorum finitimus.

The Barbarians

1. The Romans had many uncivilized neighbors.
2. The barbarians often stirred up wars and battles on account of booty.
3. The messengers warned about the danger, didn't they?
4. When they brought the message, the allies had to bring aid and arm their troops.
5. The Romans were not afraid, but they fought in barbarian lands.
6. They used to attack many towns there and conquer them.
7. The German people were not friendly to the Romans.
8. They were uncivilized and neighboring to the native country of the Romans.

Barbari	The Barbarians
9. Victoriae copiarum Romanarum erant clarae et magnae.	9. The victories of the Roman troops were famous and great.
10. Copiis praemia dabant, cum nuntii famas bonas de gloria in provinciis narrabant.	10. They gave the troops rewards, when the messengers related good reports about their glory in the provinces.

READING VOCABULARY

Nouns

barbarus, barbari, m., barbarian (barbarous)
finitimus, finitimi, m., neighbor

Adjectives

propinquus, propinqua, propinquum, near (propinquity)
finitimus, finitima, finitimum, neighboring
idoneus, idonea, idoneum, fit, suitable
amicus, amica, amicum, friendly (amicable)
gratus, grata, gratum, pleasing (grateful)
inimicus, inimica, inimicum, unfriendly (inimical)
barbarus, barbara, barbarum, savage, uncivilized, barbarian (barbarous)

Verbs

moneo, monere, warn, advise (monition, monitor)
incito, incitare, arouse, stir up, incite (incitement)

Adverb

cras, tomorrow (procrastinate)

Preposition

ob, on account of, because of With the Accusative Case

Conjunction

atque or ac, and also, also ac is used only before consonants.

READING GRAMMAR

A. Some Adjectives are followed by the Dative Case. They are translated with the Preposition *to* or *for* in English. Some of these Adjectives are **propinquus** (near), **idoneus** (fit), **amicus** (friendly), **inimicus** (unfriendly), **gratus** (pleasing), and **finitimus** (neighboring).

Est propinquus agro.	He is near to the field.
Est idoneum bello.	It is fit for war.
Est amicus puero.	He is friendly to the boy.
Est inimicus populo.	He is unfriendly to the people.
Est gratus viris.	He is pleasing to the men.
Est finitimum oppido.	It is neighboring to the town.

B. 1. The Future Tense shows action going on in the future and is translated "shall" or "will". All but the first and last forms have **-bi-** to show the future tense. In the first form, **-bo**, and in the last form, **-bu-** show the future tense.

2. Future Tense of **a-conjugation** Verbs.

SINGULAR		PLURAL	
amabo	I shall love; like	amabimus	we shall love; like
amabis	you will love; like	amabitis	you will love; like
amabit	he, she, it will love; like	amabunt	they will love; like

3. Future Tense of **e-conjugation** Verbs.

SINGULAR		PLURAL	
habebo	I shall have; hold	habebimus	we shall have; hold
habebis	you will have; hold	habebitis	you will have; hold
habebit	he, she, it will have; hold	habebunt	they will have; hold

4. The Future Tense of **sum** is irregular, but is recognized by the Stem, **eri-**.

SINGULAR		PLURAL	
ero	I shall be	erimus	we shall be
eris	you will be	eritis	you will be
erit	he, she, it will be	erunt	they will be

LEGAL TERMS

Latin is used extensively in legal phrases and terminology. Some of the more common Latin legal terms are given below.

ius civile, civil law, referring to the laws of legal systems modeled after the Roman law.

ius gentium, the law of nations, referring to International Law.

lex scripta, written law. Written laws are those passed and put into effect by a legislative body or corporation.

lex non scripta, unwritten law. Unwritten law develops out of common practice, custom, and usage. It is sometimes called common law.

sub iudice, before the judge, referring to a case under consideration by the judge, or court, but not yet decided.

corpus iuris, the body of law, comprised of all the laws of a sovereign power or legislative body collectively.

subpoena, under penalty or punishment. A **subpoena** is a writ naming a person and ordering him to appear in court, under penalty for failure to do so.

corpus delicti, the body of the crime or offense. The **corpus delicti** refers to the circumstances necessary to a crime. In murder, the **corpus delicti** is the fact of a criminal agent or of the death of the victim. It does not refer to the victim's body.

onus probandi, the burden of proof. The burden of proving its case rests with the side that makes the affirmation in a suit.

prima facie, on or at first appearance. **Prima facie** evidence is evidence that, at first presentation, is adequate enough to establish a fact.

PRACTICE EXERCISES

No. 50. Give the English for these Verb forms.

1. oppugnat	9. habebitis	17. pugnabis	24. sumus
2. liberabant	10. pugnabas	18. superabimus	25. oppugnabamus
3. videbo	11. dabant	19. parabamus	26. incitabit
4. manebit	12. erit	20. erunt	27. natabant
5. erant	13. incitabunt	21. narrabunt	28. locabatis
6. sunt	14. monebit	22. incitabat	29. servabis
7. debent	15. portare	23. monebatis	30. iuvabitis
8. amare	16. timebit		

No. 51. Give the English for these phrases.

1. de caelo claro	6. in fossis latis	11. inimici reginae
2. finitimus patriae meae	7. gratus socio suo	12. de victoria tua
3. propinquum insulis	8. ante agros	13. per proelia multa
4. cum amico nostro	9. amicus servis	14. idoneus viro
5. ad aedificia alta	10. post bellum	15. sine praeda

No. 52. Give the tense of the following Verbs.

1. sum	6. dabat	11. iuvabis	16. liberabam
2. monebunt	7. narrabit	12. natabas	17. debebit
3. manebat	8. oppugnant	13. amabunt	18. narrabant
4. debet	9. pugnabis	14. timebat	19. pugnabamus
5. erat	10. erit	15. incitabis	20. erunt

No. 53. Translate the following into English.

1. Ad vias angustas ambulabit.
2. Ante templa stabant.
3. Ex oceano natabatis.
4. In aqua pugnabunt.
5. Feminis grata est.
6. Patriam liberam habere debebunt.
7. Puellae natabunt.
8. Finitimos suos amabat.
9. Avunculos tuos servabis.
10. Reginam laudabunt.
11. Ubi esse debetis?
12. Puerum vocabas.
13. Erit inimicus nuntio.
14. Non est provinciae propinquum.
15. Gladios tuos non timebimus.
16. Servi vestri iuvant.
17. Vir ibi manebit.
18. Fossam altam parabamus.
19. Dominus fabulam narrabit.
20. Agrum arabimus.

CHAPTER 13

READING

Gallia	Gaul
1. Patria Gallorum erat Germaniae et Hispaniae finitima.	1. The native country of the Gauls was neighboring to Germany and Spain.
2. Galli proelia et bella non amabant, sed bellum non timebant.	2. The Gauls did not like battles and wars, but they did not fear war.
3. Romani contra Gallos saepe pugnabant et Galli pro patria sua tum bene pugnabant.	3. The Romans often fought against the Gauls and the Gauls then fought hard for their native country.
4. Romani in Gallia legatos habebant quod Galli Romanis amici non erant.	4. The Romans had lieutenants in Gaul because the Gauls were not friendly to the Romans.
5. Legati bellum cum Gallis pugnare saepe parabant.	5. The lieutenants often got ready to fight with the Gauls.
6. Caesar ob victorias suas in Gallia gloriam magnam habebat.	6. Caesar had great glory because of his victories in Gaul.
7. Oppida in Gallia erant clara.	7. The towns in Gaul were famous.
8. Ibi erant oppida multa et pulchra ac silvae multae et agri boni.	8. There were many and beautiful towns there, and also many forests and good fields.
9. Ob periculum belli Romani in multis terris finitimis legatos habebant.	9. On account of the danger of war the Romans had legates in many neighboring lands.
10. Romani pro patria etiam sine praemiis magnis et praeda pugnabant.	10. The Romans fought for their country even without large rewards and booty.
11. Erant in Gallia multi agri lati atque agricolis idonea erat.	11. There were many wide fields in Gaul and it was suitable for farmers.
12. Cum in Gallia habitabant, Romani linguam Latinam tenebant.	12. When they were living in Gaul, the Romans kept the Latin language.

READING VOCABULARY

Nouns

memoria, memoriae, f., memory (memorize)
legatus, legati, m., lieutenant, legate (legation)
Gallia, Galliae, f., Gaul (the country) (Gallic)
Gallus, Galli, m., a Gaul (person)
Germanus, Germani, m., a German (person) (Germanic)

Verbs

teneo, tenere, hold, keep, have (tenable)
memoria tenere, to remember (literally, to keep by memory)

Prepositions

contra, against   With the Accusative Case (contradict)
pro, for, in behalf of, on behalf of (procurator)

READING GRAMMAR

A. A Noun in apposition (that is, the same position or use in the sentence) with another Noun must be in the same case, and the same number.

> **Puella, filia legati, ibi est.**   The girl, the daughter of the lieutenant, is there.

In this sentence, **filia** is in apposition with **puella**. **Filia** is, therefore, also in the Nominative Case and also singular number.

B. The Vocative Case is the case of address and is used for the person or thing addressed directly. It is spelled the same as the Nominative Case, with these exceptions:

o-declension Nouns in the singular end in **-e** instead of **-us**. Thus,

puella, girl	**puellae**, girls
amice, friend	**amici**, friends
puer, boy	**pueri**, boys
bellum, war	**bella**, wars

The vocative singular of **filius** and proper Nouns ends in **-i**. Thus,

> **fili**, son   **filii**, sons   **Mercuri**, Mercury

The vocative singular of **meus** is **mi**. Thus,

mea puella, my girl	**meae puellae**, my girls
mi puer, my boys	**mei pueri**, my boys

C. The Imperative of a Verb is used for a direct command. It is used with the second person singular and plural understood (you or ye not expressed).

1. **a-conjugation** Verbs form the Imperative:

SINGULAR	PLURAL
ama love; like	**amate** love; like

2. **e-conjugation** Verbs form the Imperative:

SINGULAR	PLURAL
habe have; hold	**habete** have; hold

FAMILIAR QUOTATIONS

Virginibus puerisque, For boys and girls. Horace

Non scholae sed vitae discimus, We learn not for school but for life. Seneca

Parvum parva decent, Small things become the small. Horace

Eheu fugaces anni, Alas the fleeting years. Horace

Vera amicitia est inter bonos, There is true friendship only among good men. Cicero

Ave atque vale, Hail and farewell. Catullus

Da dextram misero, Give your right hand to the wretched. Virgil

PRACTICE EXERCISES

No. 54. Translate these Imperatives.

1. ambula	5. laudate	9. timete	13. tene	17. sta
2. amate	6. navigate	10. vide	14. regna	18. iuvate
3. natate	7. date	11. state	15. tenete	19. monete
4. pugna	8. habita	12. habete	16. superate	20. mane

No. 55. Translate these Appositives.

1. vir, agricola
2. viri, nautae
3. patria, Britannia
4. puer, amicus
5. regina, puella
6. Galli, socii nostri
7. nuntius, puer
8. Gallos, inimicos
9. dominum, amicum
10. filiorum, puerorum

No. 56. Translate these Vocatives.

1. amici
2. bella
3. deae
4. deus
5. domine
6. domina
7. fili
8. gloria
9. nuntii
10. mi serve
11. bone vir
12. bona lingua
13. multi amici
14. bone agricola
15. amice noster

No. 57. Translate these sentences into English.

1. Puer aeger, filius tuus, in oppido manebit.
2. In proelio, amice, socios habere debes.
3. Contra bellum, popule Romane, viros tuos incita.
4. Incolas Galliae, nuntii, monete.
5. Sabinos, finitimos nostros, ad ludos vocabo.
6. Templa, puellae, aedificia pulchra, videte.
7. Roma, oppidum in Italia, clara erit.
8. Galliam, fili mi, memoria tene.
9. Habebimusne, amici, forum magnum?
10. Avunculos meos, nuntios, exspectabo.

THIRD REVIEW SECTION (CHAPTERS 10–13)

VOCABULARY REVIEW

NOUNS

1. aedificium	9. Germanus	17. populus	1. building	9. a German	17. people
2. arca	10. Latinus	18. praemium	2. chest, box	10. Latinus	18. reward
3. avunculus	11. Latium	19. ripa	3. uncle	11. Latium	19. river bank
4. barbarus	12. legatus	20. Roma	4. barbarian	12. lieutenant, legate	20. Rome
5. finitimus	13. lingua	21. Romanus	5. neighbor	13. language	21. a Roman
6. forum	14. ludus	22. Sabini	6. forum, market place	14. game	22. the Sabines
7. Gallia	15. lupa	23. Troia	7. Gaul	15. wolf	23. Troy
8. Gallus	16. memoria	24. vita	8. a Gaul	16. memory	24. life

ADJECTIVES

1. amicus	3. finitimus	6. inimicus	1. friendly	3. neighboring	6. unfriendly
2. barbarus	4. gratus	7. latinus	2. savage, uncivilized, barbarian	4. pleasing	7. Latin
	5. idoneus	8. propinquus		5. fit, suitable	8. near

VERBS

1. debeo	6. paro	1. owe, ought	6. prepare, get ready
2. incito	7. propero	2. arouse, stir up, incite	7. hurry, hasten
3. loco	8. servo	3. place, put	8. save, preserve
4. maneo	9. teneo	4. remain, stay	9. hold, keep, have
5. moneo	10. memoria tenere	5. warn, advise	10. remember

ADVERBS

1. certe	6. num	1. certainly, indeed, surely	6. expects the answer "no"
2. cras	7. nunc	2. tomorrow	7. now
3. ita	8. tum	3. thus, so; yes	8. then
4. minime	9. vero	4. not at all, by no means	9. truly, in truth
5. nonne		5. expects the answer "yes"	

PREPOSITIONS

1. contra	3. pro	1. against	3. for, in behalf of
2. ob	4. sine	2. on account of, because of	4. without

CONJUNCTION

1. atque, ac	1. and also, also

PRACTICE EXERCISES

No. 58. Tell whether these questions are simple questions, expect the answer yes, or expect the answer no.

1. Estne aeger?
2. Ubi est puer?
3. Cur times?
4. Nonne memoria tenent?
5. Num manebat?
6. Nonne amici sunt?
7. Num manetis?
8. Properatne?
9. Cur debent?
10. Ubi arcam locat?

No. 59. Change these Verbs to the Imperfect Tense.

1. debeo
2. locas
3. incitat
4. properant
5. paratis
6. tenemus
7. servas
8. teneo
9. manemus
10. monet

No. 60. Change these Verbs to the Future Tense.

1. videbam
2. stabant
3. timebas
4. regnabat
5. necabatis
6. habebamus
7. aedificabam
8. superabas
9. curabamus
10. nuntiabant

No. 61. Give the Singular and Plural Imperatives of these Infinitives.

1. servare
2. monere
3. incitare
4. manere
5. navigare
6. parare
7. tenere
8. properare
9. necare
10. pugnare

No. 62. Give the Singular and Plural Vocative of these Nouns.

1. populus
2. memoria
3. legatus
4. amicus
5. femina
6. bellum
7. avunculus
8. vir
9. puer
10. puella
11. filius
12. agricola

GAIUS IULIUS CAESAR

Caesar was born in Rome, of a noble family, in 100 B.C. He was educated as an orator and lawyer, but soon turned to politics and became consul in 59 B.C. For the next seven years he was proconsul in Gaul, where he was successful in subduing and conquering the Gallic tribes. The **Commentaries on the Gallic War** are a military history of this period. Caesar's refusal to surrender the command of his army led to Civil War, his long dictatorship, and political turmoil, resulting in his assassination in 44 B.C.

Natio est omnis Gallorum admodum dedita religionibus . . . Deum maxime Mercurium colunt. Huius sunt plurima simulacra; hunc omnium inventorem artium ferunt, hunc viarum atque itinerum ducem, hunc ad quaestus

The entire nation of the Gauls is quite devoted to religious rites . . . They worship the god Mercury especially. There are very many statues of him; they say he is the inventor of all the arts, they believe he is the guide on roads pecuniae mercaturasque habere vim maximam arbitrantur. Post hunc Apollinem et Martem et Iovem et Minervam. De his eandum fere, quam reliquae gentes, habent opinionem: Apollinem morbos depellere, Minervam operum atque artificiorum initia tradere, Iovem imperium caelestium tenere, Martem bella regere.

Commentarii de Bello Gallico, VI, xvi, xvii

and journeys, and that he has the greatest power over money transactions and merchants. After him come Apollo and Mars and Jupiter and Minerva. About these, they have almost the same idea as other races: Apollo dispels diseases, Minerva hands down the skills of handcrafts and arts, Jupiter holds the power over the gods, and Mars rules over wars.

Commentaries on the Gallic War, 6, 16, 17

THE BIBLE

In principio creavit Deus caelum et terram. Terra autem erat inanis et vacua, et tenebrae erant super faciem abyssi, et spiritus Dei ferebatur super aquas.

Dixitque Deus: Fiat lux. Et facta est lux. Et vidit Deus lucem quod esset bona et divisit lucem a tenebris. Appellavitque lucem diem et tenebras noctem. Factumque est vespere et mane, dies unus.

Dixit quoque Deus: Fiat firmamentum in medio aquarum et dividit aquas ab aquis. Et fecit Deus firmamentum, divisitque aquas, quae erant sub firmamento, ab his quae erant super firmamentum. Et factum est ita. Vocavitque Deus firmamentum caelum. Et factum est vespere et mane, dies secundus.

Dixit vero Deus: Congregentur aquae, quae sub caelo sunt, in locum unum, et appareat arida. Et factum est ita. Et vocavit Deus aridam terram congregationesque aquarum appellavit maria. Et vidit Deus quod esset bonum. Et ait: Germinet terra herbam virentem et facientem semen et lignum pomiferum faciens fructum iuxta genus suum, cuius semen in semetipso sit super terram. Et factum est ita. Et protulit terra herbam virentem et facientem semen iuxta genus suum lignumque faciens fructum et habens unumquodque sementem secundum speciem suam. Et vidit Deus quod esset bonum. Et factum est vespere et mane, dies tertius.

Liber Genesis I, i–xiii

In the beginning God created the heaven and the earth. And the earth was without form, and void; and darkness was upon the face of the deep. And the Spirit of God moved upon the face of the waters.

And God said: Let there be light. And there was light. And God saw the light, that it was good; and God divided the light from the darkness. And God called the light Day, and the darkness he called Night. And the evening and the morning were the first day.

And God said: Let there be a firmament in the midst of the waters, and let it divide the waters from the waters. And God made the firmament, and divided the waters which were under the firmament from the waters which were above the firmament. And it was so. And God called the firmament Heaven. And the evening and the morning were the second day.

And God said: Let the waters under the heaven be gathered together unto one place, and let the dry land appear. And it was so. And God called the dry land Earth; and the gathering together of the waters called he Seas. And God saw that it was good. And God said: Let the earth bring forth grass, the herb yielding seed, and the fruit tree yielding fruit after his kind, whose seed is in itself, upon the earth. And it was so. And the earth brought forth grass, and herb yielding seed after his kind, and the tree yielding fruit, whose seed was in itself, after his kind. And God saw that it was good. And the evening and the morning were the third day.

Genesis I, 1–13

CHAPTER 14

READING

Germani

1. Germania Galliae finitima erat et Italiae propinqua.
2. Incolae Germaniae, terrae magnae, non in oppidis magnis et pulchris, sed in silvis aut in casis parvis habitabant, quod barbari erant.
3. Inter Germanos erant multi sagittarii boni et in silvis lupae multae sagittis Germanorum necabantur.
4. Multae terrae et patriae a Vandiliis oppugnabantur atque superabantur.
5. Germani populis Galliae et Italiae non erant amici.
6. Vandilii robusti Italiam oppugnabant et populus certe terrebatur quod pro vita sua timebat.
7. Ubi Vandilii populum superabant, multi vero erant miseri.

The Germans

1. Germany was neighboring to Gaul and near Italy.
2. The inhabitants of Germany, a big country, did not live in large and beautiful towns, but in the forests or in small cottages, because they were uncivilized.
3. Among the Germans there were many good archers and in the forests many wolves used to be killed by the arrows of the Germans.
4. Many lands and native countries used to be attacked by the Vandals and conquered.
5. The Germans were not friendly to the peoples of Gaul and Italy.
6. The strong Vandals attacked Italy and the people were indeed frightened because they feared for their lives.
7. When the Vandals conquered the people, many were truly wretched.

READING VOCABULARY

Nouns

pecunia, pecuniae, f., money (pecuniary)
donum, doni, n., gift, present (donation)
sagitta, sagittae, f., arrow (sagittal)
sagittarius, sagittarii or sagittari, m., archer (Sagittarius)
littera, litterae, f., letter (of the alphabet) In the plural, a letter or epistle (literal, literature)

Adjective

robustus, robusta, robustum, strong, robust

Adverb

mox, soon, presently

Verbs

moveo, movere, move (movable)
castra movere, to break camp
doleo, dolere, grieve, be sorry (dolorous)
terreo, terrere, frighten, scare, terrify (terrorize)

Prepositions

a or ab, by; away from, from With the Ablative Case (absent)
inter, between, among With the Accusative Case (interlinear)

Conjunction

aut, or

READING GRAMMAR

A. The Passive Voice of a Verb shows the subject as the receiver of the action.

Puer amatur.,   The boy is loved.

The Passive Voice of the Present, Imperfect, and Future Tenses is formed in the same way as the Active Voice, except that the personal endings are passive instead of active.

1. Present Passive Tense

a-conjugation		e-conjugation	
amor	I am loved; being loved	habeor	I am held; being held
amaris	you are loved; being loved	haberis	you are held; being held
amatur	he, she, it is loved; being loved	habetur	he, she, it is held; being held
amamur	we are loved; being loved	habemur	we are held; being held
amamini	you are loved; being loved	habemini	you are held; being held
amantur	they are loved; being loved	habentur	they are held; being held

2. Imperfect Passive Tense

a-conjugation		e-conjugation	
amabar	I was loved; being loved	habebar	I was held; being held
amabaris	you were loved; etc.	habebaris	you were held; etc.
amabatur	he, she, it was loved; etc.	habebatur	he, she, it was held; etc.
amabamur	we were loved; etc.	habebamur	we were held; etc.
amabamini	you were loved; etc.	habebamini	you were held; etc.
amabantur	they were loved; etc.	habebantur	they were held; etc.

3. Future Passive Tense

a-conjugation		e-conjugation	
amabor	I shall be loved	habebor	I shall be held
amaberis	you will be loved	habeberis	you will be held
amabitur	he, she, it will be loved	habebitur	he, she, it will be held
amabimur	we shall be loved	habebimur	we shall be held
amabimini	you will be loved	habebimini	you will be held
amabuntur	they will be loved	habebuntur	they will be held

The only irregularities are in the Future Tense: **amaberis, habeberis.**
The Passive Voice of **video** often means "seem".

B. The doer of the action expressed by a Passive Verb is in the Ablative Case with the Preposition **a** or **ab.** It is always a person.

Puer ab agricola amatur.   The boy is loved by the farmer.

C. The thing by which the action of either an Active or a Passive Verb is done is in the Ablative Case, without any Preposition.

Puer sagitta necatur.   The boy is killed by an arrow.
Puer sagitta lupam necat.   The boy kills the wolf with an arrow.

FAMILIAR PHRASES

vi et armis, by force and arms.
pax vobiscum, peace be with you.
tempus fugit, time flies.
agenda, things that have to be done.
sic passim, thus everywhere.
multum in parvo, much in little.
senatus populusque Romanus, the Senate and the Roman people. Abbr. S.P.Q.R.

res gestae, things done; acts or deeds.
alter idem, another self, referring to a close friend.
apparatus criticus, critical apparatus or material; reference material used in the critical study of a piece of literature.

PRACTICE EXERCISES

No. 63. Give the English for the following.

1. timeberis	6. stabo	11. necabat	16. monstrabar
2. laudabam	7. armabatur	12. aedificabuntur	17. ambulabant
3. curor	8. aras	13. superabo	18. dabitur
4. laudantur	9. occupabitur	14. navigabit	19. iuvamini
5. narrabuntur	10. stabitis	15. habitabam	20. vocabor

No. 64. Change these Verbs to the Passive Voice.

1. exspectabam	6. habet	11. laudabunt	16. monebas
2. tenent	7. videbatis	12. locatis	17. servas
3. monebit	8. portabit	13. properabunt	18. debebat
4. videbat	9. movebitis	14. timemus	19. vident
5. amabit	10. parant	15. incito	20. monebant

No. 65. Give the English for these phrases, in the Ablative Case.

1. cum legato	6. a nuntio	11. equis	16. sapientia
2. gladio	7. cum avunculis	12. sagittis	17. a populo
3. a pueris	8. bellis	13. a sagittario	18. cum inimicis
4. fossis	9. ab dominis	14. a dea	19. aqua
5. ab amicis	10. cum socio	15. cum servo	20. ab viro

No. 66. Translate the following into English.

1. Pecunia viro atque puellae dabitur quod puer aeger est.
2. Memoria tenebar cum ad oppidum finitimum movebam.
3. Dolere videntur sed donum portabitur.
4. Ob pericula viri litteras timebant.
5. Pro Britannia, patria vestra, bene pugnate.
6. Multi ad templa deorum ambulabant.
7. Ubi ludus ab amico vestro dabitur?
8. In casa ubi puellas videtis habitabamus.
9. Num vir gladio oppugnabitur?
10. Nonne populus castra movere parabat?

CHAPTER 15

READING

Cincinnatus

1. Roma pacem saepe non habebat, sed in periculo erat et contra finitimos suos pugnabat.
2. Roma copias bonas atque arma habebat, sed oppugnabatur et populus caput habere debebat quod terrebatur.
3. Nuntii ad Cincinnatum properant et ubi Cincinnatum, agricolam Romanum, in agro vident, de bello et magno periculo narrant.
4. Cincinnatus agros suos bene amabat et bellum gratum non erat, sed Romam bene amabat et ab nuntiis movebatur.
5. Populo Romano magnum auxilium portabat quod dictator erat et Romam servabat.
6. Copiae Romanae a periculo patriam suam liberabant et Cincinnatus a Romanis semper memoria tenebatur.

Cincinnatus

1. Often Rome did not have peace, but was in danger and fought against her neighbors.
2. Rome had good troops and weapons, but she was being attacked and the people needed to have a leader because they were frightened.
3. Messengers hurry to Cincinnatus and when they see Cincinnatus, a Roman farmer, in the field they tell about the war and great danger.
4. Cincinnatus loved his fields well and war was not pleasing, but he loved Rome very much and was moved by the messengers.
5. He brought great help to the Roman people because he was dictator and he saved Rome.
6. The Roman troops freed their country from danger and Cincinnatus was always remembered by the Romans.

Horatius

1. Magnae copiae hostium Romam oppugnabant.
2. Pars urbis Romae erat in periculo quod hostes pontem ibi occupare parabant.
3. Homines Romae ab Horatio, milite bono, contra hostes incitabantur, sed pontem non tenebant.
4. Tum Horatius in ponte sine auxilio stat. Pro vita sua non timet.
5. Gladio suo multos milites hostium mox necat et hostes ab ponte tenet. Magna erat caedes.
6. Post Horatium milites Romani laborabant et mox pons non stabat.
7. Romani victoriam habent et Roma servatur quod aqua inter Romam et hostes stat.
8. Horatius trans aquam ad ripam ubi erant socii natat.
9. Horatius inter Romanos laudabatur et multi agri Horatio dabantur.

Horatius

1. Large forces of the enemy were attacking Rome.
2. Part of the city of Rome was in danger because the enemy was preparing to seize the bridge there.
3. The men of Rome were being stirred up against the enemy by Horatius, a good soldier, but they did not hold the bridge.
4. Then Horatius stood on the bridge without aid. He did not fear for his life.
5. Soon he killed many of the enemy's soldiers with his sword and held the enemy away from the bridge. The slaughter was great.
6. In back of Horatius the Roman soldiers were working and soon the bridge was not standing.
7. The Romans had the victory and Rome was saved because the water stood between Rome and the enemy.
8. Horatius swam across the water to the river bank where his comrades were.
9. Horatius was praised among the Romans and many fields were given to Horatius.

READING VOCABULARY

Nouns

miles, militis, m., soldier (military)
pax, pacis, f., peace (pacific)
caput, capitis, n., head (capital)
dictator, dictatoris, m., dictator (dictatorial)
homo, hominis, m., man (homicide)
Cincinnatus, Cincinnati, m., Cincinnatus
hostis, hostis, m., enemy (hostium) (hostile)
pars, partis, f., part (partium) (partake, particle)

mare, maris, n., sea (marium) (marine)
urbs, urbis, f., city (urbium) (suburb)
caedes, caedis, f., slaughter, murder (caedium)
pons, pontis, m., bridge (pontium) (pontoon)
Horatius, Horati, m., Horatius

Adverb

semper, always, ever (sempiternal)

Hostis in the singular means an individual enemy in war; in the plural, it is a collective noun, the enemy, and its Verb must also be plural.

READING GRAMMAR

A. i-declension Nouns.
  1. More Nouns belong to the i-declension than to any other declension.
  2. i-declension Nouns are masculine, feminine, and neuter. The masculine and feminine have the same endings.
  3. i-declension Nouns have a wide variety of spellings. The Genitive Case always ends in -is.
B. i-declension Nouns are divided into two groups—those that have -ium for the Genitive Plural ending and those that have -um. From now on those Nouns that have -ium in the Genitive Plural will be indicated in the Vocabulary. These Nouns may have -i as an alternate ending in the Ablative Singular.
  1. i-declension Nouns with -ium in the Genitive Plural.

Masculine or Feminine

SINGULAR		USE	PLURAL	
urbs	the city	subject	urbes	the cities
urbis	of the city	possession	urbium	of the cities
urbi	to, for the city	indirect object	urbibus	to, for the cities
urbem	the city	direct object	urbes	the cities
urbe,	from, with, by,	prepositional phrases	urbibus	from, with, by, in
urbi	in the city			the cities

Neuter

SINGULAR		USE	PLURAL	
mare	the sea	subject	maria	the seas
maris	of the sea	possession	marium	of the seas
mari	to, for the sea	indirect object	maribus	to, for the seas
mare	the sea	direct object	maria	the seas
mare,	from, with, by,	prepositional phrases	maribus	from, with, by, in
mari	in the sea			the seas

Notice that the Neuter Plural Nominative and Accusative end in -ia.

2. **i-declension** Nouns with **-um** in the Genitive Plural.

Masculine and Feminine

SINGULAR		USE	PLURAL	
homo	the man	subject	homines	the men
hominis	of the man	possession	hominum	of the men
homini	to, for the man	indirect object	hominibus	to, for the men
hominem	the man	direct object	homines	the men
homine	from, with, by, in the man	prepositional phrases	hominibus	from, with, by, in the men

Neuter

SINGULAR		USE	PLURAL	
caput	the head	subject	capita	the heads
capitis	of the head	possession	capitum	of the heads
capiti	to, for the head	indirect object	capitibus	to, for the heads
caput	the head	direct object	capita	the heads
capite	from, with, by, in the head	prepositional phrases	capitibus	from, with, by, in the heads

SUFFIXES

Suffixes are applied to the stems of Nouns and Adjectives to give a certain meaning to both Latin and English words or to form one part of speech from another. These are some of the more common suffixes that are added to Latin words to give them a special meaning:

-tor (masc.), **-trix** (fem.) denote the doer or agent. English, -er, -or.

>   **victor,** conqueror
>   **genitor,** father
>   **genetrix,** mother

-or denotes an action or state. English, -or.

>   **terror,** fear, terror

-tio denotes an action. English, -tion.

>   **natio,** nation

-ia, -tia, -tudo, -tas denote quality or state.

-ia becomes -y in English.

>   **miseria,** misery
>   **iniuria,** injury
>   **victoria,** victory

-tia becomes -ce, -ship, -ness in English.

>   **potentia,** force
>   **amicitia,** friendship
>   **laetitia,** happiness.

-tudo becomes -tude in English.

>   **longitudo,** longitude
>   **latitudo,** latitude
>   **altitudo,** altitude
>   **magnitudo,** magnitude

-tas becomes -ty in English.

>   **gravitas,** gravity
>   **dignitas,** dignity

PRACTICE EXERCISES

No. 67. Give the English for the following phrases.

1. pacis longae
2. pro milite
3. milites clari
4. pax Romana
5. capita vestra
6. dictatoribus suis
7. caput tuum
8. ab hominibus laetis
9. pars idonea
10. in urbe antiqua
11. maris nostri
12. milites robustos
13. homines boni
14. pacem longam
15. in capitibus suis
16. contra dictatores
17. cum hominibus
18. sine militibus tuis
19. de pace grata
20. homo amicus

No. 68. Fill in the blanks with the correct English.

1. militum, _____ the soldiers
2. pacis, _____ peace
3. caput, _____ head
4. partem, _____ part
5. in urbibus, _____ the cities
6. maria, _____ seas
7. cum milite, _____ the soldier
8. pontium, _____ the bridges
9. hostes, _____ enemy
10. de caede, _____ slaughter

No. 69. Change each of the following to the plural, and give the English.

1. pax
2. milite
3. capiti
4. partem
5. hosti
6. urbis
7. caedem
8. pons
9. homo
10. caput
11. militis
12. partis
13. hominem
14. pacis
15. dictatorem
16. ponti
17. maris
18. pontis
19. hostem
20. urbe

No. 70. Translate the following into English.

1. Cincinnatus ex agro suo vocabatur et auxilium dabat.
2. Homines in terra regnant sed dei caelum atque terram regnant.
3. Praemia homini magno ab populo Romano dabuntur.
4. Lingua Latina semper servabitur.
5. Cras non arabit sed patriam nostram mox servabit.
6. Ad ripam natabat quod pons non stabat.
7. Gladio pro patria tua, Horati, bene pugna.
8. Milites, filii mei, gladiis armabuntur.
9. Ob pericula tuam aquam servare debes.
10. Nauta mare amat sed agricola agros suos amat.

CHAPTER 16

READING

Daedalus et Icarus	Daedalus and Icarus
1. Daedalus hominem necat et cum filio suo, Icaro, ex Graecia ad Cretam, insulam in mari, properat.	1. Daedalus killed a man and with his son, Icarus, hurried from Greece to Crete, an island in the sea.
2. Parva in insula diu manebant et tum pater filiusque ad Graeciam volare parant.	2. They stayed for a long time on the small island and then the father and son prepared to fly toward Greece.
3. Bene laborant et alas parant.	3. They work hard and get wings ready.
4. Pater puerum monet: "Per caelum, sed non ad solem volabimus."	4. The father warns the boy: "We shall fly through the sky, but not toward the sun."
5. Sol erat clarus et Icarus ob alas suas erat laetus.	5. The sun was bright and Icarus was happy because of his wings.
6. Consilium patris sui non diu memoria tenebat.	6. He did not remember the advice of his father for long.
7. Cum patre suo non manebat, sed summo in caelo ante solem volebat.	7. He did not stay with his father, but flew very high in the sky in front of the sun.

Daedalus et Icarus

8. Cera in alis pueri non manebat.
9. Pater filium suum medio in mari mox videt.
10. Icarus non servatur et Daedalus vero dolebat quod puer consilio patris non bene monebatur.

Daedalus and Icarus

8. The wax did not stay on the boy's wings.
9. The father soon sees his son in the middle of the sea.
10. Icarus was not saved and Daedalus was truly grieved because the boy was not well warned by his father's advice.

READING VOCABULARY

Nouns

Daedalus, Daedali, m., Daedalus
Icarus, Icari, m., Icarus
Creta, Cretae, f., Crete
labor, laboris, m., work, toil, labor (laboratory)
magnitudo, magnitudinis, f., size, great size (magnitude)
celeritas, celeritatis, f., speed, swiftness (celerity, accelerator)
virtus, virtutis, f., courage, valor (virtue)
natio, nationis, f., nation (national)
consilium, consilii or consili, n., plan, advice (council)
pater, patris, m., father (paternal)
cera, cerae, f., wax (ceramics)
ala, alae, f., wing (alar)
sol, solis, m., sun (solar)

Adjectives

medius, media, medium, middle, middle of (medium)
summus, summa, summum, greatest, highest, top of (summit, sum)

Verb

volo, volare, fly (volatile)

Adverb

diu, long, for a long time

Conjunctions

-que, and
et...et, both...and

Preposition

circum, around, about (circumnavigate)

READING GRAMMAR

A. As you notice in the reading, the Preposition **in** (in, on) may stand after the Adjective and before the Noun.

   parva in insula, on a small island   **medio in caelo,** in the middle of the sky

B. The Conjunction **-que** (and) never stands alone, but is added to the second of two similarly used words or phrases. **-que** is the same as **et** in front of a word.

   vir feminaque, the man and the woman   **pueris puellisque,** to the boys and girls

C. The "of" in "in the middle of" or "top of" is part of the Adjective and therefore does not affect the case of the Noun. The Noun has whatever case it would have anyway and the Adjective simply agrees with the Noun.

   in caelo, in the sky   **medio in caelo,** in the middle of the sky
   in terra, on the land   **in summa terra,** on the top of the land

D. These rules are helpful in remembering the gender of some **i-declension** Nouns.
1. Nouns in -or are usually masculine. **labor**
2. Nouns in -io are usually feminine. **natio**
3. Nouns in -tudo, -tus, or -tas are feminine. **magnitudo, virtus, celeritas**

CHEMICAL ELEMENTS

The following are some of the Chemical Elements, with their Latin derivations.

Calcium Ca from **calx, calcis**, lime.

Carbon C from **carbo**, coal.

Copper Cu from **cuprum**, derived from the island Cyprus, anciently renowned for its copper mines.

Gold Au from **aurum**, gold.

Iron Fe from **ferrum**, iron.

Lead Pb from **plumbum**, lead.

Radium Ra from **radius**, ray, because of the alpha, beta, and gamma rays.

Silicon Si from **silex, silicis**, flint.

Silver Ag from **argentum**, silver.

Tellurium Te from **tellus, telluris**, earth.

PRACTICE EXERCISES

No. 71. Give the English for the following.

1. dei et deae
2. deus deaque
3. tenemus et damus
4. tenebat dabatque
5. hominem et feminas
6. hominum feminarumque
7. ad solem et lunam
8. ad solem lunamque
9. ex mare et terra
10. ex terra mareque

No. 72. Translate these phrases.

1. **in mediis viis**
2. **multis in oppidis**
3. **bello in magno**
4. **in summis aedificiis**
5. **parte in bona**
6. **in oceanis latis**
7. **multis in terris**
8. **medio in caelo**
9. **summo in mare**
10. **medio in oceano**

No. 73. Translate these phrases.

1. ad mare
2. ex urbibus
3. cum patribus suis
4. ante forum
5. post templum
6. de arca
7. sine consilio
8. trans oceanum
9. per maria
10. ob alas
11. pro regina tua
12. contra populum
13. inter hostes
14. ab viris
15. ab oppidis
16. ante castra
17. per pericula
18. ad dominum
19. trans agrum
20. de pace

No. 74. Give the English for these Verbs.

1. erit
2. terrebitur
3. volabat
4. natabit
5. dolent
6. portamur
7. tenebatur
8. amabimur
9. movebo
10. laudabantur
11. pugnabat
12. locabis
13. vocabor
14. monebamur
15. laborabunt
16. incitantur
17. debebit
18. parant
19. curabantur
20. liberaberis

No. 75. Translate these Vocatives and Appositives.

1. **Homo, avunculus meus**
2. **Amici boni**
3. **Fili bone**
4. **Nationum, Italiae Germaniaeque**
5. **Ob pecuniam, praemium**
6. **Feminarum, reginarum**
7. **Vir clare**
8. **Puer, servus**
9. **Puellis, filiis meis**
10. **Pater noster**

CHAPTER 17

READING

Proserpina

1. Ceres, dea frumenti, filiam, Proserpinam, habebat.
2. Pluto, deus Inferorum, Proserpinam in agro videt et ad Inferos Proserpinam portat.
3. Quod filiam suam non videbat, Ceres, mater, dolebat.
4. Quod Ceres misera erat, frumentum in agris agricolarum non erat.
5. Tum Iuppiter vitam populi in terra servat quod Mercurium vocat et Mercurius pro Iove ad Plutonem nuntium portat.
6. Iuppiter movebatur et agricolis auxilium dabat.
7. Tum Proserpina cum Iove non semper manebat, sed in terra partem anni habebat.
8. Cum Proserpina in terra erat, Ceres laeta erat et agricolis copiam magnam frumenti dabat, sed cum Proserpina sub terra erat Ceres misera erat et frumentum non erat.

Proserpina

1. Ceres, the goddess of grain, had a daughter, Proserpina.
2. Pluto, god of Those Below, saw Proserpina in a field and carried Proserpina to Those Below.
3. Because she did not see her daughter, Ceres, the mother, grieved.
4. Because Ceres was unhappy, there was not grain in the farmers' fields.
5. Then Jupiter saved the lives of the people on earth because he called Mercury and Mercury carried a message for Jupiter to Pluto.
6. Jupiter was moved and gave help to the farmers.
7. Then Proserpina did not always stay with Jupiter, but had part of the year on earth.
8. When Proserpina was on the earth, Ceres was happy and gave a great plenty of grain to the farmers, but when Proserpina was under the earth Ceres was unhappy and there was not grain.

Colosseum

1. Romani in urbe sua aedificia multa habebant.
2. Colosseum bene amabant quod ludos ibi spectabant.
3. Colosseum erat magnum amphitheatrum et etiam nunc stat.
4. Milites Romani bello servos captivosque obtinebant.
5. Captivi, gladiatores, gladiis suis contra homines aut contra animalia ibi pugnabant.
6. Multi captivi virtutem magnam habebant et liberabantur quod bene pugnabant.

The Colosseum

1. The Romans had many buildings in their city.
2. They liked the Colosseum very much because they watched the games there.
3. The Colosseum was a large amphitheater and is standing even now.
4. The Roman soldiers secured slaves and captives in war.
5. The captives, as gladiators, fought there with their swords against men or against animals.
6. Many captives had great courage and were freed because they fought well.

READING VOCABULARY

Verbs

specto, spectare, spectavi, spectatus, look at, watch (spectacle)

obtineo, obtinere, obtinui, obtentus, secure, obtain (obtainable)

Preposition

sub, under, below, at the foot of (subordinate)
1. With the Accusative Case after Verbs showing motion.
2. With the Ablative Case after Verbs showing rest.

Nouns

annus, anni, m., year (annual)

mater, matris, f., mother (maternal)

Inferi, Inferorum, m. pl., Those Below, the shades of Hades

Ceres, Cereris, f., Ceres (cereal)

Proserpina, Proserpinae, f., Proserpina

Mercurius, Mercuri, m., Mercury (mercurial)

Iuppiter, Iovis, m., Jupiter (jovial)

Pluto, Plutonis, m., Pluto (plutonium)

animal, animalis, n., animal (**animalium**)

captivus, captivi, m., captive (captivity)

amphitheatrum, amphitheatri, n., amphitheater (amphitheatrical)

gladiator, gladiatoris, m., gladiator (gladiatorial)

Colosseum, Colossei, n., the Colosseum (colossal)

READING GRAMMAR

You have already had two of the Principal Parts of Verbs:

1. **amo, habeo**   First Person Singular Present Active Tense.
2. **amare, habere** Present Active Infinitive.

A. The first two Principal Parts are used to form the tenses you have had so far:
1. Present Tense, Active and Passive
2. Imperfect Tense, Active and Passive
3. Future Tense, Active and Passive

B. The second Principal Part shows the conjugation to which the Verb belongs:
1. **amare**, a-conjugation
2. **habere**, e-conjugation

C. The third Principal Part is the First Person Singular Perfect Active Tense.

1. **amavi**, a-conjugation   I have loved
                              I have liked
2. **habui**, e-conjugation   I have had
                              I have held

D. The fourth Principal Part is the Perfect Passive Participle.

1. **amatus**, a-conjugation having been loved
                             having been liked
2. **habitus**, e-conjugation having been had
                             having been held

Most of the **a-conjugation** Verbs form their Principal parts like **amo**:

amo, amare, amavi, amatus

Those that do not are:

do, dare, dedi, datus   give

iuvo, iuvare, iuvi, iutus help, aid

sto, stare, steti, status stand

Many of the **e-conjugation** Verbs form their Principal Parts like **habeo**.

habeo, habere, habui, habitus

Of those you have met so far, these do not:

maneo, manere, mansi, mansus   remain, stay

moveo, movere, movi, motus   move

video, videre, vidi, visus   see

The Principal Parts of **sum** are: **sum, esse, fui, futurus**

futurus is the Future Active Participle—about to be

PREFIXES

These Latin Prepositions are commonly used as prefixes.

e, ex, out. **exspecto**, look out for, wait for, expect.

per, through; thoroughly, very. **perduco**, lead through. **pervenio**, arrive (come thoroughly).

inter, between. **interpono**, put between.

in, in, on; into; not. **invenio**, discover (come on).

infirmus, weak (not firm, not strong).

trans, across. **transmitto**, send across.

PRACTICE EXERCISES

No. 76. Give the Present Active Infinitive of these Verbs and the English translation.

1. voco	5. sum	9. curo	13. terreo	17. servo
2. debeo	6. moneo	10. doleo	14. adoro	18. laudo
3. ambulo	7. timeo	11. nuntio	15. moveo	19. do
4. sto	8. narro	12. volo	16. paro	20. video

No. 77. Give the third Principal Part, the First Person Singular Perfect Active Tense, and the translation.

1. paro	5. libero	9. habito	13. do	17. timeo
2. incito	6. loco	10. moneo	14. teneo	18. nato
3. aro	7. terreo	11. propero	15. servo	19. moveo
4. debeo	8. aedifico	12. habeo	16. monstro	20. maneo

No. 78. Give the fourth Principal Part, the Perfect Passive Participle, and the translation.

1. amo	5. moneo	9. occupo	13. servo	17. moveo
2. habeo	6. exspecto	10. porto	14. iuvo	18. specto
3. libero	7. narro	11. do	15. video	19. obtineo
4. neco	8. terreo	12. moneo	16. adoro	20. loco

No. 79. Translate the following into English.

1. Et mater tua et pater vester de virtute consilium dabant.
2. Medio in oppido erant aedificia multa.
3. Fama de natione mea ab nuntiis portabitur.
4. Puella puerque sub aqua natant.
5. Circum urbem ambulare et multa videre debemus.
6. Nonne multa mala memoria tenes?
7. Sol summa in aqua esse videbatur.
8. Nationes Europae non semper pugnabunt.
9. Nautae in maribus oceanisque navigant.
10. Milites Romani virtutem magnam habent.

FOURTH REVIEW SECTION (CHAPTERS 14–17)

VOCABULARY REVIEW

NOUNS

1. ala	16. dictator	31. miles	1. wing	16. dictator	31. soldier
2. amphitheatrum	17. donum	32. natio	2. amphitheater	17. gift	32. nation
3. animal	18. gladiator	33. pars	3. animal	18. gladiator	33. part
4. annus	19. homo	34. pater	4. year	19. man	34. father
5. caedes	20. Horatius	35. pax	5. slaughter	20. Horatius	35. peace
6. captivus	21. hostis	36. pecunia	6. captive	21. enemy	36. money
7. caput	22. Icarus	37. Pluto	7. head	22. Icarus	37. Pluto
8. celeritas	23. Inferi	38. pons	8. speed, swiftness	23. Those Below	38. bridge
9. cera	24. Iuppiter	39. Proserpina	9. wax	24. Jupiter	39. Proserpina
10. Ceres	25. labor	40. sagitta	10. Ceres	25. work, toil, labor	40. arrow
11. Cincinnatus	26. littera	41. sagittarius	11. Cincinnatus	26. letter	41. archer
12. Colosseum	27. magnitudo	42. sol	12. the Colosseum	27. size, great size	42. sun
13. consilium	28. mare	43. stella	13. plan, advice	28. sea	43. star
14. Creta	29. mater	44. urbs	14. Crete	29. mother	44. city
15. Daedalus	30. Mercurius	45. virtus	15. Daedalus	30. Mercury	45. courage, valor

ADJECTIVES

| 1. medius | 2. robustus | 3. summus | 1. middle, middle of | 2. strong, robust | 3. greatest, highest, top of |

VERBS

| 1. doleo | 3. obtineo | 5. terreo | 1. grieve | 3. secure, obtain | 5. frighten, terrify, scare |
| 2. moveo | 4. specto | 6. volo | 2. move | 4. look at, watch | 6. fly |

ADVERBS

| 1. diu | 2. mox | 3. semper | 1. long, for a long time | 2. soon, presently | 3. always |

PREPOSITIONS

| 1. a, ab | 2. circum | 3. inter | 4. sub | 1. by; away from, from | 2. around, about | 3. among, between | 4. under |

CONJUNCTIONS

| 1. aut | 2. et . . . et | 3. -que | 1. or | 2. both . . . and | 3. and |

PRACTICE EXERCISES

No. 80. Complete these Infinitives by filling in the correct vowel.

1. dol_____re	6. d_____re	11. deb_____re	16. par_____re
2. terr_____re	7. spect_____re	12. tim_____re	17. occup_____re
3. mov_____re	8. vol_____re	13. hab_____re	18. st_____re
4. voc_____re	9. laud_____re	14. vid_____re	19. iuv_____re
5. obtin_____re	10. man_____re	15. nec_____re	20. mon_____re

No. 81. Fill in the missing principal part.

1. specto, spectare, _____, spectatus
2. curo, _____, curavi, curatus
3. _____, monere, monui, monitus
4. do, dare, _____, datus
5. moveo, movere, movi, _____

6. paro, parare, _____, paratus
7. servo, servare, servavi, _____
8. terreo, terrere, terrui, _____
9. _____, habitare, habitavi, habitatus
10. laudo, _____, laudavi, laudatus

No. 82. Translate these phrases.

1. animalium hominumque
2. ab patre
3. a matribus
4. mare stellamque
5. patres matresque
6. celeritatis magnitudinisque
7. a Mercurio
8. ab militibus
9. a Plutone
10. bellum paxque

No. 83. Translate these Verb forms.

1. laudabatur	6. obtinebimus	11. occupantur	16. parabamur
2. dolebunt	7. videris	12. timebantur	17. debebitur
3. monebamur	8. iuvabatis	13. parabitur	18. curabaris
4. necantur	9. habebo	14. dabis	19. spectabamur
5. vocamini	10. moveberis	15. servaris	20. terrebunt

EUTROPIUS

Very little is known about Eutropius except that he held official positions in Rome and the provinces, and may have been a secretary to the Emperor Constantine. Of his works, the only one extant is the **Breviarium**, a brief history of Rome from the founding of the city in 753 B.C. to 364 A.D.

Hic quoque ingens bellum civile commovit cogente uxore Cleopatra, regina Aegypti, dum cupiditate muliebri optat etiam in urbe regnare. Victus est ab Augusto navali pugna clara et inlustri apud Actium, qui locus in Epiro est, ex qua fugit in Aegyptum et desperatis rebus, cum omnes ad Augustum transirent, ipse se interemit. Cleopatra sibi aspidem admisit et veneno eius exstincta est. Aegyptus per Octavianum Augustum imperio Romano adiecta est praepositusque ei C. Cornelius Gallus. Hunc primum Aegyptus Romanum iudicem habuit.

He (Antony) also stirred up a great Civil War, with his wife Cleopatra, queen of Egypt, urging it, since she hoped, with a womanly desire, to rule also in the City (Rome). He was defeated by Augustus in a famous and glorious naval battle near Actium, which is a place in Epirus, from which he escaped to Egypt and, because his future was without hope, since everyone was going over to the side of Augustus, he killed himself. Cleopatra let a snake bite her and died from its poison. Egypt was added to the Roman Empire by Octavius Augustus and Gaius Cornelius Gallus was put in command of it. Egypt had him as its first Roman judge.

Breviarii, Liber VII, vii

Breviarium, Book 7, 7

Psalmus David, cum fugeret a facie Absalom filii sui

Domine, quid multiplicati sunt qui tribulant me?
Multi insurgunt adversum me;
multi dicunt animae meae:
Non est salus ipsi in Deo eius.
Tu autem, Domine, susceptor meus es,
gloria mea et exaltans caput meum.
Voce mea ad Dominum clamavi,
et exaudivit me de monte sancto suo.
Ergo dormivi et soporatus sum
et exsurrexi, quia Dominus suscepit me.
Non timebo milia populi circumdantis me.

Exsurge, Domine, salvum me fac, Deus meus;
quoniam tu percussisti omnes adversantes mihi sine causa,
dentes peccatorum contrivisti.
Domini est salus, et super populum tuum benedictio tua.

A Psalm of David, when he fled from Absalom his son

Lord, how are they increased that trouble me!

Many are they that rise up against me;
many there be which say of my soul:
There is no help for him in God.
But thou, O Lord, art a shield for me;
my glory, and the lifter up of mine head.
I cried unto the Lord with my voice,
and he heard me out of his holy hill.
I laid me down and slept;
I awaked; for the Lord sustained me.
I will not be afraid of ten thousands of people, that have set themselves against me round about.
Arise, O Lord; save me, O my God;
for thou hast smitten all mine enemies upon the cheek bone;
thou hast broken the teeth of the ungodly.
Salvation belongeth unto the Lord; thy blessing is upon thy people.

Liber Psalmorum iii

Psalm 3

CHAPTER 18

READING

Libri Sibyllini

1. Inter antiquos erat fabula de libris Sibyllinis.
2. Tarquinius Superbus urbem Romam regnabat.
3. Femina ad Tarquinium libros novem portavit et pro libris pecuniam rogavit.
4. Tarquinius feminae pecuniam non dedit.
5. Femina in igni libros tres tum locavit.
6. Pro sex libris pretium librorum novem rogabat.
7. Tarquinius feminae pecuniam non dedit.
8. Postquam femina in igni libros sex locaverat Tarquinius feminae pro libris pecuniam dedit quod audacia feminae movebatur.
9. Libri erant libri Sibyllini.
10. Cum populus Romanus periculo incitabatur aut cum Roma oppugnabatur ad libros properabant.
11. Libri Romanis auxilium multum semper dabant.
12. Erantne libri deorum?

The Sibylline Books

1. Among the ancients there was a story about the Sibylline books.
2. Tarquin the Proud was ruling the city of Rome.
3. A woman brought nine books to Tarquin and asked for money for the books.
4. Tarquin did not give the money to the woman.
5. The woman then put three books in the fire.
6. For the six books she asked the price of the nine books.
7. Tarquin did not give the money to the woman.
8. After the woman had placed six books in the fire, Tarquin gave the money to the woman for the books because he was moved by the woman's boldness.
9. The books were the Sibylline books.
10. When the Roman people were aroused by danger or when Rome was being attacked they hurried to the books.
11. The books always gave much help to the Romans.
12. Were they the books of the gods?

READING VOCABULARY

Nouns

liber, libri, m., book (library)

ignis, ignis, m., fire (ignium) (ignite)

pretium, pretii or preti, n., price (precious)

audacia, audaciae, f., boldness, bravery, daring (audacity)

Tarquinius, Tarquini, m., Tarquin

Adjectives

Sibyllinus, Sibyllina, Sibyllinum, Sibylline

superbus, superba, superbum, proud (superb)

sex, six (sextet)

novem, nine (November)

Verb

rogo, rogare, rogavi, rogatus, ask, ask for (interrogate)

Conjunction

postquam, after, when

READING GRAMMAR

The three perfect tenses (perfect, pluperfect, and future perfect) are based on the third principal part in the Active.

A. The Perfect tense shows action completed in the past—*I have loved*—and the third principal part is the first person singular of the Perfect tense.

a-conjugation	I have loved; I loved	**e-conjugation**	I have had; I had
amavi	I have loved	habui	I have had
amavisti	you have loved	habuisti	you have had
amavit	he, she, it has loved	habuit	he, she, it has had
amavimus	we have loved	habuimus	we have had
amavistis	you have loved	habuistis	you have had
amaverunt	they have loved	habuerunt	they have had

B. The Pluperfect tense shows action completed at a definite point of time in the past—*I had loved*—.

a-conjugation	I had loved	**e-conjugation**	I had had
amaveram	I had loved	habueram	I had had
amaveras	you had loved	habueras	you had had
amaverat	he, she, it had loved	habuerat	he, she, it had had
amaveramus	we had loved	habueramus	we had had
amaveratis	you had loved	habueratis	you had had
amaverant	they had loved	habuerant	they had had

C. The Future Perfect tense shows action to be completed before a definite point of time in the future—*I shall have loved*—.

a-conjugation	I shall have loved	**e-conjugation**	I shall have had
amavero	I shall have loved	habuero	I shall have had
amaveris	you will have loved	habueris	you will have had
amaverit	he, she, it will have loved	habuerit	he, she, it will have had
amaverimus	we shall have loved	habuerimus	we shall have had
amaveritis	you will have loved	habueritis	you will have had
amaverint	they will have loved	habuerint	they will have had

D. The Verb **sum** is regular in the Perfect tenses.

PERFECT TENSE		**PLUPERFECT TENSE**		**FUTURE PERFECT TENSE**	
fui	I have been	fueram	I had been	fuero	I shall have been
fuisti	you have been	fueras	you had been	fueris	you will have been
fuit	he, she, it has been	fuerat	he, she, it had been	fuerit	he, she, it will have been
fuimus	we have been	fueramus	we had been	fuerimus	we shall have been
fuistis	you have been	fueratis	you had been	fueritis	you will have been
fuerunt	they have been	fuerant	they had been	fuerint	they will have been

FAMILIAR ABBREVIATIONS

fl. or **flor., floruit,** he (she) flourished. Used with the date at which an artist produced his work.

I.H.S., In hoc signo, In this sign. or **Iesus Hominum Salvator,** Jesus Saviour of Men.

I.N.R.I., Iesus Nazarenus, Rex Iudaeorum, Jesus of Nazareth, King of the Jews.

pinx., pinxit, he (she) painted it.

sculp., sculpsit, he (she) carved it.

op. cit., opere citato, in the work cited. Used in footnotes instead of repeating the title of the book referred to.

ibid. or **ib., ibidem,** in the same place. Used in footnotes, if the reference is the same as one made just previously.

PRACTICE EXERCISES

No. 84. Complete these principal parts.

1. ambulo, ambulare, _____, ambulatus
2. laudo, laudare, _____, laudatus
3. moneo, monere, _____, monitus
4. debeo, debere, _____, debitus
5. porto, portare, _____, portatus
6. servo, servare, _____, servatus
7. voco, vocare, _____, vocatus
8. moveo, movere, _____, motus
9. do, dare, _____, datus
10. rogo, rogare, _____, rogatus

No. 85. Translate these Perfect tenses.

1. rogavit
2. spectaverunt
3. monuimus
4. iuvi
5. fuisti
6. necavisti
7. narravistis
8. habitavi
9. vidi
10. timuerunt
11. doluisti
12. habuistis
13. debuimus
14. laboraverunt
15. superavisti
16. monstravit
17. narraverunt
18. occupavistis
19. paravimus
20. volavit

No. 86. Translate these Pluperfect tenses.

1. ambulaveram
2. adoraverant
3. araverat
4. moverant
5. manseramus
6. videratis
7. paraveras
8. dederas
9. tenueratis
10. steteram
11. paraverat
12. locaverant
13. incitaveras
14. curaveratis
15. nataveram
16. dolueramus
17. rogaverat
18. spectaverant
19. viderat
20. vocaveratis

No. 87. Translate these Future Perfect tenses.

1. amaveris
2. curaverit
3. laudavero
4. locaverimus
5. habuerint
6. terruerit
7. moverit
8. dederint
9. steteris
10. tenuerit
11. vocaverimus
12. servavero
13. portaverit
14. paraverint
15. nuntiaveris
16. narraverimus
17. habueritis
18. debuerit
19. adoraverint
20. ambulaveris

CHAPTER 19

READING

Reges Romae

1. Urbs Roma septem reges habuit. Romulus urbem parvam in monte Palatino aedificavit.
2. Urbi nomen Romam dedit. Romulus ob sapientiam suam urbem bene regnabat.
3. Populo consilium bonum dedit.
4. Quod in urbe non erant mulieres Romani finitimos suos ad ludos vocaverunt.
5. Tum feminas puellasque pugna obtinuerunt.
6. Et Sabini et socii sui contra Romanos bella multa pugnaverunt, sed copiae Romanae hostes superaverunt.
7. Postea Numa Pompilius erat rex Romanorum.
8. Pacem amavit et populo erat gratus quod Romanis leges multas bonasque dedit.
9. Aedificia templaque etiam aedificavit.
10. Tum Romani ab Anco Marcio regnabantur.
11. Multos bello superavit et murum circum montem Caelium aedificavit.
12. Postea Roma a Prisco Tarquinio regnabatur.
13. Circum Maximum, ubi Romani ludos habebant, aedificavit.
14. Contra Sabinos bellum pugnavit et agris finitimis et monte Capitolio fines urbis auxit.
15. Proximus rex, Servius Tullius, Sabinos superavit.
16. Colles Romae ad septem auxit. Circum colles murum et circum murum fossas aedificavit.
17. Multi in urbe habitaverunt et multi erant agricolae in agris et post colles et post flumen.

The Kings of Rome

1. The city of Rome had seven kings. Romulus built a small city on the Palatine mount.
2. To the city he gave the name Rome. Romulus ruled the city well because of his wisdom.
3. He gave good advice to the people.
4. Because there were not women in the city, the Romans called their neighbors to games.
5. Then they got women and girls by a fight.
6. Both the Sabines and their allies fought many wars against the Romans, but the Roman forces conquered the enemy.
7. Afterwards, Numa Pompilius was king of the Romans.
8. He liked peace and he was pleasing to the people because he gave many and good laws to the Romans.
9. He also built buildings and temples.
10. Then the Romans were ruled by Ancus Marcius.
11. He defeated many people in war and he built a wall around the Caelian mount.
12. Afterwards, Rome was ruled by Tarquinius Priscus.
13. He built the Circus Maximus, where the Romans held their games.
14. He fought a war against the Sabines and increased the territory of the city by neighboring fields and the Capitoline mount.
15. The next king, Servius Tullius, overcame the Sabines.
16. He increased the hills of Rome to seven. Around the hills he built a wall and around the wall ditches.
17. Many people lived in the city and many were farmers in the fields both in back of the hills and in back of the river.

Reges Romae	The Kings of Rome
18. Tarquinius Superbus erat ultimus rex Romae, sed bene diuque regnavit.	18. Tarquin the Proud was the last king of Rome, but he ruled well and for a long time.
19. Copiae Tarquini Superbi bella multa pugnaverunt et nationes proximas Romae superaverunt.	19. The troops of Tarquin the Proud fought many wars and defeated the nations next to Rome.

READING VOCABULARY

Nouns

collis, collis, m., hill (collium)
flumen, fluminis, n., river, stream (flume)
finis, finis, m., end, border (finium)
  In the plural, territory, boundaries. (finish)
rex, regis, m., king (regal)
nomen, nominis, n., name (nominative)
mulier, mulieris, f., woman
pugna, pugnae, f., fight
mons, montis, m., mountain, mount (montium) (monticule)
lex, legis, f., law (legal)
murus, muri, m., wall (mural)

Adjectives

proximus, proxima, proximum, next, nearest (approximate)
ultimus, ultima, ultimum, last, farthest (ultimate)
septem, seven (September)

Verb

augeo, augere, auxi, auctus, increase, enlarge (augment)

Adverb

postea, afterwards

READING GRAMMAR

A. The Perfect Passive Participle is an Adjective and therefore must agree with the word it modifies in *gender, number,* and *case.* When it is used with the Verb **sum** to form the Perfect Passive tenses, it is always in the Nominative Case, but must agree with the subject in gender and number.

> **mulier amata est,** the woman has been loved
> **mulieres amatae sunt,** the women have been loved
> **vir amatus est,** the man has been loved
> **viri amati sunt,** the men have been loved
> **nomen vocatum est,** the name has been called
> **nomina vocata sunt,** the names have been called

B. The Perfect Passive tense is formed by the fourth principal part with **sum.**

amatus sum, *I have been loved*

habitus sum, *I have been held*

a-conjugation

amatus, a, um sum	I have been loved
amatus, a, um es	you have been loved
amatus, a, um est	he, she, it has been loved
amati, ae, a sumus	we have been loved
amati, ae, a estis	you have been loved
amati, ae, a sunt	they have been loved

e-conjugation

habitus, a, um sum	I have been held
habitus, a, um es	you have been held
habitus, a, um est	he, she, it has been held
habiti, ae, a sumus	we have been held
habiti, ae, a estis	you have been held
habiti, ae, a sunt	they have been held

C. The Pluperfect Passive tense is formed by the fourth principal part and **eram**.

amatus eram, *I had been loved*   **habitus eram,** *I had been held*

a-conjugation   **e-conjugation**

amatus, a, um eram	I had been loved	**habitus, a, um eram**	I had been held
amatus, a, um eras	you had been loved	**habitus, a, um eras**	you had been held
amatus, a, um erat	he, she, it had been loved	**habitus, a, um erat**	he, she, it had been held
amati, ae, a eramus	we had been loved	**habiti, ae, a eramus**	we had been held
amati, ae, a eratis	you had been loved	**habiti, ae, a eratis**	you had been held
amati, ae, a erant	they had been loved	**habiti, ae, a erant**	they had been held

D. The Future Perfect Passive tense is formed by the fourth principal part and **ero**.

amatus ero, *I shall have been loved*   **habitus ero,** *I shall have been held*

a-conjugation   **e-conjugation**

amatus, a, um ero	I shall have been loved	**habitus, a, um ero**	I shall have been held
amatus, a, um eris	you will have been loved	**habitus, a, um eris**	you will have been held
amatus, a, um erit	he, she, it will have been loved	**habitus, a, um erit**	he, she, it will have been held
amati, ae, a erimus	we shall have been loved	**habiti, ae, a erimus**	we shall have been held
amati, ae, a eritis	you will have been loved	**habiti, ae, a eritis**	you will have been held
amati, ae, a erunt	they will have been loved	**habiti, ae, a erunt**	they will have been held

FAMILIAR PHRASES

carpe diem, seize the opportunity.

cave canem, beware the dog.

ex libris, from the library of. Used often on bookplates.

ex officio, because of an office (held previously).

in toto, in the whole; completely.

per capita, by heads; per person or individual.

post mortem, after death.

exeunt omnes, all go out. Used as a stage direction.

ultimatum, the last thing; the farthest thing. Used for the final terms offered by one party to another.

PRACTICE EXERCISES

No. 88. Give the English for these Perfect tenses.

1. fuerunt	6. laudatae sunt	11. vocati sumus	16. timuisti
2. ambulavit	7. monitus sum	12. natavi	17. paratus est
3. portatus est	8. debuimus	13. servatae estis	18. locata sunt
4. amati sunt	9. stetistis	14. nuntiatum est	19. laudaverunt
5. curata es	10. narratum est	15. moti sunt	20. movistis

No. 89. Give the English for these Pluperfect tenses.

1. dederant	6. pugnaverat	11. parati erant	16. monuerat
2. moverat	7. laudata eram	12. occupaveras	17. habueratis
3. territus erat	8. curati erant	13. liberati eratis	18. tenueras
4. manseratis	9. amata eras	14. necatus erat	19. iuti eramus
5. tenueras	10. incitati eratis	15. servati eramus	20. adoraverant

No. 90. Give the English for these Future Perfect tenses.

1. monuero	6. terrueris	11. dederimus	16. armatus eris
2. fuerit	7. moverimus	12. steterint	17. curati erunt
3. portatum erit	8. visi eritis	13. fuerimus	18. locatum erit
4. moniti erunt	9. timuerit	14. necati eritis	19. fuerint
5. habuerint	10. mota erit	15. laudatae erimus	20. servata erit

No. 91. Translate these Verb forms.

1. habitum erat	6. debitum erit	11. moniti sunt	16. monitus est
2. videro	7. debuerant	12. rogatae sumus	17. steterat
3. oppugnata erunt	8. exspectavisti	13. spectaverunt	18. dati erant
4. laudata eris	9. vidistis	14. moti sumus	19. narraverunt
5. portata eras	10. monstratum est	15. paraveramus	20. tenuero

---

CHAPTER 20

READING

Labores Herculis

1. Pythia ab Apolline docebatur et populo consilium dei dedit.
2. Hercules a femina amorem suum Apollinis demonstrare iussus est.
3. Hercules ad urbem regis, Eurysthei, properavit. Ibi Eurystheus Herculi labores duodecim dedit.
4. Sunt multae fabulae de laboribus Herculis.
5. Duodecim annos laborabat quod erat servus regis, sed Hercules de laboribus suis minime dolebat.
6. Corpus robustum habebat et regem laboremque non timebat.
7. A rege diu tenebatur, sed post duodecim annos liberatus est quod regem bene iuverat.
8. Deo Apollini amorem suum demonstraverat.

Poma Aurea Hesperidum

1. Hercules pro rege, Eurystheo, bene laboravit, sed etiam tum non erat liber et domi non mansit.

The Labors of Hercules

1. Pythia was taught by Apollo and gave the advice of the god to the people.
2. Hercules was ordered by the woman to show his love for Apollo.
3. Hercules hurried to the city of the king, Eurystheus. There Eurystheus gave Hercules twelve labors.
4. There are many stories about the labors of Hercules.
5. He labored for twelve years because he was the servant of the king, but Hercules grieved very little about his labors.
6. He had a strong body and did not fear the king and the work.
7. He was held for a long time by the king, but after twelve years he was freed because he had helped the king well.
8. He had shown the god, Apollo, his love.

The Golden Apples of the Hesperides

1. Hercules worked well for the king, Eurystheus, but even then he was not free and did not stay at home.

Poma Aurea Hesperidum	The Golden Apples of the Hesperides
2. Rex Herculem poma aurea ex horto Hesperidum obtinere iussit.	2. The king ordered Hercules to get the golden apples from the garden of the Hesperides.
3. Hesperides erant filiae pulchrae Atlantis et in loco ultimo in fini terrae ruri habitabant.	3. The Hesperides were the beautiful daughters of Atlas and lived in the country in the farthest place on the end of the earth.
4. Pro Iunone poma aurea ibi curabant.	4. They took care of the golden apples there for Juno.
5. Multi praemio pomorum moti erant, sed Hesperides poma semper bene servabant.	5. Many people had been moved by the reward of the apples, but the Hesperides always preserved the apples well.
6. Erat murus magnus altusque circum hortum ubi erant poma, atque ante hortum erat serpens.	6. There was a large and high wall around the garden where the apples were, and in front of the garden was a serpent.
7. Serpens capita multa habuit.	7. The serpent had many heads.
8. Hercules multa milia passuum ambulavit. Post annum ad hortum venit.	8. Hercules walked many miles. After a year he came to the garden.
9. Erat in fini ultimo terrae et proximus Oceano.	9. It was on the farthest end of the earth and next to the Ocean.
10. Hercules Atlantem, virum robustum et amicum, ibi vidit.	10. Hercules saw Atlas there, a strong and friendly man.
11. Auxilium rogavit.	11. He asked for help.

READING VOCABULARY

Nouns

corpus, corporis, n., body (corporal)
hora, horae, f., hour (horology)
amor, amoris, m., love (amorous)
Apollo, Apollinis, m., Apollo
Eurystheus, Eurysthei, m., Eurystheus
mille passus, a mile   milia passuum, miles
Hesperides, Hesperidum, f., the Hesperides
Atlas, Atlantis, m., Atlas
Iuno, Iunonis, f., Juno
Pythia, Pythiae, f., Pythia
Hercules, Herculis, m., Hercules
locus, loci, m., place, position. Sometimes neuter in the plural. (location, local)
serpens, serpentis, f., snake, serpent (serpentium) (serpentine)
hortus, horti, m., garden (horticulture)

Adjectives

duodecim, twelve (duodecimal)
aureus, aurea, aureum, golden, of gold (aureate)

Verbs

doceo, docere, docui, doctus, teach, show (docile, docent)
iubeo, iubere, iussi, iussus, order, command (jussive)
demonstro, demonstrare, demonstravi, demonstratus, point out, show (demonstrate)

Adverbs

domi, at home (domicile)
ruri, in the country (rural)
quam diu, how long

Preposition

in, into, onto   With the Accusative Case (in-, inhale)

READING GRAMMAR

A. Both the Accusative and Ablative Cases are used to show time.
 1. The Accusative Case shows *how long* something goes on.

> **multos annos,** for many years
> **duodecim horas,** for twelve hours

 2. The Ablative Case shows *when* something happens.

> **anno,** in (during) a year
> **hora,** in (during) an hour

B. Both the Accusative and Ablative Cases are used to show place.
 1. The Accusative Case shows *to* or *into* what place motion is directed, or *how far*.

> **ad urbem,** to the city
> **in oppidum,** into the town
> **multa milia passuum,** many miles, for many miles

 2. The Ablative Case shows *where* the place is, or *from where* the motion is directed.

> **in oppido,** in the town
> **ab oppido,** away from the town
> **de muro,** down from the wall
> **in mare,** on the sea
> **ex urbe,** out of the city

C. With the names of cities, towns, and small islands, and with the words **ruri** (in the country) and **domi** (at home), no Preposition is used.

> **Romam,** to Rome   **Roma,** from Rome

ACADEMIC DEGREES AND TERMS

The following are some of the Academic Degrees and terms used.

cum laude, with praise. Given with a diploma that has been earned with a grade of work higher than ordinary.

magna cum laude, with great praise.

summa cum laude, with highest praise.

Alumnus, pl. **Alumni,** male graduate or graduates.

Alumna, pl. **Alumnae,** female graduate or graduates.

Alma Mater, Foster Mother. Refers to one's school or college.

A.M. or **M.A., Artium Magister,** Master of Arts.

B.A. or **A.B., Baccalaureus Artium,** Bachelor of Arts.

B.Sc., Baccalaureus Scientiae, Bachelor of Science.

D.D., Divinitatis Doctor, Doctor of Divinity.

D.Litt. or **Litt.D., Doctor Litterarum,** Doctor of Literature or Letters.

M.D., Medicinae Doctor, Doctor of Medicine.

Ph.D., Philosophia Doctor, Doctor of Philosophy.

LL.D., Legum Doctor, Doctor of Laws.

D.M.D., Dentariae Medicinae Doctor, Doctor of Dental Medicine.

PRACTICE EXERCISES

No. 92. Give the English for these expressions of time.

1. multos annos
2. proximo anno
3. multas horas
4. proxima hora
5. septem horas
6. medio anno
7. sex horis
8. annos longos
9. hora
10. duodecim horas

No. 93. Give the English for these expressions of place.

1. ad urbes	6. ante forum	11. ex casa	16. sub muris
2. ex oppidis	7. post hortum	12. ruri	17. in fossam
3. Roma	8. in agro	13. domi	18. ab templo
4. Romam	9. in agros	14. ab flumine	19. e viis
5. in castra	10. de collibus	15. sub maribus	20. de sole

No. 94. Translate these Verbs.

1. videbo	5. fuerat	9. videmus	13. fuisti
2. pugnaverat	6. obtinebunt	10. spectatum est	14. oppugnabamur
3. stabatis	7. natabamus	11. movebitur	15. manserunt
4. laborabimus	8. erit	12. aedificata erant	

No. 95. Translate these sentences.

1. Proximo anno Romam movebimus.
2. Sex horas in urbe manserunt.
3. Medio in colle oppugnati erant.
4. Multas horas in Italia manebam.
5. Ibi erit horam.
6. Nonne multos annos laborabunt?
7. Ad oppidum multas horas longas ambulabat.
8. Ab rege non liberatus est.
9. Suntne in horto cum pueris?
10. Septem milia passuum ab urbe movi.

CHAPTER 21

READING

Poma Aurea Hesperidum (concl'd.)

1. Postquam Hercules auxilium petiverat, causam itineris sui ad finem terrae Atlantem docuit.
2. Atlas erat pater Hesperidum et Herculi de loco ubi erant poma aurea narravit, sed Atlas caelum in umeris suis tenebat.
3. Atlas Herculi caelum dedit et Herculem in umeris caelum tenere iussit.
4. Atlas ad hortum Hesperidum properavit.
5. Diu Hercules in umeris suis caelum tenebat. Diu Atlantem non viderat.

The Golden Apples of the Hesperides (concl'd.)

1. After Hercules had sought help, he showed Atlas the cause of his journey to the end of the earth.
2. Atlas was the father of the Hesperides and he told Hercules about the place where the golden apples were, but Atlas was holding the sky on his shoulders.
3. Atlas gave the sky to Hercules and he ordered Hercules to hold the sky on his shoulders.
4. Atlas hurried to the garden of the Hesperides.
5. For a long time Hercules held the sky on his shoulders. He had not seen Atlas for a long time.

Poma Aurea Hesperidum (concl'd.)

6. Hercules famam de Atlante non habuerat. Et timebat et dolebat.
7. Pretium pomorum erat certe magnum.
8. Post multas noctes Atlantem vidit et laetus erat.
9. Mox poma aurea habuit. Tum Atlas caelum in umeris suis locavit et Hercules erat liber.
10. Ad Graeciam cum pomis properavit.

The Golden Apples of the Hesperides (concl'd.)

6. Hercules had not had a report about Atlas. He was both afraid and grieving.
7. The price of the apples was certainly great.
8. After many nights he saw Atlas and he was happy.
9. Soon he had the golden apples. Then Atlas placed the sky on his own shoulders and Hercules was free.
10. He hurried to Greece with the apples.

Atalanta

1. Atalanta erat puella Graeciae et vero pulchra.
2. Multi viri contra eam cucurrerant, sed magnam celeritatem habebat et non superata erat.
3. Venus consilium habebat. Puella erat praemium victoriae et pedibus eos currere iussit.
4. Hippomenes contra eam currere paratus est.
5. Multi spectabant et eum incitabant.
6. Signum datum est.
7. Atalanta celeritatem suam demonstrabat. Paene volabat.
8. Quam longe ante eum currit!
9. Sed Venus Hippomeni viam ad victoriam docuerat. Ei poma aurea dederat.
10. Hippomenes pomum ad terram misit.
11. Atalanta ad moram movebatur.
12. Hippomenes celeritatem suam auxit.
13. Finis erat propinquus.
14. Venus, dea amoris, eum bene iuverat.
15. Hippomenes consilio donoque deae puellam superaverat.

Atalanta

1. Atalanta was a girl of Greece and truly beautiful.
2. Many men had raced against her, but she had great speed and had not been surpassed.
3. Venus had a plan. The girl was the reward of victory and she ordered them to run on foot.
4. Hippomenes was prepared to run against her.
5. Many were watching and urging him on.
6. The signal is given.
7. Atalanta was showing her speed. She was almost flying.
8. How far in front of him she runs!
9. But Venus had shown Hippomenes the way to victory. She had given him golden apples.
10. Hippomenes threw an apple to the ground.
11. Atalanta was moved toward delay.
12. Hippomenes increased his speed.
13. The end was near.
14. Venus, goddess of love, had helped him well.
15. Hippomenes had overtaken the girl by the plan and gift of the goddess.

READING VOCABULARY

Nouns

mora, morae, f., delay (moratorium)
nox, noctis, f., night (noctium) (nocturnal)
causa, causae, f., cause, reason (causeless)
iter, itineris, n., journey, march, way (itinerary)

umerus, umeri, m., shoulder (humerus)
pes, pedis, m., foot (pedal)
signum, signi, n., signal, standard (signify)
Atalanta, Atalantae, f., Atalanta
Hippomenes, Hippomenis, m., Hippomenes

Verbs	Adverb
duco, ducere, duxi, ductus, lead (conduct, aqueduct)	paene, almost, nearly
mitto, mittere, misi, missus, send (mission, manumit)	**Pronoun and Adjective**
peto, petere, petivi, petitus, seek, ask (petition)	is, ea, id, he, she, it; this, that
curro, currere, cucurri, cursus, run (current)	
dico, dicere, dixi, dictus, say, speak (diction)	

READING GRAMMAR

A. **e/i-conjugation** Verbs follow the same principles as those you have met so far, except in the Future Tense. The predominant vowels are **e** and **i**.

1. Principal Parts: **duco, ducere, duxi, ductus,** lead
2. Present Tense:

ACTIVE		PASSIVE	
I lead, am leading, do lead		I am being led, am led	
duco	ducimus	ducor	ducimur
ducis	ducitis	duceris	ducimini
ducit	ducunt	ducitur	ducuntur

3. Imperfect Tense:

ACTIVE		PASSIVE	
I was leading, led		I was being led, was led	
ducebam	ducebamus	ducebar	ducebamur
ducebas	ducebatis	ducebaris	ducebamini
ducebat	ducebant	ducebatur	ducebantur

4. Future Tense:

ACTIVE		PASSIVE	
I shall lead		I shall be led	
ducam	ducemus	ducar	ducemur
duces	ducetis	duceris	ducemini
ducet	ducent	ducetur	ducentur

5. Perfect Tense:

ACTIVE	PASSIVE
I have led, led	I have been led
duxi	ductus, a, um sum
duxisti, etc.	ductus, a, um es, etc.

6. Pluperfect Tense:

ACTIVE	PASSIVE
I had led	I had been led
duxeram	ductus, a, um eram
duxeras, etc.	ductus, a, um eras, etc.

7. Future Perfect Tense:

ACTIVE	PASSIVE
I shall have led	I shall have been led
duxero	ductus, a, um ero
duxeris, etc.	ductus, a, um eris, etc.

B. 1. **is, ea, id** is used as either a Pronoun or an Adjective. As a Pronoun it has the same gender and number as the Noun it replaces, but its case is determined by its use in the sentence.

Puerum video, I see the boy.   **Eum video,** I see him.
Is in casa est, He is in the house.

As a Pronoun, the singular means *he, she,* or *it* and the plural means *they.*

Nom.	is	he	ea	she	id	it
Gen.	eius	his	eius	her, hers	eius	its
Dat.	ei	to, for him	ei	to, for her	ei	to, for it
Acc.	eum	him	eam	her	id	it
Abl.	eo	from, with, by, in him	ea	from, with, by, in her	eo	from, with, by, in it

Nom.	ei or ii		eae		ea	they
Gen.	eorum		earum		eorum	their
Dat.	eis or iis		eis or iis		eis or iis	to, for them
Acc.	eos		eas		ea	them
Abl.	eis or iis		eis or iis		eis or iis	from, with, by, in them

2. As an Adjective, **is, ea, id** must be in the same gender, number and case as the noun it modifies.

is puer, this boy, that boy   **ea puella,** this girl, that girl   **id bellum,** this war, that war

As an Adjective, the singular means *this* or *that* and the plural means *these* or *those.*

Nom.	this, that	these, those
Gen.	of this, of that	of these, of those
Dat.	to, for this; to, for that	to, for these; to, for those
Acc.	this, that	these, those
Abl.	from, with, by, in this; from, with, by, in that	from, with, by, in these; from, with, by, in those

C. 1. The possessive form of the Pronoun **eius** does not refer to the subject.

> **Pomum eius videmus.**   We see his apple.

2. When the possessor is the same as the subject, the Adjective **suus** is used.

> **Pomum suum habet.**   He has his (own) apple.

ASSIMILATION

Some prefixes take on the first letter of the word to which they are attached. This process is called assimilation. Assimilation occurs with these prefixes:

> **ad**   ad and **pono** become **appono**, put to, put near
> **con**   con and **mitto** become **committo**, send together
> **in**   in and **mortalis** become **immortalis**, immortal

Sometimes there is a change to a different letter:

> **in** and **porto** become **importo**, carry in, bring in
> **con** and **pono** become **compono**, put together

You will notice that assimilation is a natural process leading to more ease in pronunciation.

PRACTICE EXERCISES

No. 96. Translate these Verb forms.

1. mittunt	6. parati erunt	11. iubebit	16. mittet
2. doctus sum	7. duxit	12. spectabamur	17. servavi
3. petimur	8. liberavisti	13. demonstratis	18. timueras
4. debet	9. adorabam	14. rogabunt	19. petiveratis
5. moniti eratis	10. miserit	15. ducebas	20. manserunt

No. 97. Translate these phrases.

1. ob iniuriam	4. in itinere	7. ab colle	10. in ripam
2. ex proeliis	5. e finibus	8. in litteris	
3. sex horas	6. ad Galliam	9. ab hominibus	

No. 98. Translate the following.

1. Eas peto.	6. Eum vidistis.	11. ea hora	16. eorum poma
2. eorum librorum	7. in eis locis	12. sua signa	17. suos reges
3. hortus eius	8. patri eius	13. ex eis urbibus	18. cum eis
4. Ea eis dedi.	9. Ab eo mittuntur.	14. eam mulierem	19. id iter
5. Is pugnabat.	10. Eos misisti.	15. Ab eis ducimur.	20. eam causam

No. 99. Change these Verb forms to the Active or Passive.

1. ducit	6. misisti	11. petiverunt	16. current
2. duxi	7. mittebantur	12. petiti erimus	17. cucurrit
3. ducebar	8. mittemini	13. petet	18. curritur
4. ducti sunt	9. missus es	14. petitur	19. currebant
5. ducam	10. miserat	15. petebaris	20. cursum erat

FIFTH REVIEW SECTION (CHAPTERS 18–21)

VOCABULARY REVIEW

NOUNS

1. amor	15. Hippomenes	29. murus	1. love	15. Hippomenes	29. wall
2. Apollo	16. hora	30. nomen	2. Apollo	16. hour	30. name
3. Atalanta	17. hortus	31. nox	3. Atalanta	17. garden	31. night
4. Atlas	18. ignis	32. pes	4. Atlas	18. fire	32. foot
5. audacia	19. iter	33. pomum	5. boldness, bravery, daring	19. journey, march, way	33. apple
6. causa	20. Iuno	34. pretium	6. cause, reason	20. Juno	34. price
7. collis	21. lex	35. pugna	7. hill	21. law	35. fight
8. corpus	22. liber	36. Pythia	8. body	22. book	36. Pythia
9. Eurystheus	23. locus	37. rex	9. Eurystheus	23. place	37. king
10. finis	24. mille passus	38. serpens	10. end, border	24. a mile	38. snake, serpent
11. fines	25. milia passuum	39. signum	11. territory	25. miles	39. signal, standard
12. flumen	26. mons	40. Tarquinius	12. river	26. mountain, mount	40. Tarquin
13. Hercules	27. mora	41. umerus	13. Hercules	27. delay	41. shoulder
14. Hesperides	28. mulier	42. Venus	14. the Hesperides	28. woman	42. Venus

ADJECTIVES

1. aureus	5. septem	9. ultimus	1. golden	5. seven	9. last, farthest
2. duodecim	6. sex	10. is, ea, id	2. twelve	6. six	10. this, that
3. novem	7. Sibyllinus		3. nine	7. Sibylline	
4. proximus	8. superbus		4. next, nearest	8. proud, haughty	

VERBS

1. augeo	5. doceo	9. peto	1. increase, enlarge	5. teach, show	9. seek
2. curro	6. duco	10. rogo	2. run	6. lead	10. ask, ask for
3. demonstro	7. iubeo		3. point out, show	7. order, command	
4. dico	8. mitto		4. speak, say	8. send	

ADVERBS

1. domi	3. postea	5. ruri	1. at home	3. afterwards	5. in the country
2. paene	4. quam diu		2. almost, nearly	4. how long	

PRONOUNS

1. is	2. ea	3. id	1. he	2. she	3. it

PREPOSITION

1. in	1. into, onto; in, on

CONJUNCTION

1. postquam	1. after, when

PRACTICE EXERCISES

No. 100. Give the English for these phrases.

1. in pedibus	4. ex agris	7. de corpore	10. Romam
2. ab colli	5. in ignem	8. ruri	11. domi
3. ad flumina	6. in muris	9. Roma	12. ex nocte

No. 101. Translate these Perfect Tenses.

1. fuerat	6. locaverunt	11. movimus	16. rogatus sum
2. regnavimus	7. data sunt	12. fuimus	17. stetit
3. rogatus est	8. misistis	13. incitati erant	18. vocavisti
4. portaveris	9. petitum erit	14. properaveratis	19. laudati erimus
5. dederunt	10. auctum erat	15. fuerint	20. habuerat

No. 102. Give the English for these phrases.

1. proximo anno	4. multo anno	7. eas noctes	10. ea hora
2. horas septem	5. sex annos	8. eos annos	
3. proximis horis	6. eo nocte	9. eo anno	

No. 103. Give the English for these Pronouns.

1. eius	4. ei	7. ea	10. eum
2. eos	5. id	8. eorum	11. ii
3. eae	6. eas	9. eis	12. eo

No. 104. Translate these Adjective phrases.

1. eum amorem	5. eis finibus	9. id corpus	13. eas leges
2. eius audaciae	6. eorum itinerum	10. eius loci	14. eo monte
3. ea nomina	7. ea poma	11. ei regi	15. eius signi
4. eas causas	8. ei mulieri	12. eam noctem	

MARCUS VALERIUS MARTIALIS

Martial was born in Spain about 40 A.D. and went to Rome as a young man. He was a master of the epigram, and his poems, depicting scenes of everyday life, are full of wit, freshness, and satire. Martial died about 103 A.D., after returning to Spain.

Non amo te, Sabidi, nec possum dicere quare; | I do not love thee, Sabidius, nor can I tell you why;

hoc tantum possum dicere: non amo te. | this only I can say: I do not love thee.

Epigrammaton Liber I, xxxii | Epigrams, 1, 32

Cras te victurum, cras dicis, Postume, semper.

Dic mihi, cras istud, Postume, quando venit?

Quam longe cras istud, ubi est? aut unde petendum?
Numquid apud Parthos Armeniosque latet?

Iam cras istud habet Priami vel Nestoris annos.

Cras istud quanti, dic mihi, posset emi?

Cras vives? Hodie iam vivere, Postume, serum est;
ille sapit, quisquis, Postume, vixit heri.

Epigrammaton Liber V, lviii

Tomorrow you will live, tomorrow you always say, Postumus.

Tell me, when, Postumus, is that tomorrow coming?

How far away is your tomorrow, where is it? or where must it be sought?
It doesn't lie hidden among the Parthians and Armenians, does it?

Already that tomorrow of yours has the years of Priam or Nestor.

Tell me, for how much could that tomorrow of yours be bought?

You will live tomorrow? Today it is already too late to live, Postumus;
he is wise, whoever has lived yesterday, Postumus.

Epigrams, 5, 58

Omnia tempus habent,
et suis spatiis transeunt universa sub caelo.
Tempus nascendi et tempus moriendi,
tempus plantandi et tempus evellendi quod plantatum est,
tempus occidendi et tempus sanandi,
tempus destruendi et tempus aedificandi,
tempus flendi et tempus ridendi,
tempus plangendi et tempus saltandi,
tempus spargendi lapides et tempus colligendi,

tempus amplexandi et tempus longe fieri ab amplexibus,
tempus adquirendi et tempus perdendi,
tempus custodiendi et tempus abiciendi,
tempus scindendi et tempus consuendi,
tempus tacendi et tempus loquendi,
tempus dilectionis et tempus odii,
tempus belli et tempus pacis.
Quid habet amplius homo de labore suo?

Liber Ecclesiastes III, i–ix

To every thing there is a season,
and a time to every purpose under the heaven:
A time to be born, and a time to die;
a time to plant, and a time to pluck that which is planted;
A time to kill, and a time to heal;
a time to break down, and a time to build up;
A time to weep, and a time to laugh;
a time to mourn, and a time to dance;
A time to cast away stones, and a time to gather stones together;

a time to embrace, and a time to refrain from embracing;
A time to get, and a time to lose;
a time to keep, and a time to cast away;
A time to rend, and a time to sew;
a time to keep silence, and a time to speak;
A time to love, and a time to hate;
a time of war, and a time of peace.
What profit hath he that worketh in that wherein he laboureth?

Ecclesiastes 3, 1–9

CHAPTER 22

READING

Midas et Aurum

1. Temporibus antiquis erat rex, Midas.
2. Nomen eius regis erat clarum quod amicus Bacchi erat.
3. Silenus Bacchum docebat, sed ab hostibus captus erat.
4. A Mida liberatus erat. Bacchus vero fuit laetus.
5. Bacchus ei nuntiavit: "Donum dabo."
6. Midas bonam fortunam, sed non multam sapientiam habebat.
7. Rex id donum accepit: Postea ea proxima ei in aurum vertebantur.

8. Rex donum dei bene amabat.
9. Midas aurum facere properavit.
10. In aurum arbores altas atque terram aquamque in eis locis ubi stabat aut ambulabat vertit.
11. Ob donum suum deum laudavit.
12. Rex superbus auro suo factus erat.
13. Nunc Midas domi est. Magno cum studio multa in aurum vertit.
14. Tum cibus aquaque ante eum a servo suo ponebantur.
15. Ea petivit, sed sine mora in aurum versa sunt.
16. Tum Midas timore magno capiebatur. Suam mortem vero timebat.
17. In locis ultimis proximisque aurum videbat.

18. Ad Bacchum vocavit: "Id donum rogavi, sed non est donum bonum. Est poena magna malaque. Nunc auxilium peto."
19. Deus ei auxilium mox dedit.
20. Corpus caputque in flumine ponere eum iussit.
21. Midas magna cum diligentia id fecit. Mox liberatus est, sed flumini suum donum dederat.

Midas and the Gold

1. In ancient times there was a king, Midas.
2. The name of this king was famous because he was a friend of Bacchus.
3. Silenus taught Bacchus, but he had been captured by the enemy.
4. He had been freed by Midas. Bacchus was indeed happy.
5. Bacchus told him: "I shall give a gift."
6. Midas had good fortune, but not much wisdom.
7. The king received this gift: Afterwards those things nearest to him were turned into gold.
8. The king liked the gift of the god very much.
9. Midas hurried to make gold.
10. He turns into gold the high trees and also the land and water in those places where he was standing or walking.
11. He praised the god because of his gift.
12. The king had been made proud by his gold.
13. Now Midas is at home. With great eagerness he turns many things into gold.
14. Then food and water were placed in front of him by his servant.
15. He sought these things, but without delay they were turned into gold.
16. Then Midas was seized with great fear. He indeed feared his death.
17. He saw gold in the farthest and nearest places.
18. He called on Bacchus: "I asked for this gift, but it is not a good gift. It is a great and evil punishment. Now I seek help."
19. The god soon gave him help.
20. He ordered him to place his body and head in a river.
21. Midas did this with great care. Soon he was freed, but he had given his own gift to the river.

Midas et Aurum	Midas and the Gold
22. Post id tempus arenae fluminis erant aureae.	22. After that time the sands of the river were golden.
23. Bacchus laetus erat quod nunc liber erat et arena ab eo tempore erat pulchra.	23. Bacchus was happy because now he was free and the sand was beautiful from that time on.

READING VOCABULARY

Nouns

studium, studii or studi, n., zeal, eagerness (studio)

diligentia, diligentiae, f., diligence, care (diligent)

timor, timoris, m., fear, dread (timorous)

mors, mortis, f., death (mortium) (mortality)

poena, poenae, f., punishment, fine (penal)

arena, arenae, f., sand (arena)

cibus, cibi, m., food

tempus, temporis, n., time (temporary, ex tempore)

aurum, auri, n., gold (auriferous)

arbor, arboris, f., tree (arboretum)

Bacchus, Bacchi, m., Bacchus (bacchanalian)

Midas, Midae, m., Midas

Silenus, Sileni, m., Silenus

Verbs

pono, ponere, posui, positus, put, place (position, postpone)

capio, capere, cepi, captus, take, seize, capture (caption)

verto, vertere, verti, versus, turn (vertical)

facio, facere, feci, factus, make, do (factory)

Preposition

propter, because of, on account of

READING GRAMMAR

A. Some **e/i-conjugation** Verbs have **-io** in the first principal part. These also have an **-i-** in most forms of the present, imperfect, and future tenses.

Present tense:

ACTIVE		PASSIVE	
I lead; I seize		I am led; I am seized	
duco	capio	ducor	capior
ducis	capis	duceris	caperis
ducit	capit	ducitur	capitur
ducimus	capimus	ducimur	capimur
ducitis	capitis	ducimini	capimini
ducunt	capiunt	ducuntur	capiuntur

Imperfect tense:

ACTIVE		PASSIVE	
I was leading; I was seizing		I was led; I was seized	
ducebam	capiebam	ducebar	capiebar
ducebas	capiebas	ducebaris	capiebaris
ducebat	capiebat	ducebatur	capiebatur
ducebamus	capiebamus	ducebamur	capiebamur
ducebatis	capiebatis	ducebamini	capiebamini
ducebant	capiebant	ducebantur	capiebantur

Future tense:

ACTIVE		PASSIVE	
I shall lead; I shall seize		I shall be led; I shall be seized	
ducam	capiam	ducar	capiar
duces	capies	duceris	capieris
ducet	capiet	ducetur	capietur
ducemus	capiemus	ducemur	capiemur
ducetis	capietis	ducemini	capiemini
ducent	capient	ducentur	capientur

The perfect tenses are all regular.

B. When **cum** is used to show how something was done, it often follows the Adjective.

Cum diligentia laborat.   He works with diligence.
Magna cum diligentia laborat.   He works with great diligence.

C. The cause of an action may be shown by either the Ablative Case alone or by **ob** or **propter** and the Accusative Case.

timore,	because of (on account of) fear
ob timorem,	because of (on account of) fear
propter timorem,	because of (on account of) fear

LATIN IN THE CONSTITUTION OF THE UNITED STATES

The following Latin phrases are used in the Constitution:

In Section 3, dealing with Officers of the Senate:

"The Senate shall choose their officers, and also a president **pro tempore**, in the absence of the Vice-President, or when he shall exercise the office of President of the United States." **pro tempore** means *for the time*.

In Section 9, dealing with Powers Forbidden to the United States:

"The privilege of the writ of **habeas corpus** shall not be suspended, unless when in cases of rebellion or invasion the public safety may require it." **habeas corpus** means *thou shalt have the body*. A writ of habeas corpus is a legal document making it mandatory that an accused person be told in court the reason for his detention.

"No bill of attainder or **ex-post-facto** law shall be passed." **ex post facto** means *from what is done afterwards*. An ex post facto law is one passed after a crime has been committed. Thus, a person who has committed a crime must be tried under the laws as they existed at the time of the commission of the crime.

PRACTICE EXERCISES

No. 105. Translate these phrases, showing cause or reason.

1. ob moram
2. cura mea
3. propter pericula
4. propter timorem
5. ob mortem
6. diligentia
7. celeritate
8. ob audaciam
9. propter moras
10. tempore

No. 106. Translate these phrases, showing manner.

1. cum studio
2. magna cura
3. magna cum diligentia
4. magno cum timore
5. cum celeritate
6. studio multo
7. magno cum studio
8. cum mora
9. magna celeritate
10. magna cum mora

No. 107. Complete these principal parts.

1. pono, ponere, —————, positus
2. supero, —————, superavi, superatus
3. do, dare, —————, datus
4. capio, —————, cepi, captus
5. servo, servare, servavi, —————
6. —————, facere, feci, factus
7. verto, vertere, —————, versus
8. terreo, terrere, —————, territus
9. —————, ducere, duxi, ductus
10. paro, parare, paravi, —————

No. 108. Translate these Verb forms.

1. iussit
2. duxisti
3. demonstraverunt
4. rogabam
5. fecimus
6. docetur
7. mitteris
8. capimini
9. spectabit
10. augebimus
11. petent
12. volabant
13. obtinebas
14. vertebatur
15. terruerat
16. petiveratis
17. ceperant
18. moti erunt
19. ducti eramus
20. capiebat

No. 109. Translate these prepositional phrases.

1. ob horam
2. propter telum
3. ante castra
4. a timore
5. de arbore
6. ab rege
7. ex arboribus
8. in eum locum
9. cum patre
10. cum cura
11. in aqua
12. sub oceano
13. circum muros
14. contra eum
15. inter oppida
16. per agrum
17. post castra
18. sine eis
19. trans mare
20. de viris

CHAPTER 23

READING

Hannibal	Hannibal
1. Adulescens, Hannibal, erat inimicus Romanis quod a patre suo ductus est.	1. The youth, Hannibal, was unfriendly to the Romans because he had been led by his father.
2. In Africa habitaverunt, sed mox Hannibal cum suis trans aquam in navibus multis ad Hispaniam navigavit.	2. They lived in Africa, but soon Hannibal with his men sailed across the water in many ships to Spain.
3. Ipse multas copias et classem bonam habuit.	3. He himself had many troops and a good fleet.
4. In Hispania multa oppida oppugnavit et praedam captivosque cepit.	4. In Spain he attacked many towns and took booty and captives.
5. Tum ad Italiam viros suos duxit, sed inter Hispaniam Italiamque erant montes.	5. Then he led his men to Italy, but between Spain and Italy there were mountains.

Hannibal

6. Eidem montes pedites equitesque eius minime iuverunt.
7. Multa impedimenta portabantur. Ad imperatorem Romanorum id nuntium portatum est.
8. Romani ad hostes iter facere properaverunt.
9. Romani proelio hostes non vicerunt, sed bellum ad Africam mox portatum est et Romani ad victoriam ab imperatore suo ibi ducti sunt.

Hannibal

6. These same mountains did not help his foot-soldiers and horsemen at all.
7. They were carrying much baggage. This message was carried to the general of the Romans.
8. The Romans hurried to travel toward the enemy.
9. The Romans did not conquer the enemy in battle, but soon the war was carried to Africa and the Romans were led to victory there by their general.

Theseus et Minotaurus

1. Populus Graeciae contra populum insulae Cretae multos annos bellum gesserat.
2. Graeci magno cum animo diu contendebant, sed ab copiis Minois, regis Cretae, victi erant.
3. Haec fuerat causa belli: Filius Minois a Graecis interfectus erat. Itaque rex ob iniuriam illam ab his poenam petebat.
4. Septem puellas et septem pueros rogavit.
5. Graeci erant miseri, sed illos miserunt.
6. Minos, rex, labyrinthum habebat. In labyrintho animal barbarum, Minotaurum, tenebat.
7. In labyrinthum puellas puerosque duxit.
8. In illo loco terrebantur quod contra eum sine armis pugnare non poterant et mortem acceperunt.

Theseus and the Minotaur

1. The people of Greece had waged war against the people of the island of Crete for many years.
2. The Greeks fought for a long time with great spirit, but they had been conquered by the forces of Minos, the king of Crete.
3. This was the cause of the war: The son of Minos had been killed by the Greeks. And so the king sought punishment from them because of that injury.
4. He asked for seven girls and seven boys.
5. The Greeks were unhappy, but they sent them.
6. Minos, the king, had a labyrinth. In the labyrinth he kept a savage animal, the Minotaur.
7. He led the girls and boys into the labyrinth.
8. In that place they were terrified because they were not able to fight against him without weapons and they accepted death.

READING VOCABULARY

Nouns

animus, animi, m., mind, spirit (animosity)

labyrinthus, labyrinthi, m., labyrinth (labyrinthal)

iniuria, iniuriae, f., injury, harm (injurious)

adulescens, adulescentis, m., youth (adulescentium) (adolescent)

classis, classis, f., a fleet (classium) (class)

imperator, imperatoris, m., general, commander, emperor (imperative)

impedimentum, impedimenti, n., hindrance In the plural, baggage (impediment)

eques, equitis, m., horseman, knight (equestrian)

pedes, peditis, m., foot soldier

navis, navis, f., ship (navium) (navy)

Minotaurus, Minotauri, m., the Minotaur

Minos, Minois, m., Minos

Hannibal, Hannibalis, m., Hannibal

Africa, Africae, f., Africa

Adjectives

hic, haec, hoc, this
ille, illa, illud, that
idem, eadem, idem, the same (identical)
ipse, ipsa, ipsum, himself, herself, itself; very

Pronouns

hic, haec, hoc, he, she, it
ille, illa, illud, he, she, it
idem, eadem, idem, he, she, it
ipse, ipsa, ipsum, he (himself), she (herself), it (itself)

Verbs

vinco, vincere, vici, victus, conquer
contendo, contendere, contendi, contentus, hasten, strive, contend (contender)
interficio, interficere, interfeci, interfectus, kill
gero, gerere, gessi, gestus, carry on, wage

Conjunction

itaque, and so, therefore

READING GRAMMAR

A. These words are used as both Pronouns and Adjectives in the same way as **is, ea, id.**

	PRONOUN	ADJECTIVE
hic, haec, hoc	he, she, it (here)	this
ille, illa, illud	he, she, it (there)	that
idem, eadem, idem	he, she, it (the same)	the same
ipse, ipsa, ipsum	he, she, it (-self)	himself, herself, itself; very

hic vir, this man	hic, he
ille homo, that man	ille, he
idem homo, the same man	idem, he
vir ipse, the man himself	ipse, he

The declension of these words is very much the same as **is, ea, id:**

Nom.	hic	he	haec	she	hoc	it	this
Gen.	huius	his	huius	her	huius	its	of this
Dat.	huic	to him	huic	to her	huic	to it	to this
Acc.	hunc	him	hanc	her	hoc	it	this
Abl.	hoc	by him	hac	by her	hoc	by it	by this

Nom.	hi		hae		haec	they	these
Gen.	horum		harum		horum	their	of these
Dat.	his		his		his	to them	to these
Acc.	hos		has		haec	them	these
Abl.	his		his		his	by them	by these

	SINGULAR			PLURAL		
Nom.	ille	illa	illud	illi	illae	illa
Gen.	illius	illius	illius	illorum	illarum	illorum
Dat.	illi	illi	illi	illis	illis	illis
Acc.	illum	illam	illud	illos	illas	illa
Abl.	illo	illa	illo	illis	illis	illis

ille, illa, illud has the same meanings (he, she, it) as **is, ea, id** or **hic, haec, hoc** when used as a Pronoun. As an Adjective, **ille, illa, illud** means *that*.

ipse, ipsa, ipsum is declined just like **is, ea, id** or **ille, illa, illud** after the first few forms:

Nom.	ipse	ipsa	ipsum	As a Pronoun, **ipse, ipsa, ipsum**
Gen.	ipsius	ipsius	ipsius	means *he* (himself), *she* (herself), *it*
Dat.	ipsi	ipsi	ipsi	(itself). As an Adjective, it means *him-*
Acc.	ipsum	ipsam	ipsum	*self, herself, itself, very.*
Abl.		regular		

idem, eadem, idem is based on **is, ea, id** and declined in much the same way:

Nom.	idem	eadem	idem	eidem, iidem	eaedem	eadem
Gen.	eiusdem	eiusdem	eiusdem	eorundem	earundem	eorundem
Dat.	eidem	eidem	eidem	eisdem, iisdem	in all genders	
Acc.	eundem	eandem	idem	eosdem	easdem	eadem
Abl.	eodem	eadem	eodem	eisdem, iisdem	in all genders	

As a Pronoun, **idem, eadem, idem** means (the same) *he,* (the same) *she,* (the same) *it.* As an Adjective it means *same.*

B. **possum, posse, potui,** *to be able, can,* is based on **sum, esse, fui.**

Present tense

possum	I am able, can	possumus	we are able, can
potes	you are able, can	potestis	you are able, can
potest	he, she, it is able, can	possunt	they are able, can

Imperfect tense

Future tense

poteram	I was able, could	potero	I shall be able, can
poteras	you were able, could	poteris	you will be able, can
etc.		etc.	

Perfect tense

potui	I have been able, could
potuisti	you have been able, could
etc.	

Pluperfect tense

Future Perfect tense

potueram	I had been able, could	potuero	I shall have been able, could
potueras	you had been able, could	potueris	you will have been able, could
etc.		etc.	

possum, posse, potui must always have a completing infinitive.

ducere potest, he is able to lead, he can lead
vincere posse debet, he ought to be able to conquer

THE PRONUNCIATION OF CHURCH LATIN

The pronunciation of Church Latin may follow the classical Latin pronunciation, or the general pattern of the Italian pronunciation. The rules are by no means fixed and standardized, but, with widened oral communication, the Italian pronunciation of liturgical Latin has increased in the Roman Catholic Church, as it has also in the singing of all Church Latin.

1. Vowels.
   The vowels have the same pronunciation, except that **u** becomes **ou**. meus, meous
2. Consonants.
   The most noticeable difference is that **c** before **e** or **i** is not k, but **ch**. cibus, chibous

If **c** before **e** or **i** is preceded by an **s**, the **s** is dropped. scio, chio

ti between two vowels is **tsi**. nationem, natsionem

ti after a consonant (except s, t, or x) is **ci**. amanti, amanci

g before **e** or **i** is soft, like **j**. gens, jens

All double consonants are pronounced definitely, with equal stress on each. anno, an-no

PRACTICE EXERCISES

No. 110. Translate these phrases which use **hic** and **ille**.

1. hic murus
2. illam urbem
3. in illo loco
4. hi duces
5. illis militibus
6. illi legato
7. hos imperatores
8. illa consilia
9. illius oceani
10. horum hominum
11. in illo horto
12. illa dea
13. illius peditis
14. de hoc domino
15. ex illa arbore
16. hunc impedimentum
17. his patribus
18. has naves
19. ille liber
20. illi puellae
21. haec arma
22. harum partium
23. de illa pace
24. illarum arenarum
25. his annis
26. illam horam
27. illud signum
28. huius equi
29. ad has feminas
30. illos nuntios

No. 111. Translate these Pronouns.

1. huius
2. ille
3. illi
4. hos
5. illis
6. harum
7. hoc
8. huic
9. illa
10. hi
11. haec
12. hanc
13. has
14. illum
15. illos

No. 112. Translate these phrases which use **idem** and **ipse**.

1. dea ipsa
2. ex templis ipsis
3. urbem eandem
4. homines ipsos
5. ab eodem adulescenti
6. idem nomen
7. eiusdem nationis
8. cum eisdem equitibus
9. eadem itinera
10. iisdem viris
11. ex agro ipso
12. annis ipsis
13. pueri ipsi
14. legati ipsius
15. eadem hora
16. lex ipsa
17. mons ipse
18. puellae ipsae
19. idem iter
20. ab mulieribus ipsis
21. eodem tempore
22. eorundem imperatorum
23. eadem oppida
24. in urbibus ipsis
25. eiusdem populi
26. iidem homines
27. ex iisdem locis
28. iisdem annis
29. nocte ipsa
30. pax ipsa

No. 113. Translate these Pronouns.

1. ipsi	4. ipsa	7. eundem	10. ipsius
2. eiusdem	5. ipsos	8. eorundem	
3. idem	6. eadem	9. ex iisdem	

No. 114. Give the English for these forms of possum.

1. ducere poterant	6. necare non potuimus	11. iuvare poterimus
2. manere potes	7. iubere potueram	12. pugnare poteris
3. adorare non potuit	8. docere potes	13. vocare non potuerunt
4. liberare poterit	9. rogare poteramus	14. laborare non possum
5. curare possunt	10. augere non potui	15. manere potuistis

CHAPTER 24

READING

Theseus et Minotaurus (concl'd.)	Theseus and the Minotaur (concl'd.)
1. Interea in Graecia Theseus fortuna misera puerorum puellarumque Graecorum incitatus est.	1. Meanwhile in Greece Theseus was aroused by the unhappy fortune of the Greek boys and girls.
2. Rogavit: "Estne nullum auxilium pro his filiis civium nostrorum?"	2. He asked: "Is there no help for these children of our citizens?"
3. Itaque ad Cretam cum sociis suis navi contendit.	3. And so he hurried to Crete by ship with his comrades.
4. Ariadne, filia regis, eum vidit et ob virtutem eius illum amavit.	4. Ariadne, the daughter of the king, saw him and loved him because of his courage.
5. Sine mora illa de labyrintho eum docuit.	5. Without delay she showed him about the labyrinth.
6. Tum Theseus solus ad labyrinthum properavit. Arma portabat et bonum consilium Ariadnes memoria tenebat.	6. Then Theseus alone hurried to the labyrinth. He carried weapons and he remembered the good advice of Ariadne.
7. Mox Minotaurum spectabat. Cum illo animali diu contendebat, sed id interficere potuit.	7. Soon he saw the Minotaur. He struggled with that animal for a long time, but was able to kill it.
8. Minotaurus necatus erat. Pueri puellaeque liberati erant.	8. The Minotaur had been killed. The boys and girls had been freed.
9. Totos annos postea populus Graeciae laetus erat quod regi malo Cretae nullas poenas dabat.	9. For all the years afterwards the people of Greece were happy because they paid no penalties to the evil king of Crete.

Ulixes et Cyclops

1. Homerus, poeta antiquus, de bello inter viros Graeciae Troiaeque in suo magno opere scripsit.
2. Post multos annos longos Troia ab Graecis capta erat.
3. Graeci ab illo loco navigabant. Apud eos erat Ulixes, homo audax, sed brevi tempore navis eius tempestate ad aliam partem maris portata est.
4. Ex navi ad terram cum sociis suis Ulixes contendit.
5. Non longe ab illo loco ubi stabant corpus magnum Polyphemi, Cyclopis, mox viderunt. Ille in colli habitabat.
6. Graeci iniuriam timebant.
7. Polyphemus eos a mari celeribus pedibus duxit.
8. Viri cibum exspectabant, sed Cyclops pro cibo suo unum hominem, tum alterum, et alium cepit.
9. Alii pro sociis suis dolebant.
10. Illine ab Polyphemo fugere poterunt?

Ulysses and the Cyclops

1. Homer, an ancient poet, wrote in his great work about the war between the men of Greece and Troy.
2. After many long years Troy had been captured by the Greeks.
3. The Greeks were sailing away from that place. Among them was Ulysses, a bold man, but in a short time his ship was carried by a storm to another part of the sea.
4. Ulysses hurried from his ship to the land with his comrades.
5. Not far from that place where they were standing they soon saw the large body of Polyphemus, the Cyclops. He lived on a hill.
6. The Greeks feared injury.
7. Polyphemus led them away from the sea at a swift pace.
8. The men waited for food, but the Cyclops, for his own food, took one man, then another, and another.
9. The others grieved for their comrades.
10. Will they be able to flee from Polyphemus?

READING VOCABULARY

Nouns

civis, civis, m. or f., citizen (civium) (civic)
Theseus, Thesei, m., Theseus
Ariadne, Ariadnes, f., Ariadne (a Greek noun)
opus, operis, n., work (opera)
tempestas, tempestatis, f., storm, bad weather (tempest)
poeta, poetae, m., poet (poetical)
Polyphemus, Polyphemi, m., Polyphemus
Cyclops, Cyclopis, m., Cyclops
Homerus, Homeri, m., Homer
Ulixes, Ulixis, m., Ulysses

Verbs

scribo, scribere, scripsi, scriptus, write (scribe)
fugio, fugere, fugi, flee, run away, escape (fugitive)

Adverb

interea, meanwhile

Adjectives

celer, celeris, celere, quick, swift (celerity)
acer, acris, acre, sharp, active, keen (acrid)
omnis, omne, all, every (omnibus)
audax, audacis, bold audacis is the Gen. Case (audacious)
brevis, breve, short, brief (brevity)
alius, alia, aliud, other, another (alien)
unus, una, unum, one (unite)
alter, altera, alterum, the one, the other (alternate)
nullus, nulla, nullum, no, none (null)
solus, sola, solum, alone, only (solitude)
totus, tota, totum, all, whole (total)

Prepositions

apud, among, in the presence of With the Acc. Case
pro, in front of; for, instead of With the Abl. Case

READING GRAMMAR

A. Some Adjectives that belong to the **a-** and **o-declensions** have the Genitive singular ending in **-ius** and the Dative singular ending in **-i**. Otherwise, they are regular.

Nom.	unus	una	unum
Gen.	unius	unius	unius
Dat.	uni	uni	uni
Acc.	unum	unam	unum
etc.			

These Adjectives are declined like **unus:**

> **alius, alia, aliud,** other, another
> **alter, altera, alterum,** the one, the other
> **neuter, neutra, neutrum,** neither
> **nullus, nulla, nullum,** no, none
> **solus, sola, solum,** alone, only
> **totus, tota, totum,** whole, all
> **ullus, ulla, ullum,** any
> **uter, ultra, utrum,** which (of two)

B. Sometimes **alius** or **alter** may be in pairs:

> **alius...alius,** one...another　　**alii...alii,** some...others
> **alter...alter,** the one...the other (of two)

Alterum iter longum est, alterum non est.　　One road is long, the other is not.
Alii sunt boni, alii sunt mali.　　Some are good, some are bad.

C. Those Adjectives that do not belong to the **a-** or **o-declensions** belong to the **i-declension**. These are of three kinds, according to the number of spellings in the Nominative singular, but all have the **i-declension** endings. The masculine and feminine genders are declined like **urbs;** the neuter like **mare.** See Chapter 15. The three kinds are:

1. one spelling for all genders:

	M.	F.	N.
Nom.	audax	audax	audax
Gen.	audacis	audacis	audacis
Dat.	audaci	audaci	audaci
etc.			

2. two spellings—one for the masculine and feminine, one for the neuter:

	M.	F.	N.
Nom.	omnis	omnis	omne
Gen.	omnis	omnis	omnis
Dat.	omni	omni	omni
etc.			

3. three spellings—one for each gender:

	M.	F.	N.
Nom.	celer	celeris	celere
Gen.	celeris	celeris	celeris
Dat.	celeri	celeri	celeri
etc.			

SUFFIXES

Some of the more common suffixes used to form Adjectives are:

-eus, denoting the material. English, of **aureus**, of gold

-osus, denoting fullness. English, full of **periculosis**, full of danger

-bilis, denoting possibility. English, able **amabilis**, able to be loved, lovable

-anus, -icus, -alis, -inus, denoting connection.
  -anus becomes -ane or -an in English. **Romanus**, Roman
  -icus becomes -ic in English. **publicus**, public
  -alis becomes -al in English. **mortalis**, mortal
  -inus becomes -in or -ine in English. **Latinus**, Latin

PRACTICE EXERCISES

No. 115. Give the English for these phrases.

1. uno anno
2. nullam curam
3. utrius doni
4. ulli navi
5. totos annos
6. cum patre solo
7. nullarum mortium
8. neutri nationi
9. in altera via
10. alio nomine
11. ad utrum flumen
12. ullius collis
13. uni libro
14. ob nullas causas
15. ab neutro homine

No. 116. Translate these Verb forms.

1. timuerant
2. fuistis
3. mittent
4. cepit
5. timebit
6. spectabant
7. tenebuntur
8. mittar
9. laudati sunt
10. factum erat
11. navigabas
12. dabantur
13. gerit
14. fuerant
15. habuerunt

No. 117. Give the English for the following.

1. alter puer est, alter non est
2. nullo tempore
3. ullius belli
4. ad utra castra
5. mulieres ipsae solae
6. neutrius adulescentis
7. alias urbes
8. unam partem
9. de neutra puella
10. aliud iter

No. 118. Give the English for these phrases.

1. hora breve
2. servi audacis
3. eques celer
4. in flumine celeri
5. ab viris audacibus
6. tempora omnia
7. a legato acri
8. vita brevis
9. omnibus horis
10. in navi celeri
11. opus audax
12. brevi tempore
13. copiae acres
14. equi celeris
15. acres feminae
16. mortem celerem
17. itinera brevia
18. audaci homini
19. brevem annum
20. omni in loco

CHAPTER 25

READING

Ulixes et Cyclops (concl'd.)

1. Postquam Cyclops haec fecerat, Graeci fortes mortem exspectabant, sed Ulixes Polyphemum interficere in animo habebat.
2. Ob magnitudinem viri non erat ullum iter facile ex periculo eorum, sed consilium parabant et suos animos bonos tenebant.

3. Ante hoc tempus alia pericula gravia superaverant et hoc periculum novum superare in animo habuerunt.
4. Uterque Cyclopem timebat, sed Polyphemus inimicus omnibus erat.
5. Eum incitare non debebant. Itaque Ulixes suum consilium eis demonstravit.
6. Partem arboris in igni posuerunt. Post breve tempus finis arboris erat acer.
7. Hoc erat telum eorum contra Cyclopem. Id magna cum diligentia paraverant.
8. Hoc telo Cyclops poenas dabit.

9. Polyphemus unum oculum solum habuit. Magna cum audacia Ulixes et socii sui in oculo eius finem arboris posuerunt.
10. Iniuria erat gravis et Cyclops postea videre non poterat.
11. Polyphemus etiam multa animalia habebat.
12. Ante portam ille saxum grave et magnum posuerat.
13. Id a Graecis moveri non potuit, sed Cyclops ab porta saxum movebat, cum animalia cibum petebant.
14. Hoc erat consilium: Ulixes et sui amici fugam suam noctu paraverunt.
15. Cyclops eos videre non potuit.
16. Saxum ab porta movit.
17. Animalia per portam cucurrerunt. Sub animalibus erant Graeci.
18. Graeci simulabant et Polyphemus eos non cognovit.
19. Tum Ulixes clamavit. Itaque Cyclops fugam eorum cognovit.

Ulysses and the Cyclops (concl'd.)

1. After the Cyclops had done these things, the brave Greeks waited for death, but Ulysses had in mind to kill Polyphemus.
2. Because of the great size of the man there was not any easy way out of their danger, but they prepared a plan and kept their good spirits.

3. Before this time they had overcome other serious dangers and they had in mind to overcome this new danger.
4. Each feared the Cyclops, but Polyphemus was unfriendly to all.
5. They ought not to arouse him. And so Ulysses showed them his plan.
6. They placed part of a tree in the fire. After a short time the end of the tree was sharp.
7. This was their weapon against the Cyclops. They had prepared it with great care.
8. With this weapon the Cyclops will pay the penalty.

9. Polyphemus had only one eye. With great boldness Ulysses and his comrades put the end of the tree in his eye.
10. The injury was serious and the Cyclops was not able to see after that.
11. Polyphemus also had many animals.
12. He had put a heavy and large stone in front of the door.
13. This could not be moved by the Greeks, but the Cyclops moved the stone away from the door, when the animals sought food.
14. This was the plan: Ulysses and his friends prepared their flight at night.
15. The Cyclops was not able to see them.
16. He moved the stone away from the door.
17. The animals ran through the door. Under the animals were the Greeks.
18. The Greeks pretended and Polyphemus did not recognize them.
19. Then Ulysses shouted. And so the Cyclops learned of their flight.

Ulixes et Cyclops (concl'd.)	Ulysses and the Cyclops (concl'd.)
20. Cyclops ad mare properavit. Saxum magnum ad Graecos iecit.	20. The Cyclops hurried to the sea. He threw a large stone toward the Greeks.
21. Polyphemus dixit: "Quis es?"	21. Polyphemus said: "Who are you?"
22. Ulixes clamavit: "Nullus homo sum.", sed Graeci in navi erant et laeti erant quod a Polyphemo fugerant et ad Graeciam navigabant.	22. Ulysses shouted: "I am no man.", but the Greeks were on the ship and were happy because they had escaped from Polyphemus and were sailing to Greece.
23. Postea de oculo suo Polyphemus dicebat: "Nullus id fecit."	23. Afterwards Polyphemus said about his eye: "No one did it."

READING VOCABULARY

Nouns

oculus, oculi, m., eye (oculist)
porta, portae, f., gate, door, entrance (portal)
saxum, saxi, n., stone, rock (saxatile)
fuga, fugae, f., flight, escape (fugue)
telum, teli, n., weapon

Adjectives

facilis, facile, easy (facility)
fortis, forte, brave, strong (fort)
gravis, grave, heavy, severe, serious (gravity)
novus, nova, novum, new (novel)
uterque, utraque, utrumque, each, every

Pronoun

quis, quid, who?, what?

Verbs

simulo, simulare, simulavi, simulatus, pretend (simulate)
clamo, clamare, clamavi, clamatus, shout, cry (clamor)
iacio, iacere, ieci, iactus, throw (project)
cognosco, cognoscere, cognovi, cognitus, learn, recognize, know (cognizance)

Adverb

noctu, at night (noctambular)

READING GRAMMAR

A. uterque, utraque, utrumque is declined just like uter, utra, utrum.

uterque vir, each man	utriusque viri, of each man
utrique viro, to each man	utrumque virum, each man

B. The declension of quis, quid, who?, what?, is quite similar to that of is, ea, id.

	SINGULAR			PLURAL			
	M.	F.	N.	M.	F.	N.	
Nom.	quis	quis	quid	qui	quae	quae	who?, what?
Gen.	cuius	cuius	cuius	quorum	quarum	quorum	of whom?, whose?, of what?
Dat.	cui	cui	cui	quibus	quibus	quibus	to, for whom?, to, for what?
Acc.	quem	quem	quid	quos	quas	quae	whom?, what?
Abl.	quo	quo	quo	quibus	quibus	quibus	from, with, by, in whom?, what?

Quis est? Who is it?   Qui sunt? Who are they?
Cuius est? Whose is it?   Quorum est? Whose is it?
Quem vides? Whom do you see?   Quid vides? What do you see?

C. When **cum** is used with the Ablative case, it is generally added to the end.

quocum, with whom   **quibuscum**, with whom

D. The Present Passive Infinitive of the **a-** and **e-conjugations** is like the Present Active Infinitive except that it ends in **-i.**

amare, to love   amari, to be loved
habere, to have   haberi, to be had

In the **e/i-conjugation**, the **-i** is added directly to the stem.

ducere, to lead   duci, to be led
capere, to take   capi, to be taken

FAMILIAR QUOTATIONS

Nil homini certum est, Nothing is certain to man. Ovid

Virtus praemium est optimum, Virtue is the best reward. Plautus

Omnia praeclara rara, All the best things are rare. Cicero

Possunt quia posse videntur, They can because they think they can. Virgil

Alea iacta est, The die is cast. Caesar

Mens sana in corpore sano, A sound mind in a sound body. Juvenal

Carmina morte carent, Songs do not die. Ovid

PRACTICE EXERCISES

No. 119. Translate these Adjective phrases.

1. solis aurei
2. ex neutro loco
3. summo in monte
4. itineris facilis
5. ullae horae
6. poenas graves
7. nationum proximarum
8. civem audacem
9. corpus robustum
10. fluminum celerium
11. libros latinos
12. homines alii
13. navis vestra
14. patrum multorum
15. utriusque regis

No. 120. Give the English for these Interrogative phrases and clauses.

1. Qui estis?
2. Cui ea dedit?
3. Quos videbo?
4. cuius oculi?
5. Quae cognoscit?
6. Quocum ambulat?
7. A quo captus est?
8. Quis clamat?
9. Quis pugnat?
10. quorum tela?
11. Quid habes?
12. Quem necavit?
13. Quibus id dabo?
14. Quid rogatum est?
15. Cui donum misisti?
16. Quem amas?
17. Quis fugit?
18. Quid facile est?
19. Cuius est?
20. quibuscum?
21. Quos mittet?
22. Quid facit?
23. Qui contendunt?
24. A quo gestum est?
25. Quis vocat?

No. 121. Give the Active form of these Present Passive Infinitives.

1. pugnari	5. laudari	9. cognosci	13. haberi	17. augeri
2. mitti	6. rogari	10. necari	14. moveri	18. servari
3. regi	7. scribi	11. capi	15. parari	19. vinci
4. dari	8. videri	12. timeri	16. duci	20. terreri

No. 122. Give the Passive form of these Present Active Infinitives.

1. demonstrare	6. armare	11. mittere	16. interficere
2. ducere	7. amare	12. gerere	17. iuvare
3. movere	8. facere	13. accipere	18. tenere
4. iubere	9. docere	14. timere	19. cognoscere
5. vertere	10. occupare	15. vocare	20. simulare

SIXTH REVIEW SECTION (CHAPTERS 22–25)

VOCABULARY REVIEW

NOUNS

1. adulescens	15. fuga	29. pedes	1. youth	15. flight, escape	29. foot soldier
2. Africa	16. Hannibal	30. poena	2. Africa	16. Hannibal	30. punishment, fine
3. animus	17. Homerus	31. poeta	3. mind, spirit	17. Homer	31. poet
4. arbor	18. impedimentum	32. Polyphemus	4. tree	18. hindrance	32. Polyphemus
5. arena	19. imperator	33. porta	5. sand	19. commander, general, emperor	33. gate, door, entrance
6. Ariadne	20. iniuria	34. saxum	6. Ariadne	20. injury, harm	34. stone, rock
7. aurum	21. labyrinthus	35. Silenus	7. gold	21. labyrinth	35. Silenus
8. Bacchus	22. Midas	36. studium	8. Bacchus	22. Midas	36. zeal, eagerness
9. cibus	23. Minos	37. telum	9. food	23. Minos	37. weapon
10. civis	24. Minotaurus	38. tempestas	10. citizen	24. the Minotaur	38. storm, bad weather
11. classis	25. mors	39. tempus	11. fleet	25. death	39. time
12. Cyclops	26. navis	40. Theseus	12. Cyclops	26. ship	40. Theseus
13. diligentia	27. oculus	41. timor	13. diligence, care	27. eye	41. fear, dread
14. eques	28. opus	42. Ulixes	14. horseman, knight	28. work	42. Ulysses

PRONOUNS

1. hic, haec, hoc	4. ipse, ipsa, ipsum	1. he, she, it	4. he himself, she herself, it itself
2. idem, eadem, idem	5. quis, quid	2. he, she, it	5. who?, what?
3. ille, illa, illud		3. he, she, it	

ADJECTIVES

1. acer	11. idem	1. sharp, active, keen	11. the same
2. alius	12. ille	2. other, another	12. that
3. alter	13. ipse	3. the one, the other	13. very, himself, herself, itself
4. audax	14. novus	4. bold	14. new
5. brevis	15. nullus	5. short, brief	15. no, none
6. celer	16. omnis	6. quick, swift	16. all, every
7. facilis	17. solus	7. easy	17. alone, only
8. fortis	18. totus	8. brave, strong	18. all, whole
9. gravis	19. unus	9. heavy, severe, serious	19. one
10. hic	20. uterque	10. this	20. each, every

VERBS

1. capio	8. iacio	1. take, seize, capture	8. throw
2. clamo	9. interficio	2. shout, cry	9. kill
3. cognosco	10. pono	3. learn, recognize, know	10. put, place
4. contendo	11. scribo	4. hasten, strive, contend	11. write
5. facio	12. simulo	5. make, do	12. pretend
6. fugio	13. verto	6. flee, run away, escape	13. turn
7. gero	14. vinco	7. carry on, wage	14. conquer

ADVERBS

1. interea	2. noctu	1. meanwhile	2. at night

PREPOSITIONS

1. apud	3. propter	1. among, in the presence of	3. because of, on account of
2. pro		2. in front of; for, instead of	

CONJUNCTION

1. itaque	1. and so, therefore

PRACTICE EXERCISES

No. 123. Translate these Verbs.

1. capiunt	5. interficiebamus	9. ponetur	13. contendent
2. cognitum erat	6. fecerunt	10. gesserint	14. positi sunt
3. victi sunt	7. ceperas	11. scribit	15. gestum est
4. vertent	8. fugiebat	12. iacis	

No. 124. Translate these Phrases.

1. propter mortem	5. propter cibum	9. ob impedimentum
2. ob iniuriam	6. ob classes	10. propter arenam
3. diligentia magna	7. parva cum poena	
4. ob imperatorem	8. magno cum studio	

No. 125. Translate these Pronouns.

1. hunc	4. illud	7. eadem	10. ipsorum	13. cuius
2. huius	5. ipse	8. eiusdem	11. quem	14. cui
3. illos	6. illorum	9. hic	12. quid	15. quocum

No. 126. Translate these Verb forms.

1. clamare potuit	6. contendere poterit
2. capere poterant	7. scribere potuerunt
3. facere potes	8. cognoscere poteramus
4. ponere possumus	9. vertere potes
5. vincere potuistis	10. gerere possunt

No. 127. Translate these Adjective phrases.

1. unius operis	5. brevi tempore	9. audaces equites
2. omnium civium	6. toti saxo	10. celeris poena
3. aliud impedimentum	7. nullius timoris	
4. nova tela	8. ullam iniuriam	

MARCUS TULLIUS CICERO

Cicero was born near Arpinum, in Latium, the province in which Rome was located, in 106 B.C., of an upper middle class family. He studied law, philosophy, and rhetoric in Rome, Athens, and Rhodes, and became consul in 63 B.C. It was in this office that he disclosed Catiline's conspiracy to overthrow the government and, in four orations delivered in the Senate, persuaded the Senators to decree the death penalty for the conspirators. After Caesar's assassination in 44 B.C. and the formation of the Second Triumvirate, Cicero was murdered in 43 B.C., while trying to escape from his political enemies.

O tempora! O mores! Senatus haec intellegit, consul videt; hic tamen vivit. Vivit? Immo vero etiam in senatum venit, fit publici consili particeps, notat et designat oculis ad caedem unum quemque nostrum. Nos autem, fortes viri, satis facere rei publicae videmur, si istius furorem ac tela vitamus. Ad mortem te, Catilina, duci iussu consulis iam pridem oportebat; in te conferri pestem, quam tu in nos machinaris.

Oh what times these are! Oh what habits we have! The Senate knows these things, the consul sees them; this man, however, lives. Does he live? Indeed, he even comes into the Senate, he becomes a participant in the public plans, he notes and designates with his eyes each single one of us for murder. We, however, brave men, seem to do enough for the Republic, if we avoid the fury and weapons of this man. You, Catiline, should have been led to your death by the order of the consul long ago; the destruction that you are plotting against us should have been brought against you.

In Catilinam Oratio Prima, ii

First Oration Against Catiline, 2

These two stories were written by Odo de Cerinton, who lived in the twelfth century and composed a work called **NARRATIONES**, which drew stories from various fables and other sources, giving a mystical interpretation to tales about animals.

De Hydro

Quoddam animal dicitur hydrus, cuius natura est se involvere luto, ut melius posset labi. Tandem in os crocodili, quando dormit, intrat et sic, ventrem eius ingrediens, cor eius mordet et sic crocodilum interimit.

Mistice: Hydrus significat filium Dei, qui assumpsit lutum nostrae carnis ut facilius laberetur in os diaboli, et sic, ventrem eius ingrediens et cor eius mordens, ipsum interficit.

About the Hydra

There is a certain animal called the hydra, whose nature it is to bury itself in the mud so that it might be better able to glide. Finally it enters the mouth of a crocodile, when it is sleeping, and thus, entering its stomach, it eats its heart and thus kills the crocodile.

Mystical interpretation: The hydra signifies the son of God, who has assumed the mud of our flesh so that it might slip more easily into the mouth of the devil, and thus, entering his stomach and eating his heart, he kills him.

De Antilope

Quoddam animal est quod vocatur antilops; quod cum virgultis ludit cum cornibus, tandem cornua eius implicantur cum virgultis quod non potest ea extrahere et tunc incipit clamare; quo audito veniunt venatores et interficiunt eum.

Mistice: Sic contigit quod plerique delectati sunt et ludunt cum negotiis huius mundi et sic in eisdem implicantur quod evelli non possunt et sic a venatoribus, id est a daemonibus, capiuntur et interficiuntur.

About the Antelope

There is a certain animal that is called the antelope; when this animal plays in a thicket with its horns, finally its horns are entangled with the thicket so that it is not able to extricate them and then it begins to cry aloud; when this is heard, hunters come and kill him.

Mystical interpretation: Thus it happens that many people are delighted and play with the occupations of this world and thus are entangled in these things so that they can not be torn away and thus by hunters, that is by demons, they are taken and killed.

CHAPTER 26

READING

Orpheus et Eurydice

1. Orpheus erat vir fortis, sed dolebat quod Eurydice morte capta erat et eum solum et miserum reliquerat.
2. Orpheus animalia omnia et naturam bene amabat et laetus esse simulabat, sed Eurydicen semper petebat.
3. Orpheus ipse sine ea esse non poterat. Itaque auxilium ab deis petivit.
4. Nihil ab Iove faci poterat. Eurydice ab terra discesserat et apud Inferos nunc habitabat.
5. Iter ad regnum Plutonis erat difficile.

6. Pluto suos non saepe tradit, sed Orpheus erat audax et paene nullum timorem habebat.
7. Sub terram magna cum celeritate contendit. Ante regem, Plutonem, mox stat.
8. Orpheus ab Plutone petivit: "Cur Eurydicen hic tenes? Non solum ei amorem summum semper docebam sed etiam mors ei non est idonea. Eurydice ipsa nihil fecerat."
9. Tum Pluto ipse pro illo acriter dolebat, sed Orpheum iussit: "Eam tradam, sed iter ex regno Inferorum difficile est. Illa ad terram tuam reduci poterit, sed eam spectare non debes. Cum primus eam ad terram educes, tum eam spectare poteris."

10. Ab Plutone grate discesserunt et iter ab illo loco malo celeriter faciebant.

11. Primo ille fortiter ambulabat, sed Orpheus amore regebatur. Non diu postea ad eam oculos suos vertit.
12. Ob eam causam Pluto magna cum celeritate illam cepit et eam ad Inferos reduxit.
13. Ab illo tempore in terra non visa est.

Orpheus and Eurydice

1. Orpheus was a brave man, but he grieved because Eurydice had been taken by death and had left him alone and wretched.
2. Orpheus loved all animals and nature very much and he pretended to be happy, but he always looked for Eurydice.
3. Orpheus himself could not be without her. And so he sought help from the gods.
4. Nothing could be done by Jupiter. Eurydice had departed from the earth and was now living among Those Below.
5. The journey to the kingdom of Pluto was difficult.

6. Pluto does not often give up his own, but Orpheus was bold and had almost no fear.
7. He hurries below the earth with great speed. He soon stands before the king, Pluto.
8. Orpheus asked Pluto: "Why do you keep Eurydice here? Not only did I always show the greatest love for her, but also death is not suitable to her. Eurydice herself had done nothing."
9. Then Pluto himself felt keenly sorry for him, but he instructed Orpheus: "I shall give her up, but the way out of the kingdom of Those Below is difficult. She can be led back to your land, but you ought not to look at her. When you, going first, lead her back to earth, then you can look at her."

10. They departed from Pluto gratefully and quickly made the journey away from that evil place.

11. At first he walked bravely, but Orpheus was ruled by love. Not long afterwards he turns his eyes toward her.
12. For this reason Pluto seized her with great speed and led her back to Those Below.
13. From that time she was not seen on the earth.

READING VOCABULARY

Nouns

regnum, regni, n., kingdom (interregnum)
natura, naturae, f., nature (natural)
nihil or nil, n., nothing nihil (or nil) has the same spelling in all Cases. (nihilist)
Orpheus, Orphei, m., Orpheus
Eurydice, Eurydices, f., Eurydice (a Greek noun)

Adjectives

difficilis, difficile, difficult, hard (difficulty)
primus, prima, primum, first (prime, primary)

Adverbs

parum, too little, not enough
magnopere, greatly

Verbs

relinquo, relinquere, reliqui, relictus, leave, leave behind (relinquish)
discedo, discedere, discessi, discessus, withdraw, go away, leave
trado, tradere, tradidi, traditus, give up, surrender (tradition)
rego, regere, rexi, rectus, rule (regent)
educo, educere, eduxi, eductus, lead out (educate)
reduco, reducere, reduxi, reductus, lead back (reduce)

READING GRAMMAR

A. Adverbs are generally formed from Adjectives.

1. Adverbs based on a- and o-declension Adjectives end in -e.

altus, high — alte, high, on high
latus, wide — late, widely
longus, long — longe, far, distant
miser, wretched — misere, wretchedly
pulcher, beautiful — pulchre, beautifully

2. Adverbs based on i-declension Adjectives end in -ter.

acer, keen — acriter, keenly
audax, bold — audacter, boldly
celer, swift — celeriter, swiftly
fortis, brave — fortiter, bravely

3. Some Adverbs are irregular.

bonus, good — bene, well
difficilis, difficult — difficile, with difficulty
facilis, easy — facile, easily
magnus, great — magnopere, greatly

malus, bad — male, badly
parvus, little — parum, too little, not enough
primus, first — primum, first, or primo, at first
solus, alone — solum, alone, only

4. Other Adverbs are not based on any Adjective. nunc, semper, non, etc.

B. i-conjugation Verbs have i as the predominant vowel.

1. Principal Parts: audio, audire, audivi, auditus, hear

2. Present Tense:

ACTIVE		PASSIVE	
I hear, do hear, am hearing		I am being heard, am heard	
audio	audimus	audior	audimur
audis	auditis	audiris	audimini
audit	audiunt	auditur	audiuntur

3. Imperfect Tense:

ACTIVE	PASSIVE
I was hearing, heard	I was being heard, was heard
audiebam	audiebar
audiebas	audiebaris
audiebat	audiebatur
audiebamus	audiebamur
audiebatis	audiebamini
audiebant	audiebantur

4. Future Tense:

ACTIVE		PASSIVE	
I shall hear		I shall be heard	
audiam	audiemus	audiar	audiemur
audies	audietis	audieris	audiemini
audiet	audient	audietur	audientur

5. Perfect Tense:

ACTIVE	PASSIVE
I have heard, heard	I have been heard
audivi	auditus, a, um sum
audivisti, etc.	auditus, a, um es, etc.

6. Pluperfect Tense:

ACTIVE	PASSIVE
I had heard	I had been heard
audiveram	auditus, a, um eram
audiveras, etc.	auditus, a, um eras, etc.

7. Future Perfect Tense:

ACTIVE	PASSIVE
I shall have heard	I shall have been heard
audivero	auditus, a, um ero
audiveris, etc.	auditus, a, um eris, etc.

FAMILIAR PHRASES

status quo or **status in quo**, the state in which. That is, the existing conditions.

mirabile dictu, wonderful to tell, relate.

per se, by itself, of itself; by its own force.

cum grano salis, with a grain of salt.

modus vivendi, manner of living (often temporary).

post scriptum, written after. Abbreviated, **P.S.** or **p.s.**

inter nos, among us, among ourselves.

sine qua non, something indispensable or necessary. Literally, without which not.

PRACTICE EXERCISES

No. 128. Form the Adverbs and give the English meanings.

1. pulcher	4. novus	7. brevis	10. audax	13. fortis
2. longus	5. acer	8. altus	11. miser	14. celer
3. magnus	6. gravis	9. gratus	12. proximus	15. liber

No. 129. Translate these Verb forms.

1. portas	8. auditi sunt	15. audiunt	22. fecit
2. habeo	9. acceptus es	16. iuvabamini	23. rogabunt
3. ducunt	10. auditus eram	17. audiebamur	24. audivimus
4. iacit	11. audiebant	18. vertebamus	25. auditi erant
5. audivistis	12. paratus erit	19. capientur	
6. liberatus est	13. audiet	20. audieris	
7. visi erant	14. petiverunt	21. audiris	

No. 130. Give the English for these phrases, and clauses.

1. fortiter pugnant
2. proxime vidimus
3. difficile gessit
4. late accipientur

5. bene docemur
6. longe ambulat
7. bene stant
8. facile cognovit

9. magnopere amabat
10. parum acriter

No. 131. Translate these sentences.

1. Locus facile defendetur.
2. Primo nihil parari poterat.
3. Ob timorem non fortiter contendistis.
4. Utramque portam amas?
5. Terra natura difficile defensa est.

6. Non solum rex sed etiam regina id audivit.
7. De quo audacter scripsit?
8. Illo anno multa parabamus.
9. Eurydice sub terra misere habitabat.
10. Longe ab hoc loco eos duxit.

CHAPTER 27

READING

Hero et Leander

1. Sunt multae fabulae de amore Leandri Herusque.
2. Haec fuit puella pulchra, quae in Graecia habitabat et quae omnia in templo, quod erat in oppido suo, curabat.
3. Ille in altera regione, quae erat trans Hellespontum, pontem Graeciae, habitabat, sed, cum eam videre cupiebat, trans mare quod non erat latum natabat.
4. Ob leges templi cum ea videri non poterat, sed illa lex eum non impedivit. Itaque ad eam semper noctu veniebat.

5. Etiam longum et difficile iter trans aquam ab puella eum non prohibuit.
6. Hero ad mare de alto turri omnibus noctibus spectabat.
7. Leander sine periculo ullo saepe veniebat et tum Hero ipsa vero laeta erat, quod eum bene amabat.
8. Diu Leander bonam fortunam habebat et omnibus noctibus ad Graeciam facile natabat atque ad illam terram sine ullo periculo pervenit.

Hero and Leander

1. There are many stories about the love of Hero and Leander.
2. She was a beautiful girl, who used to live in Greece and who took care of everything in the temple, that was in her town.
3. He lived in another region, which was across the Hellespont, the sea of Greece, but, when he wished to see her, he used to swim across the sea, which was not wide.
4. Because of the laws of the temple he could not be seen with her, but that law did not hinder him. And so he used to come to her always at night.
5. Even the long and difficult journey across the water did not keep him from the girl.
6. Hero used to watch every night from a high tower toward the sea.
7. Leander often came without any danger and then Hero herself was truly happy, because she loved him well.
8. For a long time Leander had good fortune and swam easily to Greece every night and came to that land without any danger.

Hero et Leander	Hero and Leander
9. Nullam inopiam celeritatis aut studi habebat. Ut accidit tamen uno tempore, cum natabat, tempestate magna victus est.	9. He had no lack of speed or eagerness. As it happened, however, one time, when he was swimming, he was overcome by a great storm.
10. Primo trans aquam turris Herus ab illo videri poterat, sed iam iter erat difficile et mox tempestate sub mare mittebatur.	10. At first Hero's tower could be seen by him across the water, but already the way was difficult and soon he was sent under the sea by the storm.
11. Hero totam noctem eum misere exspectabat.	11. Hero waited for him unhappily all night.
12. Tum ad mare contendit et corpus illius petebat. Id primo non conspexit.	12. Then she hurried to the sea and sought his body. She did not see it at first.
13. Tum in loco non longe ab mari corpus Leandri repperit.	13. Then in a place not far from the sea she found the body of Leander.
14. Misera Hero in mare cucurrit et illa eum morte sua repperit.	14. The unhappy Hero ran into the sea and she found him by her own death.

READING VOCABULARY

Nouns

turris, turris, f., tower (turrium) (turret)
regio, regionis, f., region, boundary (regional)
Hero, Herus, f., Hero (a Greek noun)
Leander, Leandri, m., Leander
Hellespontus, Hellesponti, m., Hellespont
inopia, inopiae, f., want, scarcity

Prounoun and Adjective

qui, quae, quod, who, which, that; which, what

Adverbs

tamen, however, nevertheless
iam, already, now

Conjunction

ut, as

Verbs

impedio, impedire, impedivi, impeditus, hinder (impede)
prohibeo, prohibere, prohibui, prohibitus, keep off, hinder, prohibit, prevent (prohibition)
cupio, cupere, cupivi, cupitus, desire, wish, want (cupidity)
venio, venire, veni, ventus, come (venture)
pervenio, pervenire, perveni, perventus, arrive
accido, accidere, accidi, happen (accident)
conspicio, conspicere, conspexi, conspectus, observe (conspectus)
reperio, reperire, repperi, repertus, find, discover (repertory)

READING GRAMMAR

A. A Relative Clause is used to tell something about its antecedent. It is, therefore, introduced by a Relative Pronoun in the same number and gender as its antecedent.

vir qui, the man, who   **puella quae**, the girl, who
bellum quod, the war, that

The case of a Relative Pronoun, however, is determined by its use, in its own clause.

> **vir quem video,** the man, whom I see
> **puella quam video,** the girl, whom I see

	SINGULAR			PLURAL			
	M.	**F.**	**N.**	**M.**	**F.**	**N.**	
Nom.	qui	quae	quod	qui	quae	quae	who, which, that
Gen.	cuius	cuius	cuius	quorum	quarum	quorum	whose, of which
Dat.	cui	cui	cui	quibus	quibus	quibus	to, for whom, which
Acc.	quem	quam	quod	quos	quas	quae	whom, which, that
Abl.	quo	qua	quo	quibus	quibus	quibus	from, with, by, in which, whom

Cum is added to the end of the Ablative: **quocum, quacum, quibuscum**

B. An Interrogative Adjective modifies a noun and asks a question. It is therefore in the same gender, number, and case as the noun it modifies.

> **qui vir?** which man? 　　　**quae puella?** which girl?
> 　　　**quod bellum?** what war?

The Interrogative Adjective in Latin is spelled the same as the Relative Pronoun. Only its use is different.

PREFIXES

prae, before. **praepono,** put before.
re, again, back. **remitto,** send back.
con, together, with; very, thoroughly.

convoco, call together.
conficio, finish (do thoroughly).
pro, out, forth. **provoco,** call forth.

PRACTICE EXERCISES

No. 132. In the following sentences translate (1) the relative clause, and (2) the whole sentence.

1. Homines qui cum copiis suis iter faciunt sunt fortes.
2. Turris quam aedificavit ex oppido barbaros prohibebat.
3. Femina quacum ambulabam mater mea est.
4. Navis cuius nomen conspicere non possumus ad Italiam navigat.
5. Puer cui litteras dedi celeriter veniet.
6. Timor quem habebitis mox non memoria tenebitur.
7. Flumen ad quod fugiebant erat altum latumque.
8. Locus de quo scripsit longe est ab urbe.
9. Omnia quae habuit nunc mea sunt.
10. Viri quorum pueros vides sunt amici.

No. 133. Translate these phrases containing interrogative adjectives.

1. in quibus locis?
2. qui homo?
3. quod oppidum?
4. quae praeda?
5. quos viros?
6. qua celeritate?
7. quo anno?
8. cuius nominis?
9. qua hora?
10. quo tempore?
11. cum quibus militibus?
12. quorum civium?
13. quae impedimenta?
14. cuius magnitudinis?
15. quo consilio?

No. 134. Give the English for these Verb forms.

1. faciunt
2. iubebit
3. repperisti
4. perveniet
5. haberi
6. currebat
7. fuerat
8. cepit
9. conspexerunt
10. accidebat
11. auditis
12. pervenisti
13. contendebat
14. dederant
15. videri
16. prohibuerunt
17. erunt
18. videbor
19. rogari
20. habebo

No. 135. Translate these phrases and clauses.

1. non potuit
2. illius loci
3. filios tuos
4. alii veniunt
5. venire cupit
6. fortis populus
7. ob tempestatem
8. magno studio
9. domi mansit
10. eius nationis
11. proximo anno
12. mi amice
13. omnes homines
14. nihil timet
15. non solum mater tua

CHAPTER 28

READING

Equus Troiae

1. Graeci novem annos Troiam oppugnaverant et iam domi esse cupiebant.
2. Bellum diu et fortiter gesserant, sed neque urbem ceperant neque illum locum relinquere potuerant.
3. Itaque consilium ceperunt. Magno studio laboreque equum magnum fecerunt. Multi milites Graeci, qui bene pugnare poterant, a sociis suis in equo ipso noctu locati sunt.

The Trojan Horse

1. The Greeks had attacked Troy for nine years and now they wanted to be at home.
2. They had carried on war for a long time and bravely, but they had neither captured the city nor had they been able to leave that place.
3. And so they decided on a plan. With great zeal and work they made a large horse. Many Greek soldiers, who were able to fight well, were placed in the horse itself by their comrades at night.

Equus Troiae

4. Exercitus urbis Troiae, qui post muros urbis erat, equum illa nocte non vidit.

5. Cives Troiae tamen, adventu solis in caelo, equum viderunt et eum in urbem duxerunt, sed mox Graeci, qui in equo positi erant, clamabant et in cives exercitumque Troiae impetum faciebant.
6. Populus terrebatur.
7. Graeci telis suis et igni urbem ceperunt. Tum Graeci ad mare, ubi alii Graeci naves suas instruxerant, cucurrerunt.

8. Post breve tempus, manus Graecorum cum captivis multis a Troia navigavit.

The Trojan Horse

4. The army of the city of Troy, which was behind the walls of the city, did not see the horse that night.
5. The citizens of Troy, however, at the arrival of the sun in the sky, saw the horse and led it into the city, but soon the Greeks, who had been placed in the horse, shouted and made an attack on the citizens and army of Troy.
6. The people were terrified.
7. With their weapons and fire the Greeks took the city. Then the Greeks ran to the sea, where the other Greeks had drawn up their ships.
8. After a short time, the band of Greeks sailed from Troy with many captives.

Proelium Marathonium

1. Anno XD Ante Christum, Graecia ab exercitu Persarum graviter oppugnabatur.
2. Persae trans mare ad Graeciam navigaverant et multa oppida occupaverant.
3. Hostes ad locum, qui non multa milia passuum Athenis erat, iam iter fecerant, et ob hanc rem cives Athenarum et in aliis urbibus propinquis illi loco adventum hostium timebant.
4. Populus Athenarum ad Spartam virum misit.
5. Ille totum iter cucurrit et ab populo Spartae auxilium petivit, sed Sparta legem habebat. Hac lege, illi sine luna in caelo bellum gerere non poterant, et illo tempore luna non erat.
6. Itaque milites soli Athenarum aciem suam instruxerunt et sagittis ac telis gravibus hostes vicerunt. Illo die populus Athenarum spem victoriae magnae videbat.

7. Postea ob virtutem viri, qui Athenis Spartam cucurrerat, ludos habebant. His ludis nomen proeli, quod in agro Marathonio fuerat, dederunt.

8. Etiam hodie ludo pedibus id nomen damus.

The Battle of Marathon

1. In the year 490 B.C., Greece was heavily attacked by the army of the Persians.
2. The Persians had sailed across the sea to Greece and had seized many towns.
3. The enemy had already made the journey to a place, which was not many miles from Athens, and for this reason the citizens of Athens and in other cities near to that place feared the arrival of the enemy.
4. The people of Athens sent a man to Sparta.

5. He ran the whole way and sought help from the people of Sparta, but Sparta had a law. By this law, they were not able to carry on war without a moon in the sky, and at that time there was no moon.
6. And so the soldiers of Athens drew up their battle line alone and conquered the enemy with arrows and heavy weapons. On that day the people of Athens saw the hope of a great victory.
7. Afterwards because of the courage of the man, who had run from Athens to Sparta, they held games. To these games they gave the name of the battle, that had been on the field of Marathon.
8. Even today we give this name to a contest on foot.

READING VOCABULARY

Nouns

domus, domus, f., house, home (domicile)

exercitus, exercitus, m., army (exercise)

cornu, cornus, n., horn, wing (of an army) (cornucopia)

adventus, adventus, m., arrival, approach (advent, adventure)

impetus, impetus, m., attack (impetuous)

manus, manus, f., hand, group (manual)

passus, passus, m., pace (passage)

dies, diei, m. or f., day (Diet)

res, rei, f., thing (re)

spes, spei, f., hope

acies, aciei, f., line of battle

Persae, Persarum, m., the Persians

Athenae, Athenarum, f., Athens

Sparta, Spartae, f., Sparta

Adjective

Marathonius, Marathonia, Marathonium, of Marathon

Verb

instruo, instruere, instruxi, instructus, draw up, form, train (instruct)

Conjunction

neque, and . . . not   neque . . . neque, neither . . . nor

READING GRAMMAR

A. Nouns that end in **-us** in the Genitive singular are **u-declension**. Those that end in **-us** in the Nominative singular are masculine, with a few exceptions; those in **-u** are neuter.

Nom.	exercitus	the army	cornu	the horn, wing
Gen.	exercitus	of the army	cornus	of the horn, wing
Dat.	exercitui	to, for the army	cornu	to, for the horn, wing
Acc.	exercitum	the army	cornu	the horn, wing
Abl.	exercitu	from, with, by, in the army	cornu	from, with, by, in the horn, wing

Nom.	exercitus	the armies	cornua	the horns, wings
Gen.	exercituum	of the armies	cornuum	of the horns, wings
Dat.	exercitibus	to, for the armies	cornibus	to, for the horns, wings
Acc.	exercitus	the armies	cornua	the horns, wings
Abl.	exercitibus	from, with, by, in the armies	cornibus	from, with, by, in the horns, wings

B. Nouns that end in **-ei** in the Genitive singular are **e-declension**. They are all feminine, except **dies** (day), which is generally masculine.

Nom.	res	the thing	res	the things
Gen.	rei	of the thing	rerum	of the things
Dat.	rei	to, for the thing	rebus	to, for the things
Acc.	rem	the thing	res	the things
Abl.	re	from, with, by, in the thing	rebus	from, with, by, in the things

C. **Domus** (house, home) has endings in both the **o-declension** and the **u-declension**.

Nom.	**domus**	house	**domus**	houses
Gen.	**domus, domi**	of the house	**domuum, domorum**	of the houses
Dat.	**domui, domo**	to, for the house	**domibus**	to, for the houses
Acc.	**domum**	house	**domos, domus**	houses
Abl.	**domo, domu**	from, with, by, in the house	**domibus**	from, with, by, in the houses

FAMILIAR ABBREVIATIONS

A.D., Anno Domini, in the year of (our) Lord.
a.m., ante meridiem, before noon.
p.m., post meridiem, after noon.
cf., confer, compare.

et al., et alibi, and elsewhere; **et alii,** and others.
vs., versus, against.
c., circ., circa, circum, about. Used with dates.
@, ad, to or at.

PRACTICE EXERCISES

No. 136. Give the English for these phrases.

1. multos passus
2. vestra manus
3. longum impetum
4. ob adventum eius
5. utrumque cornu
6. exercituum nostrorum
7. in cornu tuo
8. ex exercitu
9. in domum
10. sex milia passuum
11. contra exercitus
12. ob adventum tuum
13. impetus hostium
14. manus militum
15. ab exercitu

No. 137. Give the English for these phrases.

1. acies suas
2. multo die
3. proximo die
4. ob has res
5. ullius spei
6. totam rem
7. unam diem
8. quarum rerum?
9. nostrae acies
10. quas res?
11. in qua acie?
12. utriusque diei
13. ob eam rem
14. in his aciebus
15. multam spem

No. 138. Translate these Verb forms.

1. ambulavit
2. videmur
3. erant
4. fecerat
5. fugiebat
6. reperit
7. datum erat
8. potest
9. instructum est
10. videri
11. relicti sunt
12. pugnabunt
13. instruxit
14. iter facit
15. audientur

No. 139. Translate these sentences.

1. Omnes res faciles esse videntur.
2. Post sex dies neuter miles ullam spem habebat.
3. Captivi quos reduxisti ex eorum exercitu venerunt.
4. Quis fortem impetum magnopere impedivit?
5. Una hora homines domum venient.
6. Quam ob rem aciem suam in colli instruebat?
7. Inter has res quas habemus est parva copia aquae.
8. Milites in illo cornu equos suos ad agrum vertunt.
9. Neque cornu neque acies spem videbat.
10. Qui inter hos populos regnum tenent?

CHAPTER 29

READING

Proelium Thermopylarum

1. Post decem annos Persae ad Graeciam navibus suos reduxerunt.
2. Proelium Marathonium anno XD Ante Christum fuerat.
3. Hic annus erat XXD Ante Christum et hoc proelium appellatur Proelium Thermopylarum.
4. Persae magnam copiam et cibi et frumenti, quam trans mare portare in animo habebant, decem annos paraverant atque exercitum fortem acremque habuerunt.
5. Illi in impetu hoc omnem spem suam posuerant, sed illo tempore erat apud Graecos nulla pax. Alia civitas contra aliam contendebat.
6. Itaque Athenae Spartaque Graeciam totam aegre defendere poterant.
7. Exercitus hostium ad partem montium quae Thermopylae appellata est pervenit.
8. Hic locus natura fortis est quod iter parvum inter montes ab non multis militibus teneri poterat.
9. In eo loco manus parva Graecorum conlocata erat et adventum hostium exspectabat.
10. Graeci in montibus facile pugnare poterant. Ei enim patriam suam bene sciebant.
11. Iter per montes erat et difficile et angustum. Itaque Graeci praesidium ibi conlocaverant.
12. Hi contra milites fortes hostium, qui spem iam relinquebant, diu et fortiter contenderunt, sed erat unus homo, qui Persis auxilium dedit.
13. Hic vir hostibus iter, quod erat post locum ubi praesidium Graecum instructum erat, trans montes demonstravit.

The Battle of Thermopylae

1. After ten years the Persians led their men back to Greece by ship.
2. The Battle of Marathon had been in the year 490 B.C.
3. This year was 480 B.C. and this battle is called the Battle of Thermopylae.
4. The Persians for ten years had prepared a great supply both of food and grain, which they intended to carry across the sea, and they also had a brave and keen army.
5. They had placed all their hope in this attack, but at that time there was no peace among the Greeks. One state was fighting against another.
6. And so Athens and Sparta were able to defend all Greece with difficulty.
7. The army of the enemy came to the part of the mountains which is called Thermopylae.
8. This place is strong by nature because the small road between the mountains was able to be held by a few soldiers.
9. In this place a small group of Greeks had been stationed and was waiting for the arrival of the enemy.
10. The Greeks were able to fight easily in the mountains. For they knew their native country well.
11. The way through the mountains was both difficult and narrow. And so the Greeks had stationed a garrison there.
12. They fought for a long time and bravely against the brave soldiers of the enemy, who were already giving up hope, but there was one man, who gave help to the Persians.
13. This man pointed out to the enemy a way across the mountains, which was in back of the place where the Greek guard had been drawn up.

Proelium Thermopylarum	The Battle of Thermopylae
14. Exercitus hostium ad locum post aciem Graecam noctu iter fecit.	14. The army of the enemy made its way at night to a place in back of the Greek battle line.
15. Alii Graeci fugere potuerunt, sed alii milites Spartae et sociorum eius nullum timorem demonstraverunt.	15. Some Greeks were able to escape, but other soldiers of Sparta and her allies showed no fear.
16. Hi gladiis et aliis telis diu pugnabant, sed post breve tempus Graeci omnes ab hostibus interfecti erant et Persae trans corpora eorum Athenas iter fecerunt.	16. These men fought for a long time with swords and other weapons, but after a short time all the Greeks had been killed by the enemy and the Persians made their way to Athens over their bodies.

READING VOCABULARY

Nouns

civitas, civitatis, f., state
Thermopylae, Thermopylarum, f. pl., Thermopylae
praesidium, praesidii or praesidi, n., guard, garrison (presidial)

Pronouns

ego, mei, I (egotist)
nos, nostrum, we (nostrum)
tu, tui, you (sing.)
vos, vestrum, you (pl.)

Verbs

appello, appellare, appellavi, appellatus, address, call, name (appellation)
conloco, conlocare, conlocavi, conlocatus, place, station (collocate)
scio, scire, scivi, scitus, know (sciolist)

Adjective

decem, ten (decimal)

Conjunction

enim, for Never the first word in a Latin sentence.

READING GRAMMAR

A. Personal Pronouns are used to show emphasis or to make a clear distinction.

Emphasis: **ego scio,** I (myself) know
Clarity: **ego et tu scimus,** I and you know

1. Personal Pronouns of the First Person.

	SINGULAR		PLURAL	
Nom.	ego	I	nos	we
Gen.	mei	of me	nostrum or nostri	of us
Dat.	mihi	to, for me	nobis	to, for us
Acc.	me	me	nos	us
Abl.	me	from, with, by, in me	nobis	from, with, by, in us

2. Personal Pronouns of the Second Person.

	SINGULAR		PLURAL	
Nom.	tu	you	vos	you
Gen.	tui	of you	vestrum or vestri	of you
Dat.	tibi	to, for you	vobis	to, for you
Acc.	te	you	vos	you
Abl.	te	from, with, by, in you	vobis	from, with, by, in you

3. You have already met the Personal Pronouns of the Third Person.

SINGULAR		PLURAL	
is, ea, id	he, she, it	ei, eae, ea	they
ille, illa, illud	he, she, it	illi, illae, illa	they
hic, haec, hoc	he, she, it	hi, hae, haec	they

B. Adjectives are more commonly used to show possession than is the Genitive Case of the Personal Pronouns, except in the Third Person.

1st Person	meus, mea, meum	my, mine
	noster, nostra, nostrum	our, ours
2nd Person	tuus, tua, tuum	your, yours
	vester, vestra, vestrum	your, yours

But

3rd Person	eius, eius, eius	his, her, its
	eorum, earum, eorum	their
or		
	illius, illius, illius	his, her, its
	illorum, illarum, illorum	their
or		
	huius, huius, huius	his, her, its
	horum, harum, horum	their

When the Third Person possessor is the same as the subject:

suus, sua, suum   his, her, its, their (own)

Cum is added to the end of the Personal Pronouns.

mecum, with me	nobiscum, with us
tecum, with you	vobiscum, with you

C. Reflexive Pronouns reflect back to the subject and therefore have no Nominative Case.

Me video, I see myself   **Te vides,** you see yourself

1. Reflexive Pronouns of the First Person.

	SINGULAR		PLURAL	
Gen.	mei	of myself	nostri	of ourselves
Dat.	mihi	to, for myself	nobis	to, for ourselves
Acc.	me	myself	nos	ourselves
Abl.	me	from, with, by, in myself	nobis	from, with, by, in ourselves

2. Reflexive Pronouns of the Second Person.

	SINGULAR			PLURAL	
Gen.	**tui**	of yourself		**vestri**	The meanings are the
Dat.	**tibi**	to, for yourself		**vobis**	same as the singular.
Acc.	**te**	yourself		**vos**	
Abl.	**te**	from, with, by, in yourself		**vobis**	

3. Reflexive Pronouns of the Third Person.

	SINGULAR	
Gen.	**sui**	of himself, herself, itself
Dat.	**sibi**	to, for himself, herself, itself
Acc.	**se**	himself, herself, itself
Abl.	**se**	from, with, by, in himself, herself, itself

In the plural, the Latin is the same—sui, sibi, se, se—but the meaning is plural—themselves.

LEGAL TERMS

a vinculo matrimoni, from the bond of marriage. Used in a decree of absolute divorce.

caveat emptor, let the buyer beware. The buyer buys at his own risk.

inter vivos, between the living. Used to indicate a gift from a living person to another living person.

compos mentis, sound or sane of mind. **non compos mentis** or **non compos,** not sound or sane of mind.

nolo contendere, I do not wish to contend. A plea by which a defendant is subject to conviction, but does not admit his guilt.

nolle prosequi, to be unwilling to prosecute. Abbr. **nol pros.** A court record stating that the prosecutor will not carry his suit further.

non prosequitur, he does not prosecute. Abbr. **non pros.** Used to indicate a decision against a plaintiff who does not appear in court to prosecute.

obiter dictum, something said along the way. Used of remarks made by a judge that are not part of the legal decision, but are his personal comments and observations on matters relating to the case and decision.

nisi, if not, unless. Used to indicate that an order or decree will go into effect at a specified time unless modified by further evidence or cause presented before that time.

sui iuris or **suo iure,** of one's own right or in one's own right. Used of a person who has full capacity and ability to act for himself in legal proceedings.

PRACTICE EXERCISES

No. 140. Give the English for these Personal Pronouns.

1. vos	7. te	13. vobis	19. illorum	25. illis
2. nos	8. ego	14. eos	20. ad vos	26. de his
3. a te	9. eum	15. illud	21. tibi	27. illa
4. eorum	10. mihi	16. huic	22. vestrum	28. cum ea
5. ea	11. nobiscum	17. eius	23. nostri	29. horum
6. ei	12. tu	18. tecum	24. de me	30. illos

No. 141. Give the English for these Reflexive Pronouns.

1. sibi	3. a me	5. se	7. mihi	9. me
2. te	4. vos	6. vobis	8. nobis	10. nos

No. 142. Translate these sentences.

1. Homo ipse nos scit.
2. Ego tibi auxilium misi.
3. Nos in hoc loco te repperimus.
4. Venietisne vos mecum?
5. Tu nobis libros das.
6. Vos eum non auditis.
7. Illi ad nos fugiebant.
8. Is mihi haec misit.
9. Tecum domum ambulare non poterit.
10. Haec est patria nostra.
11. Tu id illis narrabis.
12. Nos hanc domum reducemus.
13. Illi ab his pacem petebant.
14. Ego a te et tuo gladio terrebar.
15. Nos illo tempore nos servaveramus.
16. Nonne tu nos iuvare potes?
17. Ille urbem eorum vidit.
18. Nos ipsi eos venire iubebimus.
19. Vos nobis ea demonstrabitis.
20. Animus eius me non diu terrebat.

SEVENTH REVIEW SECTION (CHAPTERS 26–29)

VOCABULARY REVIEW

NOUNS

1. acies	11. Hero	21. praesidium	1. line of battle	11. Hero	21. guard, garrison
2. adventus	12. impetus	22. regio	2. arrival, approach	12. attack	22. region, boundary
3. Athenae	13. inopia	23. regnum	3. Athens	13. want, scarcity	23. kingdom
4. civitas	14. Leander	24. res	4. state	14. Leander	24. thing
5. cornu	15. manus	25. Sparta	5. horn, wing	15. hand, group	25. Sparta
6. dies	16. natura	26. spes	6. day	16. nature	26. hope
7. domus	17. nihil, nil	27. Thermopylae	7. house, home	17. nothing	27. Thermopylae
8. Eurydice	18. Orpheus	28. turris	8. Eurydice	18. Orpheus	28. tower
9. exercitus	19. passus		9. army	19. pace	
10. Hellespontus	20. Persae		10. Hellespont	20. the Persians	

ADJECTIVES

1. decem	3. Marathonius	1. ten	3. of Marathon
2. difficilis	4. primus	2. difficult, hard	4. first

PRONOUNS

1. ego	3. qui	4. tu	1. I	3. who, which, that; which, what	4. you(s.)
2. nos		5. vos	2. we		5. you(pl.)

VERBS

1. accido	10. pervenio	1. happen	10. arrive
2. appello	11. prohibeo	2. address, call, name	11. keep off, hinder, prohibit, prevent
3. conloco	12. reduco	3. place, station	12. lead back
4. conspicio	13. rego	4. observe	13. rule
5. cupio	14. relinquo	5. desire, wish, want	14. leave, leave behind
6. discedo	15. reperio	6. withdraw, go away, leave	15. find, discover
7. educo	16. scio	7. lead out	16. know
8. impedio	17. trado	8. hinder	17. give up, surrender
9. instruo	18. venio	9. draw up, form, train	18. come

ADVERBS

1. iam	4. primum, primo	1. now, already	4. first, at first
2. magnopere	5. solum	2. greatly	5. alone, only
3. parum	6. tamen	3. too little, not enough	6. however, nevertheless

CONJUNCTIONS

1. enim	3. neque … neque	1. for	3. neither … nor
2. neque	4. ut	2. and not	4. as

PRACTICE EXERCISES

No. 143. Give the Adverbs of these Adjectives, with their meanings.

1. latus
2. acer
3. difficilis
4. miser
5. longus
6. magnus
7. laetus
8. liber
9. parvus
10. angustus

No. 144. Translate these Verbs.

1. veniam	4. perveniebamus	7. audiebaris	10. audieris
2. sciebat	5. impedientur	8. scitum erat	
3. auditus est	6. reperiunt	9. cupiverunt	

No. 145. Translate these Pronouns.

1. cuius	4. qui	7. mihi	10. tibi	13. eorum
2. quem	5. quibuscum	8. me	11. tecum	14. illum
3. quae	6. nos	9. vestrum	12. eius	15. hanc

No. 146. Translate these Nouns.

1. exercitui	4. aciem	7. die	10. domum	13. exercituum
2. res	5. spem	8. impetibus	11. rebus	14. manui
3. cornus	6. manuum	9. adventum	12. cornua	15. spei

PUBLIUS VERGILIUS MARO

Virgil was born in 70 B.C. near Mantua, in the north of Italy, and was educated in Milan, Rome, and Naples, where he studied philosophy and rhetoric. During the latter part of his life, he lived near Naples, where he composed his epic poem, **The Aeneid.** Virgil died in 19 B.C. at Brundisium, while returning from Greece.

Ibant obscuri, sola sub nocte, per umbram	They walked obscured by darkness, in the lonely night, through the shadows
perque domos Ditis vacuas, et inania regna;	and through the vacant kingdoms of Pluto, and the empty homes;
quale per incertam lunam sub luce maligna est iter in silvis, ubi caelum condidit umbra	just as under the dim light of a wavering moon is a journey in the woods, when Jupiter has hidden the sky in shadows
Iuppiter, et rebus nox abstulit atra colorem.	and black night has taken away the color from things.
Vestibulum ante ipsum primisque in faucibus Orci	Before the very entrance and in the very jaws of Orcus
Luctus et ultrices posuere cubilia Curae,	Grief and avenging Cares have placed their couches,
pallentesque habitant Morbi, tristisque Senectus,	and pale Diseases dwell, and sad Old Age,
et Metus, et malesuada Fames, ac turpis Egestas,	and Fear, and Hunger persuading-evil, also base Want,
terribiles visu formae, Letumque Labosque,	forms terrible to see, both Death and Toil,
tum consanguineus Leti Sopor, et mala mentis	then Sleep the kinsman of Death, and evil Pleasures
Gaudia, mortiferumque adverso in limine Bellum,	of the mind, and death-bearing War on the threshold opposite,
ferreique Eumenidum thalami, et Discordia demens,	and the iron chambers of the Furies, and mad Discord,
vipereum crinem vittis innexa cruentis.	entwining her snaky hair with bloody fillets.
Aeneidos VI, 268–281	Aeneid 6, 268–281

These two stories are found in the sermons of James of Vitry, who was the Cardinal Bishop of Tusculum and died in 1240 A.D. The stories were used to illustrate a point as well as to entertain the listeners.

De Arbore In Qua Se Suspendebant Mulieres

De quodam alio audivi, qui habebat arborem in horto suo, in qua duae eius uxores suspenderant semetipsas. Cui quidam eius vicinus ait: "Valde fortunata est arbor illa et bonum omen habet. Habeo autem uxorem pessimam; rogo te, da mihi surculum ex ea, ut plantem in horto meo."

De Bachone Qui Pendebat In Quadam Villa

Aliquando transivi per quandam villam in Francia, ubi suspenderant pernam seu bachonem in platea hac condicione ut, qui vellet iuramento firmare quod uno integro anno post contractum matrimonium permansisset cum uxore ita quod de matrimonio non paenituisset, bachonem haberet. Et cum per decem annos ibi pependisset non est unus solus inventus qui bachonem lucraretur, omnibus infra annum de matrimonio contracto paenitentibus.

About a Tree on Which Women Were Hanging

I have heard about a certain other man, who had a tree in his garden, on which two of his wives had hung themselves. A certain one of his neighbors said to him: "Certainly that tree is lucky and holds a good omen. I, however, have a very bad wife; I ask you, give me a young shoot from it, so that I may plant it in my garden."

About a Side of Bacon Which Was Hanging in a Certain Town

Once I passed through a certain town in France, where they had hung a ham or side of bacon in the street with this condition that, whoever might wish to swear on oath that he had lived one whole year with his wife after the marriage had been contracted in such a way that he had not regretted the marriage, might have the side of bacon. And although it had hung there for ten years not one single man was found who might win the side of bacon, because all inside of a year from the contract of marriage regretted it.

CHAPTER 30

READING

Aeneas in Igni Troiae

1. Aeneas in vias Troiae una nocte cucurrit et multitudinem militum Graecorum, qui vero laeti erant, quod urbem vicerant, ibi videbat.
2. Aeneas cum parva manu sociorum suorum contra hostes primo contendit, sed nihil faci poterat.
3. Tum patrem suum, qui domi erat, memoria tenuit et domum properavit.

Aeneas in the Fire of Troy

1. Aeneas ran into the streets of Troy one night and he saw there a great number of Greek soldiers, who were truly happy, because they had conquered the city.
2. Aeneas with a small band of his comrades at first struggled against the enemy, but nothing could be done.
3. Then he remembered his father, who was at home, and he hurried home.

Aeneas in Igni Troiae

4. Troia eo tempore acriter incendebatur. Populus Troiae dediderat. Bellum contra Graecos pugnatum erat.

5. Aeneas patrem suum secum venire coegit et in umeris suis totum onus corporis eius portabat. Hi tres, Aeneas atque pater suus atque suus filius parvus, ex igni contendebant.

6. Ob victoriam hostium magnopere opprimebantur.

7. Post breve tempus, Aeneas matrem fili sui, Creusam, memoria tenuit. Illa enim erat in urbe. Itaque in urbem celeriter cucurrit.

8. Bis centum tempora eam appellabat, sed illa ibi non erat. A Morte educta erat.

Aeneas in the Fire of Troy

4. Troy at that time was being fiercely burned. The people of Troy had surrendered. The war against the Greeks had been finished.

5. Aeneas forced his father to come with him and he carried the whole burden of his body on his shoulders. These three, Aeneas and his father and his small son, hurried from the fire.

6. Because of the victory of the enemy they were greatly oppressed.

7. After a short time, Aeneas remembered the mother of his son, Creusa. For she was in the city. And so he ran quickly into the city.

8. He called her twice a hundred times, but she was not there. She had been carried off by Death.

Iter Ulixis

1. Decem annos Ulixes ab portu Troiae ad patriam suam navigabat. Ipse et socii sui ad multa loca illo tempore pervenerunt.

2. Primus locus erat eis acriter gratus idoneusque.

3. Secundus locus erat terra in qua Polyphemus habitabat.

4. Tertio in loco, venti eis ab rege ventorum dati sunt.

5. Quarto in loco, multi viri ab illo, quem ibi reppererunt, necati sunt.

6. Ob feminam pulchram ab quinto loco difficile se recipere potuerunt.

7. Sexto in loco, omnes qui apud Inferos convenerant viderunt.

8. Septimo in loco, multas res pulchras audiverunt et ibi manere cupiverunt.

9. Ab octavo loco celeriter fugerunt. Nam duo animalia ibi habitabant. Unum ex his erat serpens et alterum erat magnum saxum.

10. Nono in loco animalia dei solis tenebantur.

11. Tum omnes socii eius in mari necati sunt. Itaque ille solus ad decimum locum pervenit.

12. Iter difficile susceperat, sed post decem aestates atque decem hiemes servatus erat et domum venit.

The Journey of Ulysses

1. Ulysses sailed for ten years from the harbor of Troy to his native country. He and his comrades arrived at many places during that time.

2. The first place was keenly pleasing and suitable to them.

3. The second place was the land in which Polyphemus lived.

4. In the third place, winds were given to them by the king of the winds.

5. In the fourth place, many of the men were killed by him, whom they found there.

6. They were able to depart from the fifth place with difficulty because of a beautiful woman.

7. In the sixth place, they saw all those who had come together among Those Below.

8. In the seventh place, they heard many beautiful things and wished to stay there.

9. They fled from the eighth place quickly. For two animals lived there. One of these was a serpent and the other was a large rock.

10. In the ninth place the animals of the god of the sun were held.

11. Then all his comrades were killed on the sea. And so he arrived alone at the tenth place.

12. He had undertaken a difficult journey, but after ten summers and ten winters he had been saved and he came home.

READING VOCABULARY

Nouns

multitudo, multitudinis, f., great number, multitude (multitudinous)

Creusa, Creusae, f., Creusa

onus, oneris, n., burden, weight (onerous)

aestas, aestatis, f., summer

ventus, venti, m., wind (vent)

hiems, hiemis, f., winter

portus, portus, m., harbor, port

Adverb

bis, twice (bicycle)

Conjunction

nam, for

Verbs

incendo, incendere, incendi, incensus, set fire to, burn (incendiary)

opprimo, opprimere, oppressi, oppressus, overcome, crush (oppressive)

dedo, dedere, dedidi, deditus, give up, surrender

cogo, cogere, coegi, coactus, collect, drive, compel (cogent)

recipio, recipere, recepi, receptus, take back, receive (reception)

convenio, convenire, conveni, conventus, come together, assemble (convention)

suscipio, suscipere, suscepi, susceptus, take up, undertake (susceptible)

READING GRAMMAR

A. The Cardinal Numbers one to twenty, one hundred, and one thousand:

1—unus, una, unum	11—undecim
2—duo, duae, duo	12—duodecim
3—tres, tria	13—tredecim
4—quattuor	14—quattuordecim
5—quinque	15—quindecim
6—sex	16—sedecim
7—septem	17—septendecim
8—octo	18—duodeviginti
9—novem	19—undeviginti
10—decem	20—viginti

100—centum

1000—mille

These Cardinal Numbers are declined:

1—

	M.	F.	N.
Nom.	unus	una	unum
Gen.	unius	unius	unius
Dat.	uni	uni	uni
Acc.	unum	unam	unum
Abl.	uno	una	uno

2—

	M.	F.	N.
Nom.	duo	duae	duo
Gen.	duorum	duarum	duorum
Dat.	duobus	duabus	duobus
Acc.	duos, duo	duas	duo
Abl.	duobus	duabus	duobus

3—

	M. and F.	N.
Nom.	tres	tria
Gen.	trium	trium
Dat.	tribus	tribus
Acc.	tres, tris	tria
Abl.	tribus	tribus

1000—

	SINGULAR	PLURAL
Nom.	mille	milia
Gen.	mille	milium
Dat.	mille	milibus
Acc.	mille	milia
Abl.	mille	milibus

1. Mille is an Adjective in the singular and a Noun in the plural.

   mille homines, a thousand men
   milia hominum, thousands of men

2. The other Cardinal Numbers may be used as Adjectives or Nouns.

   tres homines, three men
   tres hominum, three of the men
   tres de hominibus, three (from the) men
   tres ex hominibus, three (from the) men

B. The Ordinal Numbers first to tenth:

   first—primus, prima, primum
   second—secundus, secunda, secundum
   third—tertius, tertia, tertium
   fourth—quartus, quarta, quartum
   fifth—quintus, quinta, quintum
   sixth—sextus, sexta, sextum
   seventh—septimus, septima, septimum
   eighth—octavus, octava, octavum
   ninth—nonus, nona, nonum
   tenth—decimus, decima, decimum

All Ordinal Numbers are a- and o-declension Adjectives.

   sexto die, on the sixth day
   quartum annum, for the fourth year

LATIN MOTTOES

E Pluribus Unum, One from Many, United States

Nil sine numine, Nothing without divine power, Colorado

Qui transtulit sustinet, He who has transplanted sustains, Connecticut

Scuto bonae voluntatis tuae coronasti nos, You have crowned us with the shield of Thy Will, Maryland

Si quaeris peninsulam amoenam circumspice, If you seek a pleasant peninsula, look around, Michigan

Crescit eundo, It increases as it goes, New Mexico

Esse quam videri, To be rather than to seem, North Carolina

Labor omnia vincit, Labor conquers all, Oklahoma

Alis volat propriis, It flies on its own wings, Oregon

Animis opibusque parati, Prepared in mind and resources, South Carolina

Sic semper tyrannis, Thus always to tyrants, Virginia

PRACTICE EXERCISES

No. 147. Give the meanings of these Cardinal Numbers.

1. quindecim	7. tres	13. octo	19. duodeviginti
2. novem	8. septendecim	14. undeviginti	20. mille
3. viginti	9. quattuor	15. duo	21. duodecim
4. quinque	10. undecim	16. tredecim	22. sex
5. sedecim	11. centum	17. septem	
6. decem	12. quattuordecim	18. unus	

No. 148. Give the meanings of these Ordinal Numbers.

1. quartus	4. tertius	7. quintus	10. sextus
2. octavus	5. septimus	8. nonus	
3. decimus	6. secundus	9. primus	

No. 149. Translate these phrases which contain Cardinal Numbers.

1. mille naves
2. tres homines
3. milium militum
4. quattuordecim dies
5. unius viri
6. viginti milia passuum
7. centum pueros
8. quinque annos
9. sex de militibus
10. septem horis
11. centum annis
12. octo ex pueris
13. duos dies
14. decem legum
15. tria loca
16. duae de provinciis
17. duodecim diebus
18. sex animalium
19. duodeviginti ex regibus
20. tribus annis

No. 150. Translate these phrases which contain Ordinal Numbers.

1. decimae puellae
2. octavo die
3. sexta hora
4. septima navis
5. quinta aestate
6. tertium diem
7. decima hieme
8. septimus impetus
9. nonae horae
10. primo anno

CHAPTER 31

READING

Cupido et Psyche

1. Erant olim tres sorores pulchrae, quae erant filiae regis reginaeque. Harum Psyche erat clarissima. Itaque fama eius in regionibus, quae finitimae erant domui suae, erat aequa illi Veneris.

2. Venus non solum immortalis sed etiam superbissima erat. Itaque contra puellam, quae neque dea neque immortalis erat, poenam reperire constituit.

3. Dea pulchra nullam inopiam consili habebat. Postquam ipsa iter ex hac difficultate delegerat, filium suum, Cupidem, deum amoris, ad se vocavit.

4. Ei difficultatem suam demonstrat et dicit: "Omnes Psychen petunt et illi nunc me adorare non etiam simulant. Ob iniurias, quas matri tuae fecit, poenas dare debet. Hoc opus tibi idoneum est."

5. Cupido matrem suam iuvare celeriter parabat.

6. Ad hortum Veneris, in quo erant duo fontes, quorum alter dulcis erat alterque non dulcis, properavit.

Cupid and Psyche

1. There were once three beautiful sisters, who were daughters of the king and queen. Of these Psyche was the most famous. And so her reputation in the regions, that were neighboring to her home, was equal to that of Venus.

2. Venus was not only immortal but also very proud. And so she decided to find a punishment against the girl, who was neither a goddess nor immortal.

3. The beautiful goddess had no lack of plan. After she had chosen a way out of this difficulty, she called her son, Cupid, the god of love, to her.

4. To him she pointed out her difficulty and said: "All seek Psyche and they do not even pretend to worship me now. Because of the injuries, which she has done to your mother, she ought to pay penalties. This work is suitable to you."

5. Cupid quickly prepared to help his mother.

6. He hurried to the garden of Venus, in which there were two fountains, one of which was sweet and the other not sweet.

Cupido et Psyche

7. Postquam ex utroque fonte aquam obtinu-
erat, Psychen, quae domi dormiebat, petivit.

8. Ipse, ubi illam vidit, paene motus est quod
pulcherrima erat, sed deus matrem memoria
tenebat et puellam aqua, quae non dulcis
erat, et sagitta sua tetigit.

9. Psyche incitata est, sed Cupidinem videre
non poterat. Ipse territus est et in illa
aquam dulcem posuit.

10. Postea Psyche, quamquam pulchra erat,
miserrima quoque erat. Quod illa a Venere
non amabatur nullus eam in matrimonium
ducere cupiebat.

11. Itaque Psyche domi manebat et pater
materque puellae simillimam inopiam spei
demonstrabant.

12. Hoc ab oraculo dictum erat: "Non a viro,
sed ab uno contra quem nullus stare potest
tu in matrimonium duceris."

Cupid and Psyche

7. After he had obtained water from each fountain, he sought Psyche, who was asleep at
home.

8. He himself, when he saw her, was almost
moved because she was very pretty, but the
god remembered his mother and touched
the girl with the water, that was not sweet,
with his arrow.

9. Psyche was aroused, but she was not able
to see Cupid. He was frightened and placed
the sweet water on her.

10. Afterwards Psyche, although she was pretty,
was also very unhappy. Because she was not
loved by Venus, no one wanted to marry
her.

11. And so Psyche remained at home and the
father and mother of the girl showed a very
similar lack of hope.

12. This had been said by the oracle: "You will
be married not by a man, but by one against
whom no one can stand."

READING VOCABULARY

Nouns

fons, fontis, m., spring, fountain (fontium)
(font)
matrimonium, matrimonii or matrimoni, n.,
marriage (matrimony) in matrimonium ducere, marry
oraculum, oraculi, n., oracle (oracular)
soror, sororis, f., sister (sorority)
difficultas, difficultatis, f., difficulty
Cupido, Cupidinis, m., Cupid (cupidity)
Psyche, Psyches, f., Psyche (a Greek noun) (psy-
chic)

Adjectives

similis, simile, like, similar (similarity)
dulcis, dulce, sweet (dulcet)
aequus, aequa, aequum, equal, level, fair (equal-
ity)
immortalis, immortale, immortal (immortality)

Verbs

dormio, dormire, dormivi, dormitus, sleep
(dormant, dormitory)
tango, tangere, tetigi, tactus, touch (tangent)
deligo, deligere, delegi, delectus, choose, select
constituo, constituere, constitui, constitutus, decide, establish (constitution)

Adverbs

olim, formerly, once upon a time
quoque, also

Conjunction

quamquam, although

READING GRAMMAR

A. Adjectives have three degrees of comparison—positive, comparative, and superlative.
  1. The Positive degree is always the simple form of the Adjective.

> **longus, longa, longum,** long
> **fortis, forte,** brave
> **miser, misera, miserum,** wretched
> **pulcher, pulchra, pulchrum,** pretty
> **acer, acris, acre,** keen
> **facilis, facile,** easy

  2. The Comparative degree of all Adjectives ends in **-ior** or **-ius.**

> **longior, longius,** longer, rather long, too long, quite long
> **fortior, fortius,** braver, rather brave, too brave, quite brave
> **miserior, miserius,** more wretched, rather wretched, quite wretched
> **pulchrior, pulchrius,** prettier, more pretty, rather pretty, quite pretty
> **acrior, acrius,** keener, more keen, rather keen, quite keen
> **facilior, facilius,** easier, more easy, rather easy, quite easy

  3. The Superlative degree endings are:
  a. for those Adjectives that end in **-er,**

> **miserrimus, a, um,** very wretched, most wretched
> **pulcherrimus, a, um,** very pretty, most pretty, prettiest
> **acerrimus, a, um,** very keen, most keen, keenest

  b. for **facilis, difficilis,** and **similis,**

> **facillimus, a, um,** very easy, most easy, easiest
> **difficillimus, a, um,** very difficult, most difficult
> **simillimus, a, um,** very similar, most similar

  c. for all other Adjectives, the ending is **-issimus, a, um**

> **longissimus, a, um,** very long, most long, longest
> **fortissimus, a, um,** very brave, bravest, most brave

B. 1. The Positive degree of an Adjective is declined regularly in the **a-** and **o-declensions** or in the **i-declension.**

  2. The Comparative degree is declined:

	SINGULAR		PLURAL	
	M. and F.	**N.**	**M. and F.**	**N.**
Nom.	longior	longius	longiores	longiora
Gen.	longioris	longioris	longiorum	longiorum
Dat.	longiori	longiori	longioribus	longioribus
Acc.	longiorem	longius	longiores	longiora
Abl.	longiore	longiore	longioribus	longioribus

  3. The Superlative degree is declined regularly in the **a-** and **o-declensions.**

FAMILIAR QUOTATIONS

Laudator temporis acti. A praiser of past times. Horace

Abeunt studia in mores. Pursuits pass over into habits. Ovid

Factum fieri infectum non potest. What is done can not be undone. Terence

O tempora! O mores! Oh the times! Oh the customs! Cicero

Tu ne cede malis. Do not yield to misfortunes. Virgil

Docendo discitur. We learn by teaching. Seneca

In hoc signo vinces. By this sign thou shalt conquer. Constantine

Non datur ad Musas currere lata via. It is not granted to run to the Muses on a wide road. Propertius

Est modus in rebus. There is a middle course in things. Horace

Forsan et haec olim meminisse iuvabit. Perhaps some time it will be pleasant to remember even these things. Virgil

PRACTICE EXERCISES

No. 151. Translate these Positive degree Adjectives.

1. iter difficile
2. domum miseram
3. virorum liberorum
4. timores acres
5. exercitus similes
6. diem longum
7. in monte alto
8. flumina celeria
9. vias latas
10. puellarum pulchrarum

No. 152. Translate these Comparative degree Adjectives.

1. viae angustiores
2. puer altior
3. puellarum laetiorum
4. populus amicior
5. iter longius
6. in locis gratioribus
7. sororum clariorum
8. hiemem longiorem
9. flumina latiora
10. virum audaciorem

No. 153. Translate these Superlative degree Adjectives.

1. fontis dulcissimi
2. ex hortis pulcherrimis
3. templum angustissimum
4. ob memorias miserrimas
5. oracula clarissima
6. civis laetissimus
7. ex agro latissimo
8. cum matribus pulcherrimis
9. in navi novissima
10. nomina brevissima

No. 154. Translate these sentences.

1. Is est locus miserrimus.
2. Fortissimi homines ad insulam pervenerunt.
3. Acerrimi equi erant inter primos.
4. Quid ad Graeciam est iter facilius?
5. Populus Italiae est liberrimus.
6. Haec est angustior pars aquae.
7. Hae res sunt quoque simillimae.
8. Flumen altissimum et latius vidimus.
9. Nostri ad urbem viam breviorem delegerunt.
10. Aedificium altum ab hoc loco videre potestis.

CHAPTER 32

READING

Cupido et Psyche (cont'd.)

1. Locus, quem oraculum demonstraverat et in quo maritus illam exspectabat, summo in monte erat.
2. Illa ipsa etiam miserior aut patre aut matre erat. Itaque ad suam fortunam malam se dedere constituit.
3. Mox postea puella, cum matre patreque atque multis ex amicis suis, ad montem a populo oppidi, in quo habitabat, ducta est.
4. Hi eam solam ibi reliquerunt, quamquam pro ea magnopere dolebant, et se receperunt.
5. Psyche, quae summo in monte diu steterat et omnia in eo loco timebat, ab uno ex ventis, Zephyro, a monte ad terram pulcherrimam celeriter portata est.
6. Postquam breve tempus dormiverat, circum se spectabat et in silvam, quae propinqua erat agro, in quo a Zephyro relicta erat, audacter ambulavit.
7. In silva domum, quae pulchrior erat ulla quam antea viderat, repperit. Ad domum cucurrit.
8. Omnia in domo ei erant gratissima et ipsa tum vero laetissima erat.
9. Mox vocem audivit, sed neque virum neque mulierem vidit. Vox dixit: "Haec domus tua est et nos servi tui erimus. Omnia quae rogabis faciemus."
10. Postea in domo habitabat et laetior erat quam ulla puella in terra illa. Nil cupiebat.
11. Domum, servos, omnia bona, et maritum habebat, sed hunc non videbat. Noctu veniebat et ab ea ante diem properabat.

Cupid and Psyche (cont'd.)

1. The place, which the oracle had pointed out and in which her husband was waiting for her, was on the top of a mountain.
2. She herself was more unhappy than either her father or mother. And so she decided to surrender herself to her bad fortune.
3. Soon afterwards the girl, with her mother and father and many of her friends, was led to the mountain by the people of the town, in which she lived.
4. They left her there alone, although they felt very sorry for her, and departed.
5. Psyche, who had stayed on the top of the mountain for a long time and was afraid of everything in that place, was carried quickly from the mountain to a very beautiful land by one of the winds, Zephyr.
6. After she had slept for a short time, she looked around her and boldly walked into the forest, which was near the field, in which she had been left by Zephyr.
7. In the forest she found a house, which was prettier than any that she had seen before. She ran toward the house.
8. All the things in the house pleased her very much and she herself was then truly very happy.
9. Soon she heard a voice, but she saw neither man nor woman. The voice said: "This house is yours and we shall be your servants. We shall do everything that you ask."
10. Afterwards she lived in the house and she was happier than any girl in that land. She wished for nothing.
11. She had a house, servants, all good things, and a husband, but she did not see him. He came at night and hurried away from her before day.

Cupido et Psyche (cont'd.)	Cupid and Psyche (cont'd.)
12. Quam ob rem maxime dolebat, sed maritum suum bene amabat. Ipse dixit: "Me nunc amas quod aequi sumus. Hoc iter optimum est."	12. For this reason she grieved greatly, but she loved her husband well. He said: "You love me now because we are equal. This way is best."
13. Diu tamen laetissima erat, sed posteriore tempore matrem patremque sororesque quoque memoria tenebat et oppressa est quod ibi non erant.	13. For a long time, however, she was very happy, but at a later time she remembered her mother and father and also her sisters and was oppressed because they were not there.
14. Una nocte, ubi maritus eius venit, ab eo viam e difficultate sua petivit.	14. One night, when her husband came, she sought from him a way out of her difficulty.

READING VOCABULARY

Nouns

maritus, mariti, m., husband (marital)
Zephyrus, Zephyri, m., Zephyr, west wind
vox, vocis, f., voice (vocal)

Adjective

posterus, postera, posterum, next, following (posterior)

Adverbs

quam, than
antea, before
multo, much, by much
magis, more
maxime, most, especially (maximum)

Conjunction

aut . . . aut, either . . . or

READING GRAMMAR

A. There are two ways to show the comparison between two things.

1. quam, with the same case for the two things being compared.

    Ego altior sum quam tu, I am taller than you
    amicior illi quam huic, more friendly to that one than this

2. the Ablative Case after the Comparative degree, without quam.

    Ego altior sum te, I am taller than you
    amicior illi hoc, more friendly to that one than this

B. Some Adjectives have an irregular comparison.

bonus, a, um	melior, melius	optimus, a, um
good	better	best
magnus, a um	maior, maius	maximus, a, um
large	larger	largest
malus, a, um	peior, peius	pessimus, a, um
bad	worse	worst
parvus, a, um	minor, minus	minimus, a, um
small	smaller	smallest

multus, a, um	——, plus	plurimus, a, um
much	more	most
multi, ae, a	plures, plura	plurimi, ae, a
many	more	most

The Superlative degree of posterus is postremus, a, um, or postumus, a, um.

C. Most Adjectives ending in a vowel and -us are compared this way:

idoneus, a, um	magis idoneus, a, um	maxime idoneus, a, um
suitable	more suitable	most suitable

D. **Plus** is a neuter noun in the singular; an adjective in the plural.

		M. and F.	N.
Nom.	plus	plures	plura
Gen.	pluris	plurium	plurium
Dat.	——	pluribus	pluribus
Acc.	plus	plures, pluris	plura
Abl.	plure	pluribus	pluribus

MATHEMATICAL TERMS BASED ON LATIN

plus, more, increased by.

minus, less, diminished by.

multiplication, from **multiplicare**, to make manifold or many fold.

division, from **dividere**, divide.

subtraction, from **subtrahere**, withdraw, draw from beneath.

addition, from **addere**, add to, or **additio**, adding.

ratio, from **ratio**, reason.

quotient, from **quotiens**, how often, how many times.

sum, from **summa**, sum or total, or **summus**, highest.

number and numeral, from **numerus**, number.

integer, from **integer**, whole, untouched.

fraction, from **frangere**, break.

percent and per centum, from **per centum**, by the hundred, in the hundred.

PRACTICE EXERCISES

No. 155. Translate these sentences.

1. Hae turres altiores sunt quam illae.
2. Es altior patre tuo.
3. Illa itinera aliis faciliora non sunt.
4. Patri tuo quam matri similior es.
5. Homines multo fortiores mulieribus sunt.
6. Domus eius ruri novior est illa in urbe.
7. Puer laetior est quam soror.
8. Barbari multo audaciores sunt finitimis suis.
9. Ille vobis amicior quam mihi erit.
10. Estne manus celerior quam oculus?

No. 156. Give the English for these Verb forms.

1. erunt
2. demonstratum est
3. constituit
4. parabitur
5. ducebant
6. relictus est
7. mittetur
8. portaris
9. videbamus
10. ambulavit

No. 157. Give the English for these Adjectives.

1. plura
2. melior
3. pessimorum
4. maioris
5. minorum
6. plurimorum
7. pluribus
8. posteros
9. magis idonei
10. maxime idoneum

No. 158. Translate these Adjective phrases.

1. in pluribus urbibus
2. ex fontibus minoribus
3. virtutem maximam
4. vox optima
5. de muris altioribus
6. plus aquae
7. tempus magis idoneum
8. rei pessimae
9. ad partem meliorem
10. cum maiore exercitu
11. die longiore
12. plurimas civitates
13. finem peiorem
14. annos optimos
15. soror minima
16. plurium difficultatum
17. iter melius
18. aestatis pessimae
19. dona plurima
20. navis minoris

CHAPTER 33

READING

Cupido et Psyche (cont'd.)

1. Postridie ad Zephyrum quam celerrime contendit et illi id quod maritus suus dixerat narrabat.
2. Imperia Cupidinis facillime confecit et brevi tempore duae sorores eius ad domum eius a Zephyro celeriter portatae sunt.
3. Psyche adventu earum laetissima erat et illis omnia sua demonstravit. Ipsae tamen postquam domum atque servos illius viderant inopiam eius bonae fortunae acerrime cognoverunt.
4. Multa rogabant: "Esne uxor laeta?" "Quis es maritus tuus?"
5. Magno cum studio verba eius audiebant. Vita eius melior quam vita earum esse videbatur.
6. Eam miserrime conspiciebant. Eodem tempore spem maiorem videbant: "Num tu maritum tuum umquam vidisti? Maritus quem uxor numquam vidit optimus maritus esse non potest. Nonne verba oraculi memoria tenes? Ille aut serpens aut animal est."

7. Psyche consilio sororum suarum coacta est quod ab eis semper facillime ducebatur. Itaque lucem ac gladium cepit et haec in loco idoneo conlocavit.

Cupid and Psyche (cont'd.)

1. On the next day she hurried as quickly as possible to Zephyr and told him what her husband had said.
2. He very easily carried out the commands of Cupid and in a short time her two sisters were carried quickly to her house by Zephyr.
3. Psyche was very happy at their arrival and showed them all her possessions. They, however, after they had seen her house and servants, clearly recognized her lack of good fortune.
4. They asked many things: "Are you a happy wife?" "Who is your husband?"
5. They listened to her words with great eagerness. Her life seemed to be better than their life.
6. They looked at her most unhappily. At the same time they saw a greater hope: "You haven't ever seen your husband, have you? A husband whom his wife has never seen can not be the best husband. You remember the words of the oracle, don't you? He is either a serpent or an animal."
7. Psyche was convinced by the plan of her sisters because she was always very easily influenced by them. And so she took a light and a sword and placed these things in a suitable place.

Cupido et Psyche (cont'd.)

8. Psyche consilium sororum suarum minime amabat, sed verba earum quam verba sua plus poterant. Illae plus facile quam ipsa dicere poterant.
9. Itaque ipsa lucem gladiumque paravit et maritus eius ad eam noctu venit. Ipsa maxime timebat, sed ei timorem suum non demonstrabat.
10. Dum ille dormit, lucem cepit et supra eum id tenebat. Quid vidit? Neque serpentem neque animal ante se conspexit. Erat unus ex deorum pulcherrimus atque gratissimus.

11. A timore liberata erat. Eum non diutius timebat, sed magis amabat.
12. Ut accidit tamen umerum eius luce tetigit et ille excitatus est. Ipse nullum verbum dixit, sed oculis suis eam monuit et alis celeribus eam reliquit.
13. Psyche ad terram cecidit. Cupido supra eam breve tempus volabat et dixit: "Contra imperia matris meae te amavi. Immortales mortales non saepe amant, sed te in matrimonium duxi et me interficere nunc cupis. Amor tuus minus fortis meo est."
14. His verbis puellam miserrimam reliquit et ad caelum volavit.

Cupid and Psyche (cont'd.)

8. Psyche did not like her sisters' plan at all, but their words were more powerful than her own. They were able to talk more easily than she.
9. And so she got the light and the sword ready and her husband came to her at night. She was very much afraid, but she did not show her fear to him.
10. While he slept, she took the light and held it above him. What did she see? She saw in front of her neither a serpent nor an animal. He was one of the most handsome and pleasing of the gods.
11. She had been freed from fear. She no longer feared him, but loved him more.
12. As it happened, however, she touched his shoulder with the light and he was aroused. He said no word, but warned her with his eyes and left her on swift wings.
13. Psyche fell to the ground. Cupid flew above her for a short time and said: "I have loved you against the commands of my mother. Immortals do not often love mortals, but I married you and now you want to kill me. Your love is less strong than mine."
14. With these words he left the very unhappy girl and flew to the sky.

READING VOCABULARY

Nouns

imperium, imperii or imperi, n., command (imperial)

uxor, uxoris, f., wife (uxorial)

verbum, verbi, n., word (verb)

lux, lucis, f., light (lucent)

Adjective

mortalis, mortale, mortal (mortality)

Conjunction

dum, while   With the Present tense.

Verbs

excito, excitare, excitavi, excitatus, arouse, stir up (excitement)

cado, cadere, cecidi, casurus, fall (cadence)

conficio, conficere, confeci, confectus, finish, complete, carry out (confection)

plus posse, be more powerful

plurimum posse, be most powerful

Adverbs

supra, over, above   Also a Preposition with the Accusative Case.

quam, as possible   With the Superlative degree.

numquam, never

umquam, ever

postridie, on the next day

READING GRAMMAR

A. Adverbs are compared in much the same way as Adjectives, but have only one form for each degree.

1. Regular Adverbs are compared:

longe	longius	longissime
far	farther	farthest
misere	**miserius**	**miserrime**
unhappily	more unhappily	most unhappily
pulchre	**pulchrius**	**pulcherrime**
beautifully	more beautifully	most beautifully
acriter	**acrius**	**acerrime**
keenly	more keenly	most keenly
fortiter	**fortius**	**fortissime**
bravely	more bravely	most bravely
facile	**facilius**	**facillime**
easily	more easily	most easily

2. These Adverbs are irregular:

bene	**melius**	**optime**
well	better	best
magnopere	**magis**	**maxime**
greatly	more	most
male	**peius**	**pessime**
badly	worse	worst
multum	**plus**	**plurimum**
much	more	most
parum	**minus**	**minime**
little	less	least
diu	**diutius**	**diutissime**
long	longer	longest
saepe	**saepius**	**saepissime**
often	more often	most often

B. When **quam** is used with the superlative degree of an Adjective or Adverb it means *as . . . as possible*.

> **quam pulcherrimus**, as pretty as possible
> **quam pulcherrime**, as beautifully as possible

GEOMETRICAL TERMS BASED ON LATIN

perpendicular, from **per**, through, and **pendere**, hang.

circumference, from **circum**, around, and **ferre**, carry.

circle, from **circus**, circle.

radius, from **radius**, staff, rod, ray.

arc, from **arcus**, bow, arc.

tangent, from **tangere**, touch.

angle, from **angulus**, angle, corner.

obtuse, from **obtundere**, strike.

acute, from **acuere**, sharpen.

triangle, from **tri**, three, and **angulus**, angle.

rectangle, from **rectus**, right, and **angulus**, angle.

square, from **ex**, out, and **quadra**, square.

Q.E.D., abbreviation of **quod erat demonstrandum**, which was to be demonstrated.

PRACTICE EXERCISES

No. 159. Give the English for these Adjectives and Adverbs.

1. latus	9. liberior	17. pulchrius	25. acer
2. late	10. liberrimus	18. pulcherrime	26. acriter
3. latior	11. liberius	19. celer	27. acrior
4. latius	12. liberrime	20. celeriter	28. acrius
5. latissimus	13. pulcher	21. celerior	29. acerrimus
6. latissime	14. pulchrior	22. celerius	30. acerrime
7. liber	15. pulcherrimus	23. celerrimus	
8. libere	16. pulchre	24. celerrime	

No. 160. Translate these sentences, containing Adverbs.

1. Gravissime oppugnabantur.	8. Superbe ambulant.	15. Nove videbantur.
2. Fortius pugnat.	9. Gratius dabat.	16. Pulchrius movent.
3. Celeriter incensi sunt.	10. Altissime laudatur.	17. Acerrime timebit.
4. Multo brevius dicent.	11. Latius missi sunt.	18. Audacter capti sunt.
5. Audacissime monebitur.	12. Liberrime dedit.	19. Brevissime dicebat.
6. Difficile aciem instruxerunt.	13. Longissime navigat.	20. Fortiter pugnant.
7. Acrius bellum gessit.	14. Miserius movet.	

No. 161. Give the English for these Adverbs.

1. bene	6. diu	11. melius	16. plurimum	21. minime
2. magnopere	7. saepe	12. peius	17. diutissime	
3. male	8. diutius	13. minus	18. saepissime	
4. multum	9. plus	14. saepius	19. optime	
5. parum	10. magis	15. maxime	20. pessime	

No. 162. Translate these sentences, containing Adverbs.

1. Saepius perveniunt.	6. Id saepissime auditum est.
2. Quam diutissime pugnavit.	7. Minus difficile ambulat.
3. Magis excitatus est.	8. Apud nos plurimum possunt.
4. Plus impediebatur.	9. Plus celeriter volat.
5. Optime amatus es.	10. Multum diutius manebit.

EIGHTH REVIEW SECTION (CHAPTERS 30–33)

VOCABULARY REVIEW

NOUNS

1. aestas	8. lux	15. portus	1. summer	8. light	15. harbor, port
2. Creusa	9. maritus	16. Psyche	2. Creusa	9. husband	16. Psyche
3. Cupido	10. matrimonium	17. soror	3. Cupid	10. marriage	17. sister
4. difficultas	11. multitudo	18. uxor	4. difficulty	11. great number, multitude	18. wife
5. fons	12. onus	19. ventus	5. spring, fountain	12. burden, weight	19. wind
6. hiems	13. oraculum	20. verbum	6. winter	13. oracle	20. word
7. imperium	14. plus	21. vox	7. command	14. more	21. voice
		22. Zephyrus			22. Zephyr, west wind

ADJECTIVES

1. aequus	7. minimus	13. plurimus	1. equal, level, fair	7. smallest	13. most
2. dulcis	8. minor	14. posterus	2. sweet	8. smaller	14. next, following
3. immortalis	9. mortalis	15. postumus	3. immortal	9. mortal	15. next, following
4. maior	10. optimus	16. similis	4. larger	10. best	16. like, similar
5. maximus	11. peior		5. largest	11. worse	
6. melior	12. pessimus		6. better	12. worst	

VERBS

1. cado	9. excito	1. fall	9. arouse, stir up
2. cogo	10. incendo	2. collect, drive, compel	10. set fire to, burn
3. conficio	11. opprimo	3. finish, complete, carry out	11. overcome, crush
4. constituo	12. plurimum posse	4. decide, establish	12. be most powerful
5. convenio	13. plus posse	5. come together, assemble	13. be more powerful
6. dedo	14. recipio	6. give up, surrender	14. take back, receive
7. deligo	15. suscipio	7. choose, select	15. take up, undertake
8. dormio	16. tango	8. sleep	16. touch

ADVERBS

1. antea	7. olim	1. before	7. formerly, once upon a time
2. bis	8. postridie	2. twice	8. on the next day
3. magis	9. quam	3. more	9. as possible; than
4. maxime	10. supra	4. most, especially	10. over, above
5. multo	11. umquam	5. much, by much	11. ever
6. numquam		6. never	

CONJUNCTIONS

1. aut . . . aut	3. nam	5. quoque	1. either . . . or	3. for	5. also
2. dum	4. quamquam		2. while	4. although	

PRACTICE EXERCISES

No. 163. Translate these phrases.

1. una ex sororum	6. centum verba	11. secundo anno
2. tria flumina	7. unius vocis	12. septimum verbum
3. duos annos	8. viginti fontes	13. primum oraculum
4. mille anni	9. quarta hora	14. in quarto portu
5. duas uxores	10. quinto die	15. ex sexta porta

No. 164. Translate these Adjective phrases.

1. longiorem hiemem	5. onus simillimum	9. difficultatis acerrimae
2. pulcherrima aestas	6. vocis immortalis	10. maritorum fortiorum
3. longissimorum annorum	7. iter facilius	
4. dulcius verbum	8. luces clariores	

No. 165. Give the English for these Adjectives.

1. dulcis, dulcior, dulcissimus	6. liber, liberior, liberrimus
2. acer, acrior, acerrimus	7. celer, celerior, celerrimus
3. longus, longior, longissimus	8. latus, latior, latissimus
4. similis, similior, simillimus	9. clarus, clarior, clarissimus
5. altus, altior, altissimus	10. audax, audacior, audacissimus

No. 166. Give the English for these Adjectives.

1. magnus, maior, maximus	5. multus, plus, plurimus
2. parvus, minor, minimus	6. multi, plures, plurimi
3. bonus, melior, optimus	7. idoneous, magis idoneus, maxime idoneus
4. malus, peior, pessimus	

No. 167. Translate into English.

1. longius ambulabat	5. acrius excitati sunt	9. plus poterit
2. misere oppressus est	6. magis tangebant	10. minus facile cogentur
3. parum dormit	7. facilius dediderunt	
4. diutissime incendet	8. plurimum possunt	

PHAEDRUS

Phaedrus was a freedman of Augustus, who lived in the first half of the first century A.D. Five books of his **Fables** are extant. These are based on early folk tales and on the Greek fables of Aesop. Phaedrus, in turn, furnished the material for the French fabulist, La Fontaine.

Qui se laudari gaudet verbis subdolis,	He who rejoices that he is praised by words of flattery,
sera dat poenas turpes paenitentia.	too late pays his penalty with lowly repentance.
Cum de fenestra corvus raptum caseum	When a crow started to eat the cheese
comesse vellet, celsa residens arbore,	he snatched from a window, perching in a lofty tree,
vulpes hunc vidit; deinde sic coepit loqui:	a wolf saw him; thus, with flattery, he began to speak:
"O qui tuarum, corve, pinnarum est nitor.	"Oh what a brightness, crow, your feathers have.
Quantum decoris corpore et vultu geris.	What grace of body, what charm of looks you possess.
Si vocem haberes, nulla prior ales foret."	If you should have a voice, no bird would be above you."
At ille stultus, dum vult vocem ostendere,	Then he, foolish one, while he tried to show off his voice,
emisit ore caseum, quem celeriter	dropped the cheese from his mouth. This quickly
dolosa vulpes avidis rapuit dentibus.	the tricky fox snatched in his greedy teeth.
Tum demum ingemuit corvi deceptus stupor.	Then the crow, deceived by his stupidity, groaned, but too late.
Phaedrus I, xiii	Phaedrus I, 13

The **Stabat Mater** was composed by an unknown author, although Saint Bonaventure is sometimes given the credit for its composition, probably in the thirteenth century, and has been set to music by many musicians since the eighteenth century.

Stabat mater dolorosa	At the Cross her station keeping,
iuxta crucem lacrimosa,	Stood the mournful Mother weeping,
dum pendebat filius,	Close to Jesus at the last.
cuius animam gementem,	Through her soul, of joy bereaved,
contristantem et dolentem	Bowed with anguish, deeply grieved,
pertransivit gladius.	Now at length the sword hath passed.

O quam tristis et afflicta
fuit illa benedicta
mater unigenti,
quae maerebat et dolebat
et tremebat, dum videbat
nati poenas incliti!

Quis est homo qui non fleret,
matrem Christi si videret
in tanto supplicio?
Quis non posset contristari
piam matrem contemplari
dolentem cum filio?

Pro peccatis suae gentis
vidit Iesum in tormentis
et flagellis subditum;
vidit suum dulcem natum
morientem, desolatum,
dum emisit spiritum.

Eia mater, fons amoris!
Me sentire vim doloris
fac, ut tecum lugeam.
Fac ut ardeat cor meum
in amando Christum Deum,
ut sibi complaceam.

Sancta mater, istud agas,
crucifixi fige plagas
cordi meo valide;
tui nati vulnerati,
tam dignati pro me pati,
poenas mecum divide.

Fac me vere tecum flere,
crucifixo condolere,
donec ego vixero;
iuxta crucem tecum stare,
meque tibi sociare
in planctu desidero.

Virgo virginum praeclara,
mihi iam non sis amara,
fac me tecum plangere;
fac ut portem Christi mortem,
passionis fac consortem
et plagas recolere.

Fac me plagis vulnerari,
cruce hac inebriari,
et cruore filii;
per te, Virgo, sim defensus
inflammatus et accensus,
in die iudicii.

Oh how sad and sore distressed
Was that Mother, highly blest,
Of the sole begotten One!
Oh that silent, ceaseless mourning,
Oh those dim eyes, never turning
From that wondrous, suffering Son!

Who on Christ's dear Mother gazing,
In her trouble so amazing,
Born of woman, would not weep?
Who on Christ's dear Mother thinking,
Such a cup of sorrow drinking,
Would not share her sorrow deep?

For the sins of his own nation,
Saw him hang in desolation
Till his Spirit forth he sent;
Bruised, derided, cursed, defiled,
She beheld her tender Child,
All with bloody scourges rent.

O, thou Mother, fount of love!
Touch my spirit from above,
Make my heart with thine accord.
Make me feel as thou hast felt;
Make my soul to glow and melt
With the love of Christ my Lord.

Holy Mother, pierce me through.
In my heart each wound renew
Of my Saviour crucified;
Let me share with thee his pain,
Who for all my sins was slain,
Who for me in torment died.

Let me mingle tears with thee,
Mourning him who mourned for me,
All the days that I may live.
By the cross with thee to stay,
There with thee to weep and pray,
Is all I ask of thee to give.

Virgin of all virgins blest,
Listen to my fond request:
Let me share thy grief divine.
Let me to my latest breath,
In my body bear the death
Of that dying Son of thine.

Wounded with his every wound,
Steep my soul till it hath swooned
In his very blood away.
Be to me, O Virgin, nigh,
Lest in flames I burn and die
In his awful judgment day.

Fac me cruce custodiri
morte Christi praemuniri,
confoveri gratia.
Quando corpus morietur,
fac ut animae donetur
paradisi gloria.

Christ, when thou shalt call me hence,
Be thy Mother my defense,
Be thy cross my victory.
While my body here decays
May my soul thy goodness praise
Safe in Paradise with thee.

CHAPTER 34

READING

Cupido et Psyche (cont'd.)

1. Postquam Cupido uxorem suam tam celeriter reliquerat, illa circum se spectavit. Omnis spes ab ea interea cecidit atque sua vita laeta discessit, nam horti pulchri ac domus magna nunc ibi non erant.
2. Non longe ab urbe, ubi antea habitaverat, erat sola. Maxime dolebat.
3. Sorores fabulam eius magno cum studio audiverunt. Sibi dixerunt: "Cupido unam ex nobis nunc certe deliget."
4. Prima luce postridie illae duae ad montem properaverunt et Zephyrum audacissime appellabant. Utraque tamen ad terram sub monte cecidit et interfecta est, quod deus venti eam non iuvit.
5. Psyche interea maritum suum noctu dieque petebat. Montem altissimum, in quo templum magnum erat, conspexit. Eratne templum Cupidinis?
6. In templo aliud genus rei invenit. Omnibus in partibus aedifici frumentum videbat.
7. Quo modo multa genera frumenti in ordine ponere poterit.
8. Nunc etiam magis dolebat, sed erat puella fortissima.

Cupid and Psyche (cont'd.)

1. After Cupid had left his wife so quickly, she looked around her. All hope fell from her meanwhile and her happy life departed, for the beautiful gardens and large house were not there now.
2. She was alone, not far from the city, where she had lived before. She grieved very much.
3. Her sisters heard her story with great eagerness. They said to themselves: "Cupid will now certainly choose one of us."
4. At dawn the next day those two hurried to the mountain and very boldly called Zephyr by name. Each, however, fell to the ground at the foot of the mountain and was killed, because the god of the wind did not help her.
5. Psyche meanwhile sought her husband night and day. She saw a very high mountain, on which there was a large temple. Was it the temple of Cupid?
6. In the temple she found another kind of thing. In all parts of the building she saw grain.
7. How will she be able to put many kinds of grain in order?
8. Now she grieved even more, but she was a very brave girl.

Cupido et Psyche (cont'd.)

9. Dum illa laborat, Ceres, dea frumenti, in templum venit, nam id erat templum Cereris. Ceres puellam miserrimam iuvare cupiebat quod Psyche bene laboraverat et frumentum in templo in ordine bene posuerat.

10. Dea ei auxilium dare cupiebat quod illa pro ea satis iam fecerat. Dixit: "Venus tibi auxilium non dat. Dea bona est, sed filium suum, maritum tuum, maxime amat et eum dedere non cupit."

11. Psyche nullam spem habebat, sed tamen ad domum deae pulcherrimae properavit.

12. Ibi Venerem superbam invenit, quae dixit: "Nonne tu me tandem memoria tenes? Maritus tuus vulnus quod tu luce ei dedisti nunc curat. Postquam hunc laborem confecisti tibi eum dare cupio."

13. Hoc opus erat: Magnum numerum et multa genera frumenti sine ordine ante se videbat.

14. Mors melior quam hoc opus esse videbatur. Ipsa nil fecit. Labor maximus erat, sed Cupido uxorem suam mox vidit et ei auxilium misit.

15. Parva formica, quae erat dux sociorum amicorumque suorum, ad eam venit.

16. Omnes hae formicae brevissimo tempore frumentum in ordine conlocaverunt. Fugerunt postquam hoc fecerant.

Cupid and Psyche (cont'd.)

9. While she was working, Ceres, the goddess of grain, came into the temple, for this was the temple of Ceres. Ceres wished to help the very unhappy girl because Psyche had worked well and had put the grain in the temple in order well.

10. The Goddess wished to give help to her because she had already done enough for her. She said: "Venus does not give help to you. The goddess is good, but she loves her son, your husband, very much and does not want to give him up."

11. Psyche had no hope, but nevertheless she hurried to the house of the very beautiful goddess.

12. There she found the proud Venus, who said: "You finally remember me, don't you? Your husband is now caring for the wound that you gave him with the light. After you have finished this work I want to give him to you."

13. This was the task: She saw in front of her a great amount and many kinds of grain without order.

14. Death seemed to be better than this task. She did nothing. The work was very great, but Cupid soon saw his wife and sent help to her.

15. A small ant, that was the leader of his comrades and friends, came to her.

16. All these ants placed the grain in order in a very short time. They fled after they had done this.

READING VOCABULARY

Nouns

dux, ducis, m., leader (duke)
numerus, numeri, m., number (numeral)
vulnus, vulneris, n., wound (vulnerable)
satis, n., enough   Same spelling in all cases. (satisfy)
formica, formicae, f., ant (formic)
modus, modi, m., manner, way (mode)
genus, generis, n., kind, class (genus)
ordo, ordinis, m., rank, order (order, ordinal)

Verb

invenio, invenire, inveni, inventus, find, come upon (invent)

Adverbs

tam, so
satis, enough (satisfaction)
tandem, finally (tandem)

READING GRAMMAR

A. All Infinitives are formed on the same pattern.
   1. The Present Active Infinitive is the second principal part.

amare, to love	**ducere**, to lead	**esse**, to be
habere, to have	**capere**, to seize	**posse**, to be able
	audire, to hear	

   2. The Present Passive Infinitive ends in **-i**. Note the **e/i-conjugation** drops the **-er-**.

amari, to be loved	**duci**, to be led	**audiri**, to be heard
haberi, to be had	**capi**, to be seized	

   3. The Perfect Active Infinitive is the third principal part ending in **-isse**.

amavisse, to have loved	**duxisse**, to have led	**fuisse**, to have been
habuisse, to have had	**cepisse**, to have seized	**potuisse**, to have been able
	audivisse, to have heard	

   4. The Perfect Passive Infinitive is the fourth principal part in the Accusative case with **esse**.

amatum, am, um esse, to have been loved	**captum, am, um esse**, to have been seized
habitum, am, um esse, to have been had	**auditum, am, um esse**, to have been heard
ductum, am, um esse, to have been led	

   5. The Future Active Infinitive is the fourth principal part ending in **-urum** with **esse**.

amaturum, am, um esse, to be about to love	**capturum, am, um esse**, to be about to seize
habiturum, am, um esse, to be about to have	**auditurum, am, um esse**, to be about to hear
ducturum, am, um esse, to be about to lead	**futurum, am, um esse**, to be about to be

B. You have already met the completing Infinitive.

   Id capere cupit.   He wants to take it.

   The Infinitive is also used to express:

   1. A Subject.

   Id invenire difficile est.   It is difficult to find it.

   2. A Direct Object.

   Natare amat.   He likes to swim.

   3. An Indirect Statement after a Verb showing mental processes such as saying, thinking, knowing, hearing.

   Virum laborare dico.   I say that the man is working.

C. All Subjects of Infinitives are in the Accusative case.

virum laborare	**viros laborare**
agrum arari	**agros arari**

D. The Perfect Passive and Future Active Infinitives must be Accusative to agree with their Accusative subjects.

Agrum aratum esse dicit.	He says the field has been plowed.
Agros aratos esse dicit.	He says the fields have been plowed.
Virum laboraturum esse dicit.	He says the man is going to work.
Viros laboraturos esse dicit.	He says the men are going to work.

MEDICAL ABBREVIATIONS

The following are some of the more common medical and pharmaceutical abbreviations of Latin terms.

Ŗ, recipe, take
bib., bibe, drink
d., da, give
cap., capsula, capsule
gtt., guttae, drops
gr., granum, grain
Lb., libra, pound
mist., mistura, mixture
ol., oleum, oil
ung., unguentum, ointment
pulv., pulvis, powder
aq., aqua, water
c̄, cum, with
no., numero, number
os., os, ora, mouth
p.o., per os, by mouth
Q.s., quantum sufficiat, a sufficient quantity
Q.v., quantum vis, as much as you wish
a.c., ante cibum, before food, before meals
p.c., post cibum, after food, after meals
stat., statim, immediately

quotid., quotidie, every day
alt. dieb., alternis diebus, every other day, on alternate days
t.i.d., ter in die, three times a day
q.i.d., quater in die, four times a day
H., hora, hour
h.s., hora somni, at the hour of sleep, bedtime
Q.h., quaque hora, every hour   Q.2h., every two hours
omn. hor., omni hora, every hour
noct., nocte, at night
omn. noct., omni nocte, every night
t.i.n., ter in nocte, three times a night, q.i.n., quater in nocte, four times a night
rep. repetatur, let it be repeated
non rep., non repetatur, do not repeat
p.r.n., pro re nata, as the occasion arises, as needed
Sig., S., signetur, let it be marked (directions to patient)

PRACTICE EXERCISES

No. 168. Give the English for these Infinitives.

1. monere
2. auxisse
3. iaci
4. positurum esse
5. fugisse
6. impedire
7. natavisse
8. territurum esse
9. mansisse
10. auditurum esse
11. scripsisse
12. pugnaturum esse
13. laudaturum esse
14. excitari
15. petitum esse
16. mittere
17. tangi
18. oppugnatum esse
19. sciri
20. gesturum esse
21. accipi
22. victum esse
23. dici
24. ambulaturum esse
25. timuisse

No. 169. Change these Infinitives to the Active, and give the English.

1. peti
2. captum esse
3. haberi
4. rectum esse
5. portari
6. vocatum esse
7. faci
8. datum esse
9. instrui
10. verti

No. 170. Change these Infinitives to the Passive, and give the English.

1. narrare
2. defendisse
3. videre
4. iuvare
5. pugnavisse
6. movisse
7. vocare
8. invenire
9. necavisse
10. relinquere

No. 171. Give the Future Active Infinitive of these Verbs, and the English.

1. esse
2. iubere
3. facere
4. defendere
5. oppugnare
6. properare
7. capere
8. invenire
9. dare
10. ponere

No. 172. Translate these sentences.

1. Illi milites viros auxilium portaturos esse dixerunt.
2. Putatisne opus vestrum factum esse?
3. Nos hostes quam celerrime venturos esse sperabamus.
4. Puellae laetae esse videntur.
5. Hic rex bene regere cupiebat.
6. Ille appellari non cupiet.
7. Oppidum nostrum defendere optimum est.
8. Spem habuisse melius erat quam se recepisse.
9. Celeritatem augeri posse nuntiavit.
10. Nos locum meliorem invenire iussit.

CHAPTER 35

READING

Cupido et Psyche (cont'd.)

1. Venus ad templum suum multo die venit et ad illam partem templi ubi puellam reliquerat sine mora properavit. Ipsa puellam miseram ante se etiam tum laborem difficile habere sperabat.
2. Ubi laborem confectum esse vidit, filium suum id fecisse putabat et puellae cibum minimum dedit.
3. Postridie puellam ad se venire iussit. Dea ad silvam in qua erant multae oves, quarum lana erat aurea, currere et lanam reportare illam iussit.
4. Cum illa ad flumen pervenit non solum oves sed etiam deum fluminis invenit.
5. Ille dixit flumen celerrimum esse atque oves die maxime inimicas esse, sed demonstravit oves noctu futuras esse dulciores. Quam ob rem illa ad noctem exspectavit et oves dormire invenit.
6. Labor eius facillimus erat quod lana ovium in arboribus erat. Oves non etiam tetigerat, sed auxilio dei multam lanam auream ab arboribus obtinuit et eodem die ad Venerem, dominam suam, properavit, quod pro illa omnia bene facere cupiebat.
7. Postquam ad Veneram venerat et sub pedibus illius lanam posuerat, Psyche deam eam liberaturam esse atque se maritum suum recepturam esse sperabat.

Cupid and Psyche (cont'd.)

1. Venus came to her temple late in the day and hurried without delay to that part of the temple where she had left the girl. She hoped that the unhappy girl had difficult work ahead of her even then.
2. When she saw that the work had been finished, she thought her son had done it and she gave the girl very little food.
3. On the next day she ordered the girl to come to her. The goddess ordered her to run to the forest in which there were many sheep, whose wool was golden, and to bring back the wool.
4. When she came to the river, she found not only the sheep but also the god of the river.
5. He said that the river was very swift and the sheep were especially unfriendly in the daytime, but he pointed out that the sheep would be more gentle at night. For this reason she waited until night and found that the sheep were sleeping.
6. Her work was very easy because the wool of the sheep was on the trees. She had not even touched the sheep, but with the help of the god she obtained much golden wool from the trees and the same day she hurried to Venus, her mistress, because she wished to do everything well for her.
7. After she came to Venus and placed the wool at her feet, Psyche hoped that the goddess would free her and that she would get back her husband.

Cupido et Psyche (cont'd.)

8. Qua de causa spes eius celeriter fugit nam domina eius illam sine auxilio alterius lanam non obtinuisse dixit.

9. Puellam esse utilem cupiebat. Itaque eam apud Inferos iter facere iussit. Ei arcam parvam dedit.

10. Psyche miser templum Veneris reliquit et se mortem certe inventuram esse putabat quod dea partem pulchritudinis Proserpinae ex terra mortis ad se reportari cupiebat.

11. Psyche tamen fortissima erat et ad turrem altissimam venit. Celerrimum iter ad Inferos petebat, sed vox ex turre eam appellavit et ipsam illo modo se necare non debere dixit.

12. Vox quoque id ei futurum esse postremum laborem nuntiavit. Puellae iter facile celerebque ad regnum Plutonis demonstravit et illa ex timore ab eodem amico qui eam antea servaverat nunc liberata est.

Cupid and Psyche (cont'd.)

8. For this reason her hope quickly fled for her mistress said that she had not obtained the wool without the help of another.

9. She wanted the girl to be useful. And so she ordered her to make a journey among Those Below. She gave her a small box.

10. The unhappy Psyche left the temple of Venus and thought that she would certainly find death because the goddess wished a part of Proserpina's beauty to be brought back to her from the land of death.

11. Psyche, however, was very brave and came to a very high tower. She was seeking the fastest way to Those Below, but a voice out of the tower called her and said she ought not to kill herself in that manner.

12. The voice also announced that this would be the last task for her. It pointed out to the girl an easy and quick way to the kingdom of Pluto and she was now freed from fear by the same friend who had saved her before.

READING VOCABULARY

Nouns

lana, lanae, f., wool (lanate, lanolin)
ovis, ovis, f., sheep (ovium) (ovine)
pulchritudo, pulchritudinis, f., beauty (pulchritude)

Adjective

utilis, utile, useful (utility)

Verbs

puto, putare, putavi, putatus, think, believe (putative)
spero, sperare, speravi, speratus, hope (aspire)
reporto, reportare, reportavi, reportatus, carry back, bring back (reporter)

READING GRAMMAR

A. There are three Participles in Latin.

1. The Present Active Participle ends in -ns.

amans, loving   ducens, leading   audiens, hearing
habens, having   capiens, seizing

2. The Perfect Passive Participle is the fourth principal part.

amatus, a, um, having been loved   captus, a, um, having been seized
habitus, a, um, having been had   auditus, a, um, having been heard
ductus, a, um, having been led

3. The Future Active Participle is the fourth principal part ending in **-urus.**

amaturus, a, um, about to love   **capturus, a, um,** about to seize
habiturus, a, um, about to have   **auditurus, a, um,** about to hear
ducturus, a, um, about to lead

B. Participles are Adjectives and must agree with their Nouns in gender, number, and case.
1. The Present Participle is **i-declension:**

	M. and F.	N.			M. and F.	N.
Nom.	amans	amans	the loving		amantes	amantia
Gen.	amantis	amantis	of the loving		amantium	amantium
Dat.	amanti	amanti	to the loving		amantibus	amantibus
Acc.	amantem	amans	the loving		amantes	amantia
Abl.	amanti	amanti	from, with, by, in the loving		amantibus	amantibus

2. The Perfect and Future Participles are **a-** and **o-declension.**

C. Participles are best translated by a clause in English, beginning with *when, who, because, if,* or *although.*

Miles captus non timebat.   The soldier, although he was captured, was not afraid.
Miles captus timebat.   The soldier, because he was captured, was afraid.
Miles pugnans necatus est.   The soldier, when he was fighting, was killed.
            -or- The soldier, who was fighting, was killed.

FAMILIAR ABBREVIATIONS

i.e., id est, that is.
pro and con, pro et contra, for and against.
etc., et cetera, and the rest; and so forth.
e.g., exempli gratia, for (the sake of) example.
no., numero, by number.

viz., videlicet, namely, that is to say; introduces further explanation.
d.v. or D.V., Deo volente, God willing; if God is willing.
vox pop., vox populi, the voice of the people.

PRACTICE EXERCISES

No. 173. Translate these Participles.

1. vocans	4. accipiens	7. perveniens	10. nuntiatus	13. dicturus
2. motus	5. venturus	8. capturus	11. monitus	14. excitatus
3. missurus	6. spectatus	9. ponens	12. timens	15. videns

No. 174. Translate these Participial Phrases.

1. naves navigantes	5. petentes pacem	9. portus inventos
2. ducem iussurum	6. canem currentem	10. flumina currentia
3. illi oppugnati	7. urbes captae	
4. viros perventuros	8. templa aedificata	

No. 175. Translate these sentences.

1. Populus urbium captarum quam fortissimus erat.
2. Viri perventuri iter quam celerrime faciebant.
3. Rex patriam vestram nunc regens timidus esse videtur.
4. Mulier difficultatem tuam videns auxilium dabit.
5. Tempestas non auctura non acerrima erit.
6. Pater filios suos visurus magnum gaudium habebat.
7. Ei nostros timentes quam celerrime currebant.
8. Homines victi maxime territi sunt.
9. In oppido perveniens illa fabulam suam narravit.
10. Illi portam defendentes amici non erant.

No. 176. Translate these Adverbs.

1. fortiter
2. quam celerrime
3. minime
4. diutissime
5. acrius
6. difficile
7. facillime
8. melius
9. male
10. magnopere
11. saepius
12. miserrime

CHAPTER 36

READING

Cupido et Psyche (concl'd.)

1. Psyche, timida videri non cupiens, verba vocis magno cum gaudio audivit et hunc laborem difficillimum futurum esse sperabat.

2. Itaque haec omnia, quae ei demonstraverant, facere contendit. Sine plurimo periculo enim ad regnum Inferorum iter facere magnopere cupiebat.

3. Cerberus, ante portam quae ad terram mortis ducit positus, canis erat audacissimus qui tria capita habebat, sed Psyche voce monita eum non timebat.

4. Charon tum nave minima trans flumen illam, in regnum Plutonis venturam, duxit.

5. Ante Proserpinam, reginam pulcherrimam Inferorum, stans illa Venerem donum cupire nuntiavit.

6. Regina arcam a puella cepit et in eandem arcam partem parvam suae pulchritudinis posuit. Dea, puellae arcam dans, illam monuit.

Cupid and Psyche (concl'd.)

1. Psyche, who did not wish to seem timid, heard the words of the voice with great joy and hoped this task would be very difficult.

2. And so she hurried to do all these things, that they had pointed out to her. For she greatly wished to make the journey to the kingdom of Those Below without very great danger.

3. Cerberus, who was placed in front of the door that leads to the land of death, was a very bold dog who had three heads, but Psyche, because she had been warned by the voice, was not afraid of him.

4. Charon then led her, as she was about to come into the kingdom of Pluto, across the river in a very small boat.

5. Standing in front of Proserpina, the very beautiful queen of Those Below, she reported that Venus wanted a gift.

6. The queen took the box from the girl and put a small part of her own beauty into the same box. The goddess, as she gave the box to the girl, warned her.

Cupido et Psyche (concl'd.)

7. Illam, in arcam spectantem, in periculum magnum casuram esse dixit, sed Psyche, ex terra Inferorum iter facere cupiens, verbis reginae ad timorem non excitata est.

8. Ad terram mortalium eandem viam cepit, sed postquam ad lucem pervenerat in arcam spectare et pulchritudinem videre atque habere cupiebat, sed nil pulchritudinis ibi invenit, arca aperta.

9. Psyche dolens pulchritudinem ibi non invenit quod id quod Proserpina in arca posuerat somnus altus Inferorum erat.

10. Somno ex carcere suo liberato, puella somno celeriter capta est et ipsa sine ulla mora, modo simili corpori quod a Morte delectum erat, media in via cecidit. Nil sciebat atque nil faciebat. Solum dormiebat.

11. Cupido tamen, vulnere eius curato, magno cum gaudio uxorem suam vidit. Ad locum ubi illa dormiebat quam celerrime volavit.

12. Ipse, supra illam stans, somnum qui illam opprimebat cepit et, hoc in arca posito, una ex sagittis suis uxorem tetigit.

13. Ipse dixit: "Tu, multis temporibus e morte servata, omnes labores tuos conficere debes. His factis, omnia reliqua faciam."

14. Illa satis poenae habuerat. Hic ad Iovem properavit et ab eo auxilium petivit. Iuppiter ad Venerem eodem die iter fecit et illa tandem puellam dedidit.

15. Psyche, ad regnum deorum a Mercurio ducta, immortalis facta est.

16. Matrimonium ab illo tempore ad finem temporis omnis, illa immortali facta, laetissimum erat.

17. Mortales hac fabula animum esse immortalem atque se gaudium per omnes difficultates semper inventuros esse docentur.

Cupid and Psyche (concl'd.)

7. She said that she would fall into great danger, if she looked into the box, but Psyche, who wished to make the journey out of the land of Those Below, was not aroused to fear by the words of the queen.

8. She took the same road to the land of mortals, but after she had arrived at the light she wished to look into the box and to see and have the beauty, but she found no beauty there, when the box was opened.

9. The grieving Psyche did not find beauty there because what Proserpina had placed in the box was the deep sleep of Those Below.

10. When sleep had been freed from its prison, the girl was quickly overcome by sleep and without any delay, in a manner similar to a body that had been chosen by Death, she fell in the middle of the road. She knew nothing and she did nothing. She only slept.

11. Cupid, however, when his wound had been healed, saw his wife with great joy. He flew as quickly as possible to the place where she was sleeping.

12. He, standing above her, took the sleep that was oppressing her and, when this had been placed in the box, he touched his wife with one of his arrows.

13. He said: "You, because you have been saved from death many times, ought to finish all your tasks. When these have been done, I shall do all the other things."

14. She had had enough punishment. He hurried to Jupiter and begged aid from him. Jupiter made the journey to Venus the same day and she at last surrendered the girl.

15. Psyche, after she had been led to the kingdom of the gods by Mercury, was made immortal.

16. The marriage from that time to the end of all time was very happy, because she had been made immortal.

17. Mortals are taught by this story that the spirit is immortal and that they will always find joy through all difficulties.

READING VOCABULARY

Nouns	Adjectives
carcer, carceris, n., prison (incarcerate)	timidus, timida, timidum, timid (timidity)
somnus, somni, m., sleep (insomnia)	apertus, aperta, apertum, open (aperture)
gaudium, gaudii or gaudi, n., joy (gaudy)	reliquus, reliqua, reliquum, remaining, rest of
canis, canis, m. and f., dog (canine)	
Cerberus, Cerberi, m., Cerberus	
Charon, Charontis, m., Charon	

READING GRAMMAR

A Participle with a Noun or Pronoun, both in the Ablative case, may be used as a clause. The Participle may be replaced by a Noun or an Adjective.

1. The clause must have a Noun or Pronoun subject that is different from the subject of the main part of the sentence.
2. The clause may be translated with *because, when, although,* or *if.*
3. The Verb "to be" must sometimes be supplied in English.

Oppidis captis, pacem petebant.	When the towns had been captured, they sought peace.
Hoc viro duce, vincemur.	If this man is leader, we shall be conquered.
Navibus gravibus, celerius navigabant.	Although the ships were heavy, they were sailing quite quickly.

FAMILIAR QUOTATIONS

Veni, vidi, vici, I came, I saw, I conquered. Caesar	Non omnia possumus omnes, We can't all do everything. Virgil
Vae victis, Woe to the vanquished. Livy	Diem perdidi, I have lost a day. Titus
In medias res, Into the midst of things. Horace	Pares cum paribus facillime congregantur, Equals very easily congregate with equals. Cicero
Finis coronat opus, The end crowns the work. Ovid	

PRACTICE EXERCISES

No. 177. Translate these sentences.

1. Multi, oraculo audito, ad terram nostram venire constituerunt.
2. Signo dato, in agrum impetum fecerunt.
3. Homines, armis non multis, tamen fortiter pugnaverunt.
4. Militibus multis interfectis, pacem petiverunt.
5. Viri, praeda magna, magno cum gaudio domi accipientur.
6. Hac re gesta, pueri domum venient.
7. Illo duce, id sine difficultate faciemus.
8. His mihi nuntiatis, ex urbe iter facere cupiebam.
9. His necatis, populus melius regetur.
10. Die dicto, omnia quam celerrime paraverunt.
11. Porta aperta, in casam venire potuit.
12. Nullam spem habebat, oppido capto.
13. His rebus factis, rex plus poterat.
14. Reliquis visis, ad silvam curremus.
15. Patre eius duce, omnia audacter faciunt.
16. Pace facta, ab insula navigabit.
17. Multis timidis, flumina invenire non poterunt.
18. Tempore nunc brevi, nullum auxilium perveniet.
19. Loco idoneo, hic diutius manere cupitis.
20. Auxilio dato, gaudium magnum erat.

NINTH REVIEW SECTION (CHAPTERS 34–36)

VOCABULARY REVIEW

NOUNS

1. canis	7. gaudium	13. ovis	1. dog	7. joy	13. sheep
2. carcer	8. genus	14. pulchritudo	2. prison	8. kind, class	14. beauty
3. Cerberus	9. lana	15. satis	3. Cerberus	9. wool	15. enough
4. Charon	10. modus	16. somnus	4. Charon	10. manner, way	16. sleep
5. dux	11. numerus	17. vulnus	5. leader	11. number	17. wound
6. formica	12. ordo		6. ant	12. rank, order	

ADJECTIVES

1. apertus   2. reliquus   3. timidus   4. utilis   1. open   2. remaining, rest of   3. timid   4. useful

VERBS

1. invenio	3. reporto	1. find, come upon	3. carry back, bring back
2. puto	4. spero	2. think, believe	4. hope

ADVERBS

1. satis   2. tam   3. tandem   1. enough   2. so   3. finally

PRACTICE EXERCISES

No. 178. Translate these Infinitives.

1. esse	11. duci	21. moneri
2. fuisse	12. duxisse	22. monuisse
3. inventurum esse	13. habitum esse	23. dixisse
4. inveniri	14. habere	24. dici
5. putatum esse	15. cupere	25. timeri
6. putavisse	16. cupi	26. timuisse
7. reportare	17. potuisse	27. factum esse
8. reportaturum esse	18. posse	28. facturum esse
9. speravisse	19. pugnavisse	29. videri
10. speraturum esse	20. pugnatum esse	30. visurum esse

No. 179. Translate these Participles.

1. ducens	11. sperantia	21. mittens
2. ducturus	12. speratam	22. missus
3. habentes	13. moturos	23. visuris
4. habitos	14. moventes	24. videntium
5. putata	15. venientium	25. dicturos
6. putaturis	16. ventura	26. dicens
7. invenientem	17. timenti	27. monentes
8. inventa	18. territus	28. moniti
9. reportantium	19. posituros	29. positos
10. reportaturus	20. ponentibus	30. ponens

No. 180. Translate these Ablative clauses.

1. eis visis	6. puella ambulanti	11. urbe capta
2. illo capto	7. ducibus timidis	12. reliquis dicentibus
3. his dictis	8. numero parvo	13. verbo audito
4. bello facto	9. somno venienti	14. spe inventa
5. viris timentibus	10. carcere magno	15. generibus multis

QUINTUS HORATIUS FLACCUS

Horace was born in 65 B.C. at Venusia, in southern Italy, the son of a freedman, and studied in Rome and Athens. He was a friend of Virgil and of Augustus, through his literary patron, Maecenas. Before his death in 8 B.C. he had gained enduring popularity from the quality and universality of his poetry and philosophy.

Integer vitae scelerisque purus
non eget Mauris iaculis neque arcu
nec venenatis gravida sagittis, Fusce, pharetra,
sive per Syrtis iter aestuosas

sive facturus per inhospitalem
Caucasum vel quae loca fabulosus lambit
  Hydaspes.

Carminum Liber Primus, xxii

He who is upright of life and free from crime
needs neither Moorish javelins nor a bow
nor a quiver heavy with poisoned arrows, Fuscus,
whether he is going to journey through the hot
  Quicksands
or through the inhospitable
Caucasus or the places which the storied
  Hydaspes laps.

First Book of Odes, 22

CARMINA BURANA

In the early nineteenth century, a manuscript from the thirteenth century was found in the monastery of Benedictbeuren in Bavaria, from which it gets its name, **CARMINA BURANA.** These **carmina**, or songs, were mostly poems, chiefly in Latin or German, or a combination of both, composed by the goliards, or wandering students and monks, on a wide variety of topics. By the Middle Ages the classical pronunciation and meter had changed and the use of rhyme had been introduced in poetry. These poems provided both inspiration and text for the contemporary German composer Carl Orff's famous "Carmina Burana."

Omnia sol temperat	The sun, pure and clear,
purus et subtilis,	Tempers everything,
nova mundo reserat	A new world resows
facies Aprilis,	The appearance of April;
ad amorem properat	The sweetheart's spirit
animus erilis,	Hurries to love,
et iucundis imperat	And over pleasant things rules
deus puerilis.	The boyish god, Cupid.
Rerum tanta novitas	So much newness of nature
in sollemni vere	In the festive springtime
et veris auctoritas	And the power of the spring
iubet nos gaudere,	Order us to rejoice,
vias praebet solitas,	Show us the accustomed ways,
et in tuo vere	And in your own springtime

fides est et probitas	There is trust and the right
tuum retinere.	To cling to your loved one.
Ama me fideliter,	Love me faithfully,
fidem meam nota,	Mark my trust,
de corde totaliter	In my heart completely,
et ex mente tota,	And with my whole mind
sum praesentialiter	I am in your presence,
absens in remota;	Even when absent at a distance;
quisquis amat taliter,	Whoever loves in such a way,
volvitur in rota.	Is turned on a wheel of torture.
Ecce gratum	Behold, pleasing
et optatum	And longed for,
ver reducit gaudia,	The spring brings back our joys;
purpuratum	Clad in purple
floret pratum,	The meadow is in flower,
sol serenat omnia,	The sun makes all serene,
iam iam cedant tristia.	Now, now, sorrows depart,
aestas redit,	Summer returns,
nunc recedit	Now retreats
hiemis saevitia.	The severity of winter.
Iam liquescit	Now there melts
et decrescit	And disappears
grando, nix, et cetera,	All hail, snow, and such,
bruma fugit,	Winter flees,
et iam sugit	And now the spring
ver aestatis ubera;	Sucks in the richness of summer;
illi mens est misera,	His heart is wretched,
qui nec vivit,	Who neither lives,
nec lascivit	Nor plays
sub aestatis dextera.	Under the joys of summer.
Gloriantur	They glory
et laetantur	And delight
in melle dulcedinis	In the honey of sweetness
qui conantur	Who try
ut utantur	To use
praemio Cupidinis;	The favor of Cupid;
simus iussu Cypridis	Let us be, at the command of Venus,
gloriantes	Boasting
et laetantes	And rejoicing
pares esse Paridis.	To be the equals of Paris.

DICTIONARY—LATIN–ENGLISH

A

a, ab from, away from; by

accido, accidere, accidi happen

acer, acris, acre sharp, active, keen

acies, aciei, f. battle line

ad to, toward

adoro, adorare, adoravi, adoratus worship, adore

adulescens, adulescentis, m. youth

adventus, adventus, m. arrival, approach

aedificium, aedificii or aedifici, n. building

aedifico, aedificare, aedificavi, aedificatus build

aeger, aegra, aegrum sick, ill

aequus, aequa, aequum equal, level, fair

aestas, aestatis, f. summer

Africa, Africae, f. Africa

ager, agri, m. field

agricola, agricolae, m. farmer

ala, alae, f. wing

alius, alia, aliud other, another

alter, altera, alterum the one, the other

altus, alta, altum high, deep

ambulo, ambulare, ambulavi, ambulatus walk

amicus, amica, amicum friendly

amicus, amici, m. friend

amo, amare, amavi, amatus like, love

amor, amoris, m. love

amphitheatrum, amphitheatri, n. amphitheater

angustus, angusta, angustum narrow

animal, animalis, n. animal

animus, animi, m. mind, spirit

annus, anni, m. year

ante before, in front of

antea before

antiquus, antiqua, antiquum ancient, old

apertus, aperta, apertum open

Apollo, Apollonis, m. Apollo

appello, appellare, appellavi, appellatus address, call, name

apud among, in the presence of

aqua, aquae, f. water

arbor, arboris, f. tree

arca, arcae, f. chest, box

arena, arenae, f. sand

Ariadne, Ariadnes, f. Ariadne

arma, armorum, n. pl. arms, weapons

armo, armare, armavi, armatus arm

aro, arare, aravi, aratus plow

Atalanta, Atalantae, f. Atalanta

Athenae, Athenarum, f. pl. Athens

Atlas, Atlantis, m. Atlas

atque, ac and also, also

audacia, audaciae, f. boldness, bravery, daring

audax, audacis bold

augeo, augere, auxi, auctus increase, enlarge

aureus, aurea, aureum golden

aurum, auri, n. gold

aut or

aut . . . aut either . . . or

auxilium, auxilii or auxili, n. aid, help

avunculus, avunculi, m. uncle

B

Bacchus, Bacchi, m. Bacchus

barbarus, barbara, barbarum savage, uncivilized, barbarian

barbarus, barbari, m. barbarian

bellum, belli, n. war

bene well

bis twice

bonus, bona, bonum good

brevis, breve short, brief

Britannia, Britanniae, f. Britain

C

cado, cadere, cecidi, casurus fall

caedes, caedis, f. slaughter, murder

caelum, caeli, n. sky, heaven

canis, canis, m. and f. dog

capio, capere, cepi, captus take, seize, capture

captivus, captivi, m. captive

caput, capitis, n. head

carcer, carceris, n. prison

casa, casae, f. cottage

castra, castrorum, n. pl. camp

causa, causae, f. cause, reason

celer, celeris, celere quick, swift

celeritas, celeritatis, f. speed, swiftness

cera, cerae, f. wax

Cerberus, Cerberi, m. Cerberus

Ceres, Cereris, f. Ceres

certe certainly, surely, indeed

Charon, Charontis, m. Charon

cibus, cibi, m. food

Cincinnatus, Cincinnati, m. Cincinnatus

circum around, about

civis, civis, m. and f. citizen

civitas, civitatis, f. state

clamo, clamare, clamavi, clamatus shout, cry

clarus, clara, clarum clear, famous, bright

classis, classis, f. fleet

cognosco, cognoscere, cognovi, cognitus learn, recognize, know

cogo, cogere, coegi, coactus collect, drive, compel

collis, collis, m. hill

Colosseum, Colossei, n. The Colosseum

conficio, conficere, confeci, confectus finish, complete, carry out

conloco, conlocare, conlocavi, conlocatus place, station

consilium, consilii or consili, n. plan, advice

conspicio, conspicere, conspexi, conspectus observe

constituo, constituere, constitui, constitutus decide, establish

contendo, contendere, contendi, contentus hasten, strive, contend

contra against

convenio, convenire, conveni, conventus come together, assemble

copia, copiae, f. supply, abundance

copiae, copiarum, f. pl. troops

cornu, cornus, n. horn, wing

corpus, corporis, n. body

cras tomorrow

Creta, Cretae, f. Crete

Creusa, Creusae, f. Creusa

cum with; when, while

Cupido, Cupidinis, m. Cupid

cupio, cupere, cupivi, cupitus desire, wish, want

cur why

cura, curae, f. care

curo, curare, curavi, curatus care for, cure

curro, currere, cucurri, cursurus run

Cyclops, Cyclopis, m. Cyclops

D

Daedalus, Daedali, m. Daedalus

de about, concerning, down from

dea, deae, f. goddess

debeo, debere, debui, debitus owe, ought

decem ten

dedo, dedere, dedidi, deditus give up, surrender

deligo, deligere, delegi, delectus choose, select

demonstro, demonstrare, demonstravi, demonstratus point out, show

deus, dei, m. god

dictator, dictatoris, m. dictator

dies, diei, m. and f. day

difficilis, difficile difficult, hard

difficultas, difficultatis, f. difficulty

diligentia, diligentiae, f. diligence, care

discedo, discedere, discessi, discessurus withdraw, go away, leave

diu long, for a long time

do, dare, dedi, datus give

doceo, docere, docui, doctus teach, show

doleo, dolere, dolui, doliturus grieve, be sorry

domi at home

domina, dominae, f. mistress

dominus, domini, m. master

domus, domus, f. house, home

donum, doni, n. gift, present

dormio, dormire, dormivi, dormiturus sleep

duco, ducere, duxi, ductus lead

dulcis, dulce sweet

dum while

duodecim twelve

dux, ducis, m. leader

E

e, ex from, out from

educo, educere, eduxi, eductus lead out

ego, mei I

enim for

eques, equitis, m. horseman, knight

equus, equi, m. horse

et and

et . . . et both . . . and

etiam even, also

Europa, Europae, f. Europe

Eurydice, Eurydices, f. Eurydice

Eurystheus, Eurysthei, m. Eurystheus

ex, e from, out from

excito, excitare, excitavi, excitatus arouse, stir up

exercitus, exercitus, m. army

exspecto, exspectare, exspectavi, exspectatus await, expect, wait for

F

fabula, fabulae, f. story

facilis, facile easy

facio, facere, feci, factus make, do

fama, famae, f. rumor, renown, report

femina, feminae, f. woman

filia, filiae, f. daughter

filius, filii or fili, m. son

finis, finis, m. end, border

fines, finium, m. pl. territory

finitimus, finitima, finitimum neighboring

finitimus, finitimi, m. neighbor

flumen, fluminis, n. river

fons, fontis, m. fountain, spring

formica, formicae, f. ant

fortis, forte brave, strong

fortuna, fortunae, f. fortune, fate, luck

forum, fori, n. forum, market place

fossa, fossae, f. ditch

frumentum, frumenti, n. grain

fuga, fugae, f. flight, escape

fugio, fugere, fugi, fugiturus flee, run away, escape

G

Gallia, Galliae, f. Gaul

Gallus, Galli, m. a Gaul

gaudium, gaudii or gaudi, n. joy

genus, generis, n. kind, class

Germania, Germaniae, f. Germany

Germanus, Germani, m. a German

gero, gerere, gessi, gestus carry on, wage

gladiator, gladiatoris, m. gladiator

gladius, gladii or gladi, m. sword

gloria, gloriae, f. glory

Graecia, Graeciae, f. Greece

gratus, grata, gratum pleasing

gravis, grave heavy, severe, serious

H

habeo, habere, habui, habitus have, hold

habito, habitare, habitavi, habitatus dwell, live

Hannibal, Hannibalis, m. Hannibal

Hellespontus, Hellesponti, m. The Hellespont

Hercules, Herculis, m. Hercules

Hero, Herus, f. Hero

Hesperides, Hesperidum, f. pl. the Hesperides

hic here, in this place

hic, haec, hoc this; he, she, it

hiems, hiemis, f. winter

Hippomenes, Hippominis, m. Hippomenes

Hispania, Hispaniae, f. Spain

hodie today

Homerus, Homeri, m. Homer

homo, hominis, m. man

hora, horae, f. hour

Horatius, Horati, m. Horatius

hortus, horti, m. garden

hostis, hostis, m. enemy

I

iacio, iacere, ieci, iactus throw

iam now, already

ibi there, in that place

Icarus, Icari, m. Icarus

idem, eadem, idem the same; he, she, it

idoneus, idonea, idoneum fit, suitable

ignis, ignis, m. fire

ille, illa, illud that; he, she, it

immortalis, immortale immortal

impedimentum, impedimenti, n. hindrance

impedio, impedire, impedivi, impeditus hinder

imperator, imperatoris, m. commander, general, emperor

imperium, imperii or imperi, n. command

impetus, impetus, m. attack

in in, on; into, onto

incendo, incendere, incendi, incensus set fire to, burn

incito, incitare, incitavi, incitatus arouse, stir up, incite

incola, incolae, m. or f. inhabitant

Inferi, Inferorum, m. pl. Those Below

inimicus, inimica, inimicum unfriendly

inimicus, inimici, m. personal enemy

iniuria, iniuriae, f. injury, harm

inopia, inopiae, f. want, scarcity

instruo, instruere, instruxi, instructus draw up, form, train

insula, insulae, f. island

inter among, between

interea meanwhile

interficio, interficere, interfeci, interfectus kill

invenio, invenire, inveni, inventus find, come upon

ipse, ipsa, ipsum himself, herself, itself; very

is, ea, id he, she, it; this, that

ita thus, so; yes

Italia, Italiae, f. Italy

itaque and so, therefore

iter, itineris, n. journey, march, way

iubeo, iubere, iussi, iussus order, command

Iulia, Iuliae, f. Julia

Iuno, Iunonis, f. Juno

Iuppiter, Iovis, m. Jupiter

iuvo, iuvare, iuvi, iutus help, aid

L

labor, laboris, m. work, toil, labor

laboro, laborare, laboravi, laboratus work

labyrinthus, labyrinthi, m. labyrinth

laetus, laeta, laetum happy

lana, lanae, f. wool

latinus, latina, latinum Latin

Latinus, Latini, m. Latinus

Latium, Lati, n. Latium

latus, lata, latum wide

laudo, laudare, laudavi, laudatus praise

Leander, Leandri, m. Leander

legatus, legati, m. lieutenant, legate

lex, legis, f. law

liber, libera, liberum free

liber, libri, m. book

libero, liberare, liberavi, liberatus free, set free

lingua, linguae, f. language

littera, litterae, f. letter

loco, locare, locavi, locatus place, put

locus, loci, m. place

longus, longa, longum long

ludus, ludi, m. game

luna, lunae, f. moon

lupa, lupae, f. wolf

lux, lucis, f. light

M

magis more

magnitudo, magnitudinis, f. size, great size

magnopere greatly

magnus, magna, magnum large, great

maior, maius larger

male badly

malus, mala, malum bad, evil

maneo, manere, mansi, mansus remain, stay

manus, manus, f. hand; group

Marathonius, Marathonia, Marathonium of Marathon

mare, maris, n. sea

maritus, mariti, m. husband

mater, matris, f. mother

matrimonium, matrimonii or matrimoni, n. marriage

maxime most, especially

maximus, maxima, maximum largest

medius, media, medium middle, middle of

melior, melius better

memoria, memoriae, f. memory

Mercurius, Mercuri, m. Mercury

meus, mea, meum my, mine

Midas, Midae, m. Midas

miles, militis, m. soldier

mille passus mile

milia passuum miles

minime by no means, not at all

minimus, minima, minimum smallest

minor, minus smaller

Minos, Minois, m. Minos

Minotaurus, Minotauri, m. the Minotaur

miser, misera, miserum wretched, unhappy

mitto, mittere, misi, missus send

modus, modi, m. manner, way

moneo, monere, monui, monitus warn, advise

mons, montis, m. mountain, mount

monstro, monstrare, monstravi, monstratus point out, show

mora, morae, f. delay

mors, mortis, f. death

mortalis, mortale, mortal

moveo, movere, movi, motus move

mox soon, presently

mulier, mulieris, f. woman

multitudo, multitudinis, f. great number, multitude

multo much, by much

multus, multa, multum much

murus, muri, m. wall

N

nam for

narro, narrare, narravi, narratus tell, relate

natio, nationis, f. nation

nato, natare, natavi, natatus swim

natura, naturae, f. nature

nauta, nautae, m. sailor

navigo, navigare, navigavi, navigatus sail, cruise

navis, navis, f. ship

-ne indicates a question

neco, necare, necavi, necatus kill

neque and not

neque . . . neque neither . . . nor

nihil, nil, n. nothing

noctu at night

nomen, nominis, n. name

non not

nonne indicates a question expecting the answer "yes"

nos, nostrum we

noster, nostra, nostrum our, ours

novem nine

novus, nova, novum new

nox, noctis, f. night

nullus, nulla, nullum no, none

num indicates a question expecting the answer "no"

numerus, numeri, m. number

numquam never

nunc now

nuntio, nuntiare, nuntiavi, nuntiatus announce, report

nuntius, nuntii, or nunti, m. message, messenger

O

ob on account of, because of

obtineo, obtinere, obtinui, obtentus secure, obtain

occupo, occupare, occupavi, occupatus seize, take possession of

oceanus, oceani, m. ocean

oculus, oculi, m. eye

olim formerly, once

omnis, omne all, every

onus, oneris, n. burden, weight

oppidum, oppidi, n. town

opprimo, opprimere, oppressi, oppressus overcome, crush

oppugno, oppugnare, oppugnavi, oppugnatus attack

optimus, optima, optimum best

opus, operis, n. work

oraculum, oraculi, n. oracle

ordo, ordinis, m. rank, order

Orpheus, Orphei, m. Orpheus

ovis, ovis, f. sheep

P

paene almost, nearly

paeninsula, paeninsulae, f. peninsula

paro, parare, paravi, paratus prepare, get ready

pars, partis, f. part

parum too little, not enough

parvus, parva, parvum small

passus, passus, m. pace

pater, patris, m. father

patria, patriae, f. native country

pax, pacis, f. peace

pecunia, pecuniae, f. money

pedes, peditis, m. foot soldier

peior, peius worse

per through

periculum, periculi, n. danger

Persae, Persarum, m. pl. the Persians

pervenio, pervenire, perveni, perventus arrive

pes, pedis, m. foot

pessimus, pessima, pessimum worst

peto, petere, petivi or petii, petitus seek

plurimum posse be most powerful

plurimus, plurima, plurimum most

plus, pluris more

plus posse be more powerful

Pluto, Plutonis, m. Pluto

poena, poenae, f. punishment, fine

poeta, poetae, m. poet

Polyphemus, Polyphemi, m. Polyphemus

pomum, pomi, n. apple

pono, ponere, posui, positus put, place

pons, pontis, m. bridge

populus, populi, m. people

porta, portae, f. gate, door, entrance

porto, portare, portavi, portatus carry

portus, portus, m. harbor, port

post behind, in back of

postea afterwards

posterus, postera, posterum next, following

postquam after, when

postridie on the next day

postumus, postuma, postumum next, following

praeda, praedae, f. booty, plunder

praemium, praemii or praemi, n. reward

praesidium, praesidii or praesidi, n. guard, garrison

pretium, pretii or preti, n. price

primum, primo first, at first

primus, prima, primum first

pro in front of; for, instead of; for, in behalf of

proelium, proelii or proeli, n. battle

prohibeo, prohibere, prohibui, prohibitus keep off, hinder, prohibit, prevent

propero, properare, properavi, properatus hurry, hasten

propinquus, propinqua, propinquum near

propter because of, on account of

Proserpina, Proserpinae, f. Proserpina

provincia, provinciae, f. province

proximus, proxima, proximum next, nearest

Psyche, Psyches, f. Psyche

puella, puellae, f. girl

puer, pueri, m. boy

pugna, pugnae, f. fight

pugno, pugnare, pugnavi, pugnatus fight

pulcher, pulchra, pulchrum pretty, beautiful

pulchritudo, pulchritudinis, f. beauty

puto, putare, putavi, putatus think, believe

Pythia, Pythiae, f. Pythia

Q

quam as possible; than

quam diu how long

quamquam although

-que and

qui, quae, quod who, which, that; which, what

quis, quid who, what

quod because

quoque also

R

recipio, recipere, recepi, receptus take back, receive

reduco, reducere, reduxi, reductus lead back

regina, reginae, f. queen

regio, regionis, f. region, boundary

regno, regnare, regnavi, regnatus rule

regnum, regni, n. kingdom

rego, regere, rexi, rectus rule

relinquo, relinquere, reliqui, relictus leave, leave behind

reliquus, reliqua, reliquum remaining, rest of

reperio, reperire, repperi, repertus find, discover

reporto, reportare, reportavi, reportatus carry back, bring back

res, rei, f. thing

rex, regis, m. king

ripa, ripae, f. river bank

robustus, robusta, robustum strong, robust

rogo, rogare, rogavi, rogatus ask, ask for

Roma, Romae, f. Rome

Romanus, Romana, Romanum Roman

Romanus, Romani, m. a Roman

ruri in the country

S

Sabini, Sabinorum, m. pl. the Sabines

saepe often

sagitta, sagittae, f. arrow

sagittarius, sagittarii or sagittari, m. archer

sapientia, sapientiae, f. wisdom

satis enough

saxum, saxi, n. stone, rock

scio, scire, scivi, scitus know

scribo, scribere, scripsi, scriptus write

sed but

semper always

septem seven

serpens, serpentis, f. snake, serpent

servo, servare, servavi, servatus save, preserve

servus, servi, m. slave, servant

sex six

Sibyllinus, Sibyllina, Sibyllinum Sibylline

signum, signi, n. signal, standard

Silenus, Sileni, m. Silenus

silva, silvae, f. forest, woods

similis, simile like, similar

simulo, simulare, simulavi, simulatus pretend

sine without

socius, socii or soci, m. comrade, ally

sol, solis, m. sun

solum alone, only

solus, sola, solum alone, only

somnus, somni, m. sleep

soror, sororis, f. sister

Sparta, Spartae, f. Sparta

specto, spectare, spectavi, spectatus look at, watch

spero, sperare, speravi, speratus hope

spes, spei, f. hope

stella, stellae, f. star

sto, stare, steti, status stand

studium, studii or studi, n. zeal, eagerness

sub under

sum, esse, fui, futurus be

summus, summa, summum greatest, highest, top of

superbus, superba, superbum proud, haughty

supero, superare, superavi, superatus surpass, overcome, conquer

supra over, above

suscipio, suscipere, suscepi, susceptus take up, undertake

suus, sua, suum his, her, its, their

T

tam so

tamen however, nevertheless

tandem finally

tango, tangere, tetigi, tactus touch

Tarquinius, Tarquini, m. Tarquin

telum, teli, n. weapon

tempestas, tempestatis, f. storm, bad weather

templum, templi, n. temple

tempus, temporis, n. time

teneo, tenere, tenui, tentus hold, keep, have

terra, terrae, f. land, earth

terreo, terrere, terrui, territus frighten, scare, terrify

Thermopylae, Thermopylarum, f. pl. Thermopylae

Theseus, Thesei, m. Theseus

timeo, timere, timui fear, be afraid of

timidus, timida, timidum timid

timor, timoris, m. fear, dread

totus, tota, totum all, whole

trado, tradere, tradidi, traditus give up, surrender

trans across

Troia, Troiae, f. Troy

tu you

tum then

turris, turris, f. tower

tuus, tua, tuum your, yours

U

ubi where, when

Ulixes, Ulixis, m. Ulysses

ultimus, ultima, ultimum last, farthest

umerus, umeri, m. shoulder

umquam ever

unus, una, unum one

urbs, urbis, f. city

ut as

uterque, utraque, utrumque each, every

utilis, utile useful

uxor, uxoris, f. wife

V

venio, venire, veni, ventus come

ventus, venti, m. wind

Venus, Veneris, f. Venus

verbum, verbi, n. word

vero truly, in truth

verto, vertere, verti, versus turn

vester, vestra, vestrum your, yours

via, viae, f. road, way, street

victoria, victoriae, f. victory

video, videre, vidi, visus see

vinco, vincere, vici, victus conquer

vir, viri, m. man

virtus, virtutis, f. courage, valor

vita, vitae, f. life

voco, vocare, vocavi, vocatus call

volo, volare, volavi, volatus fly

vos, vestrum you

vox, vocis, f. voice

vulnus, vulneris, n. wound

Z

Zephyrus, Zephyri, m. Zephyr, west wind

ANSWERS

Practice Exercise No. 1

1. aquas, the waters
2. puellarum, of the girls
3. terrae, the lands
4. agricolis, for the farmers
5. stellis, by the stars
6. vocant, they call
7. laboratis, you work
8. portamus, we carry
9. laudamus, we praise
10. amant, they like

Practice Exercise No. 2

1. of the farmers
2. the, a girl
3. the cottages
4. for the woman
5. by the lands
6. he, she, it is praising
7. you call
8. they are working
9. we like
10. you do carry

Practice Exercise No. 3

1. we   2. he, she, it   3. I   4. you   5. they   6. you

Practice Exercise No. 4

1. direct object   2. prepositional phrase   3. subject   4. indirect object   5. possession

Practice Exercise No. 5

1. portamus
2. amat
3. porto
4. laudamus
5. vocant
6. laboratis
7. portat
8. vocas
9. amamus
10. laudatis

Practice Exercise No. 6

1. casam parvam
2. mearum filiarum
3. pulchras stellas
4. tua terra
5. filiae malae
6. casis Romanis
7. puellas parvas
8. aquam bonam
9. feminae parvae
10. casarum pulchrarum

Practice Exercise No. 7

1. you are
2. he, she, it is; there is
3. they are; there are
4. I am
5. you are
6. we are

Practice Exercise No. 8

1. natantne? Do they swim?
2. portasne? Are you carrying?
3. amamusne? Do we like?
4. laboratne? Does he (she, it) work?
5. vocatisne? Are you calling?
6. suntne? Are they? Are there?
7. natamusne? Do we swim?
8. portatne? Is he (she, it) carrying?
9. estisne? Are you?
10. laudasne? Do you praise?
11. laudatne? Does he (she, it) praise?
12. vocantne? Are they calling?
13. estne? Is he (she, it) there?
14. natasne? Do you swim?
15. amantne? Do they love?

Practice Exercise No. 9

1. you love, are loving, do love
2. we praise, are praising, do praise
3. you call, do call, are calling
4. I work, am working, do work
5. they love, are loving, do love
6. you call, are calling, do call
7. he (she, it) swims, is swimming, does swim
8. we carry, are carrying, do carry
9. you work, are working, do work
10. he (she, it) praises, is praising, does praise

Practice Exercise No. 10

1. the girl's cottage
2. a supply of water
3. the farmers' land
4. the cottages of the women
5. the sailor's native country
6. the sailor's island
7. the farmer's daughter
8. the sailors' cottages
9. an abundance of stars
10. the woman's native country

Practice Exercise No. 11

1. **Feminae,** the women
2. **Puella,** the girl
3. **Agricolae,** the farmers
4. **Copiae,** the troops
5. **Nauta,** the sailor
6. **Agricola,** the farmer
7. **Filiae,** the daughters
8. **Patria,** the native country
9. **Insulae,** the islands
10. **Filia,** the daughter

Practice Exercise No. 12

1. **magna,** big
2. **pulchrae,** pretty
3. **bonae,** good
4. **mea,** mine
5. **Romanae,** Roman
6. **mala,** bad
7. **tua,** yours
8. **parvae,** small
9. **pulchra,** beautiful
10. **bona,** good

Practice Exercise No. 13

1. **agricola,** a farmer
2. **nautae,** sailors
3. **patria mea,** my native country
4. **insula,** an island
5. **casae,** cottages
6. **nauta,** a sailor
7. **feminae,** women
8. **puella,** a girl
9. **agricolae,** farmers
10. **silva,** a forest

Practice Exercise No. 14

1. toward the road
2. in the cottage
3. with the woman
4. into the woods
5. out of the cottages
6. away from the land
7. away from the cottages
8. out of the forests
9. into the islands
10. toward the streets
11. into the forests
12. with the girl
13. in or on the water
14. toward the water
15. away from the girls
16. toward the island
17. out of the land
18. with the farmer
19. in the native country
20. with the girls

Practice Exercise No. 15

1. **aquam,** water
2. **fabulam,** a story
3. **aquam,** water
4. **Nautam,** the sailor
5. **Agricolas,** the farmers
6. **fabulam,** a story
7. **viam,** the road
8. **Terram,** the land
9. **terram,** the land
10. **Insulas,** islands

Practice Exercise No. 16

1. **Feminae**, to the woman
2. **Nautae**, to the sailor
3. **Nautis**, to the sailors
4. **Puellae**, to the girl
5. **Puellis**, to the girls
6. **Feminis**, to the women
7. **Agricolis**, to the farmers
8. **Feminae**, to the woman
9. **Puellis**, to the girls
10. **Agricolae**, to the farmer

Practice Exercise No. 17

1. you walk; you are walking; you do walk
2. he, she tells; he, she is telling; he, she does tell
3. they walk, they do walk, they are walking
4. I dwell, I am dwelling, I do dwell
5. we sail, we are sailing, we do sail
6. you give, you are giving, you do give
7. he, she, it gives; he, she, it is giving; he, she, it does give
8. they call; they are calling; they do call
9. you work; you are working; you do work
10. we carry; we are carrying; we do carry
11. you praise; you are praising; you do praise
12. they love; they are loving; they do love
13. you are
14. we are
15. they swim; they are swimming; they do swim
16. you swim; you are swimming; you do swim
17. he, she, it fights; he, she, it is fighting; he, she, it does fight
18. we fight; we are fighting; we do fight
19. I attack; I am attacking; I do attack
20. they attack; they are attacking; they do attack

Practice Exercise No. 18

1. **Europam antiquam**
2. **aquae pulchrae**
3. **silvis parvis**
4. **stellas claras**
5. **insularum multarum**
6. **terra Romana**
7. **filias bonas**
8. **famam malam**
9. **puellarum pulchrarum**
10. **incolis multis**

Practice Exercise No. 19

1. casae, f.
2. feminae, f.
3. stellae, f.
4. aquae, f.
5. fabulae, f.
6. insulae, f.
7. puellae, f.
8. copiae, f.
9. filiae, f.
10. nautae, m.
11. terrae, f.
12. Britanniae, f.
13. famae, f.
14. Italiae, f.
15. silvae, f.
16. patriae, f.
17. incolae, m. or f.
18. Europae, f.
19. agricolae, m.
20. viae, f.

Practice Exercise No. 20

1. amare
2. laudare
3. navigare
4. esse
5. vocare
6. oppugnare
7. monstrare
8. dare
9. habitare
10. portare
11. narrare
12. laborare
13. natare
14. pugnare
15. ambulare

Practice Exercise No. 21

1. Nominative Case, Subject; Predicate Noun or Adjective
   Genitive Case, Possession
   Dative Case, Indirect Object
   Accusative Case, Direct Object; Prepositional Phrases
   Ablative Case, Prepositional Phrases

2. **insula lata,** wide island
   insulae latae, of the wide island
   insulae latae, to, for the wide island
   insulam latam, wide island
   insula lata, from, with, by, in the wide island

   insulae latae, wide islands
   insularum latarum, of the wide islands
   insulis latis, to, for the wide islands
   insulas latas, wide islands
   insulis latis, from, with, by, in the wide islands

   via longa, long road
   viae longae, of the long road
   viae longae, to, for the long road
   viam longam, long road
   via longa, from, with, by, in the long road

   viae longae, long roads
   viarum longarum, of the long roads
   viis longis, to, for the long roads
   vias longas, long roads
   viis longis, from, with, by, in long roads

3. **laboro,** I work; I am working; I do work
   laboras, you work; you do work; you are working
   laborat, he, she, it works; he, she, it is working; he, she, it does work

   laboramus, we work; we are working; we do work
   laboratis, you work; you are working; you do work
   laborant, they work; they are working; they do work

   laudo, I praise; I am praising; I do praise
   laudas, you praise; you are praising; you do praise
   laudat, he, she, it praises; he, she, it is praising; he, she, it does praise

   laudamus, we praise; we are praising; we do praise
   laudatis, you praise; you are praising; you do praise
   laudant, they praise; they are praising; they do praise

sum, I am	**sumus,** we are
es, you are	**estis,** you are
est, he, she, it is; there is	**sunt,** they are; there are

Practice Exercise No. 22

1. we are
2. they conquer, they are conquering, they do conquer

3. he, she, it stands; he, she, it is standing; he, she, it does stand

4. he, she, it is; there is

5. you wait for; you are waiting for; you do wait for

6. he, she, it builds; he, she, it is building; he, she, it does build

7. they are; there are

8. we swim; we are swimming; we do swim

9. he, she, it overcomes; he, she, it is overcoming; he, she, it does overcome

10. they sail; they are sailing; they do sail

11. you give; you are giving; you do give

12. you call; you are calling; you do call

13. we build; we are building; we do build

14. they walk; they are walking; they do walk

15. you stand; you are standing; you do stand

Practice Exercise No. 23

1. in Italy
2. toward Britain
3. with the women
4. toward Italy
5. in the province
6. with the troops
7. on the peninsula
8. in front of the cottages
9. behind the cottages
10. with the girl
11. in the woods
12. toward the road
13. toward the island
14. into the cottages
15. in front of the ditch

Practice Exercise No. 24

1. of the inhabitant; to, for the inhabitant; the inhabitants

2. Why do they work?
3. You help your native country.
4. He is carrying the booty.
5. He fights well.
6. They are pretty.
7. of many victories
8. a famous native country
9. a long story
10. out of the cottage
11. away from the road
12. Where is he (she, it)?
13. Here I am.
14. in front of the island
15. after the victory
16. with the troops
17. out of the provinces
18. There are troops here.
19. toward the streets
20. There is the province.
21. There are the women.
22. There is glory.
23. There are many girls.
24. Where are they?
25. Here they are.

Practice Exercise No. 25

1. to, for, from, with, by, in the field
2. to, for, from, with, by, in the wars
3. of the battles
4. of the boy; the boys
5. the ally
6. the friends
7. the camp
8. the swords
9. the help, aid
10. to, for, from, with, by, in the message, messenger
11. the dangers
12. of the weapons, arms
13. of the town
14. the man
15. the enemies

Practice Exercise No. 26

1. **amici**, the friends
2. **puerorum**, of the boys
3. **agris**, to, for, from, with, by, in the fields
4. **bellorum**, of the wars
5. **oppida**, the towns
6. **viri**, the men
7. **pericula**, dangers
8. **gladiorum**, of the swords

9. **nuntios,** messengers
10. **auxiliis,** to, for, from, with, by, in the aids
11. **nuntiis,** to, for, from, with, by, in the messages
12. **viris,** to, for, from, with, by, in the men
13. **periculis,** to, for, from, with, by, in the dangers
14. **agri,** the fields
15. **bella,** the wars

Practice Exercise No. 27

1. of
2. the, an
3. the, a
4. about
5. through
6. of
7. of
8. the
9. the
10. of

Practice Exercise No. 28

1. out of the field
2. are they arming?
3. a narrow street
4. friends
5. with the boy
6. He plows there.
7. behind the camp
8. of the friends
9. with the man
10. They fight a war.
11. They point out the towns.
12. They give arms to the man.
13. We tell stories about the war.
14. He likes dangers.
15. The camp is in the field.
16. You walk through the fields.
17. There are towns.
18. You give aid.
19. Swords kill.
20. They live in camp.

Practice Exercise No. 29

1. My friend is there.
2. toward your cottages
3. out of the deep ditches
4. in the long road
5. with famous men
6. in front of the Roman camp
7. in back of my fields
8. about good water
9. through the large forest
10. of the bad friend; the bad friends

Practice Exercise No. 30

1. virorum mult*orum*
2. filiae me*ae*
3. frumento bon*o*
4. equis tu*is*
5. me*is* filiis
6. pueros aegr*os*
7. puellae miser*ae*
8. soci liber*i*
9. feminam miser*am*
10. agris pulchr*is*

Practice Exercise No. 31

Column I	Column I	Column II	Column II
1. many **viros**	6. good **fili**	3. **multos**	6. **boni**
2. sick **pueri**	7. bad **famam**	5. **aegri**	8. **malam**
3. pretty **oppidum**	8. wretched **equis**	1. **pulchrum**	9. **miseris**
4. many **servorum**	9. Roman **terrae**	2. **multorum**	10. **Romanae**
5. happy **puellam**	10. happy **agricola**	4. **laetam**	7. **laetus**

Practice Exercise No. 32

1. curamus
2. liberas
3. laboratis
4. laudant
5. portat
6. aro
7. necant
8. nuntiat
9. occupamus
10. statis

Practice Exercise No. 33

1. They are free.
2. of the happy mistresses
3. into deep water
4. concerning great cares
5. in wide fields
6. about good masters
7. Why are you happy?
8. There are many people.
9. We are ill.
10. with good friends
11. in free lands
12. She is pretty.
13. Are they pretty?
14. He is unhappy.
15. many things

Practice Exercise No. 34

1. nostram
2. tuas
3. sua
4. meis
5. sua
6. vestrae
7. nostram
8. sui
9. suarum
10. meam

Practice Exercise No. 35

1. I fear; I am fearing; I do fear
2. he, she, it sees; he, she, it is seeing; he, she, it does see
3. you fear; you are fearing; you do fear
4. he, she, it adores; he, she, it is adoring; he, she, it does adore
5. they rule; they are ruling; they do rule
6. you see; you are seeing; you do see
7. they fear; they are fearing; they do fear
8. we have; we are having; we do have
9. we rule; we are ruling; we do rule
10. they have; they are having; they do have
11. he, she, it fears; he, she, it is fearing; he, she, it does fear
12. you see; you are seeing; you do see
13. I have; I am having; I do have
14. you rule; you are ruling; you do rule
15. you adore; you are adoring; you do adore

Practice Exercise No. 36

1. ancient gods
2. of, to, for the Roman goddess; Roman goddesses
3. of my friends
4. of your sailor; your sailors
5. your booty
6. our daughters
7. his, her, its, their master
8. his, her, their son
9. his, her, its, their wisdom; from, with, by, in his, her, its, their wisdom
10. our glory

Practice Exercise No. 37

1. Your glory is not great.
2. Why do you kill your enemy?
3. Is the messenger telling many things?
4. The men are walking across their own fields.
5. The women are in their cottages.
6. Your daughters are sick today.
7. Many people sail across the ocean.
8. They are our goddesses.
9. They are our gods.
10. The woman cares for her daughters.
11. I am standing in front of the cottages.
12. He does not have many things.
13. We are telling about the moon.
14. Your fortune is good.
15. The slaves fear their masters.
16. Why are you not afraid?
17. We see beautiful temples.
18. He has a camp there.
19. We see the boys in back of the ditch.
20. You have great wisdom.

Practice Exercise No. 38

1. aedificare	4. superare	7. regnare	10. curare	13. timere
2. nuntiare	5. videre	8. arare	11. necare	14. habere
3. exspectare	6. liberare	9. stare	12. adorare	15. occupare

Practice Exercise No. 39

1. deae, f.	8. amici, m.	15. victoriae, f.
2. proelii or proeli, n.	9. inimici, m.	16. viri, m.
3. provinciae, f.	10. reginae, f.	17. gladii or gladi, m.
4. belli, n.	11. pueri, m.	18. curae, f.
5. oceani, m.	12. agri, m.	19. praedae, f.
6. socii or soci, m.	13. castrorum, n.	20. equi, m.
7. fortunae, f.	14. periculi, n.	

Practice Exercise No. 40

1. a. **Cur viris frumentum non datis?**
   b. **Datne incolis insularum curam bonam?**

2. sto   I stand; I am standing; I do stand

   stas   you stand; you are standing; you do stand

   stat   he, she, it stands; he, she, it is standing; he, she, it does stand

   stamus   we stand; we are standing; we do stand

   statis   you stand; you are standing; you do stand

   stant   they stand; they are standing; they do stand

   timeo   I fear; I am fearing; I do fear

   times   you fear; you are fearing; you do fear

   timet   he, she, it fears; he, she, it is fearing; he, she, it does fear

   timemus   we fear; we are fearing; we do fear

   timetis   you fear; you are fearing; you do fear

   timent   they fear; they are fearing; they do fear

Practice Exercise No. 41

1. our farmers
2. of the happy daughters
3. high sky
4. of, to, for a free country; free countries
5. your slave
6. his, her, their sons
7. wretched people
8. narrow roads
9. your messenger; your message
10. my fortune; from, with, by, in my fortune
11. many people
12. small boy
13. of the wide fields
14. good care; from, with, by, in good care
15. of the long sword

Practice Exercise No. 42

1. You have friends, haven't you? Certainly.
2. Are they building cottages? Yes. They are building cottages.
3. You are indeed afraid, aren't you? I am indeed afraid.
4. The people are not fighting, are they? The people are not fighting.

5. The roads are not long, are they? The roads are not at all long.
6. Why are they walking toward the town?
7. Is the man staying in the building? The man is staying in the building.
8. Is the province free? The province is truly free.
9. He isn't sailing on the ocean, is he? He is not sailing on the ocean.
10. Is your queen great? My queen is certainly great.

Practice Exercise No. 43

1. e	4. a	7. e	10. a	13. a
2. a	5. e	8. e	11. a	14. a
3. e	6. a	9. e	12. e	15. a

Practice Exercise No. 44

1. Ambulare
2. Pugnare
3. Necare
4. Superare
5. Vocare
6. Natare
7. Iuvare
8. Laborare
9. Oppugnare
10. Manere

Practice Exercise No. 45

1. Why is he preparing grain there?
2. You like the Latin language, don't you?
3. Where do your buildings stand?
4. You ought not to give swords to the boys.
5. The gods also have their own weapons.
6. They tell the story about the long war of Troy.
7. Aeneas is sailing with his men to Italy.
8. The god helps the people of Greece.
9. Why do the Romans fear their allies?
10. He sees the clear moon in the sky.

Practice Exercise No. 46

1. debebamus
2. parabam
3. properabant
4. manebant
5. timebat
6. videbas
7. curabam
8. adorabamus
9. locabas
10. dabatis
11. habebatis
12. stabat
13. laudabam
14. manebas
15. videbamus
16. habebas
17. portabatis
18. iuvabat
19. vocabat
20. timebamus

Practice Exercise No. 47

1. he, she, it was pointing out; used to point out, did point out
2. I call; I am calling; I do call
3. we prepare; we are preparing; we do prepare
4. you were ruling; you used to rule; you did rule; you ruled
5. you ought
6. you fear; you are fearing; you do fear
7. he, she, it was; there was
8. you fight; you are fighting; you do fight
9. I was hurrying; I used to hurry; I did hurry; I hurried
10. they saw; they used to see; they did see; they were seeing
11. you were praising; you used to praise; you did praise; you praised
12. you carry; you are carrying; you do carry

13. you were conquering; you used to conquer; you did conquer; you conquered
14. they tell; they are telling; they do tell
15. we remain; we are remaining; we do remain
16. he, she, it was saving; used to save; did save; saved
17. I was placing; I used to place; I did place; I placed
18. you were attacking; you used to attack; you did attack; you attacked
19. you were having; you used to have; you did have; you had
20. you were

Practice Exercise No. 48

1. when he was standing
2. with the daughter
3. when we work
4. when I wait for, await
5. with friends
6. when he conquers
7. with a wolf
8. when you see
9. when he was; when there was
10. when you were fighting
11. with the girl
12. when they were; when there were
13. with my uncle
14. with the Romans
15. with many women

Practice Exercise No. 49

1. He does not have men in camp, does he?
2. We were preparing today to be there.
3. Your friend has a good reputation in our town.
4. I was preparing to stay with the girls.
5. He often kills many wolves in the forests, doesn't he?
6. The Romans ought not to fear the swords of the Sabines.
7. When they build a town, they place temples and buildings there.
8. Why do they give rewards to their slaves?
9. The farmer was in the field with his friend.
10. You are without water, aren't you?

Practice Exercise No. 50

1. he, she, it attacks
2. they were setting free
3. I shall see
4. he, she, it will remain
5. they were; there were
6. they are; there are
7. they ought; they owe
8. to love; to like
9. you will have; hold
10. you were fighting
11. they were giving
12. he, she, it will be; there will be
13. they will stir up; arouse
14. he, she, it will warn; advise
15. to carry
16. he, she, it will fear
17. you will fight
18. we shall conquer; overcome
19. we were preparing; getting ready
20. they will be; there will be
21. they will tell; relate
22. he, she, it was inciting; arousing
23. you were warning
24. we are
25. we were attacking
26. he will arouse; incite; stir up
27. they were swimming
28. you were placing
29. you will save; preserve
30. you will help; aid

Practice Exercise No. 51

1. down from a clear sky
2. neighboring to my country
3. near to the islands
4. with our friend
5. toward the high buildings
6. in the wide ditches
7. pleasing to his comrade
8. in front of the fields
9. friendly to the slaves
10. after the war
11. unfriendly to the queen
12. concerning your victory
13. through many battles
14. suitable to the man
15. without booty

Practice Exercise No. 52

1. present
2. future
3. imperfect
4. present
5. imperfect
6. imperfect
7. future
8. present
9. future
10. future
11. future
12. imperfect
13. future
14. imperfect
15. future
16. imperfect
17. future
18. imperfect
19. imperfect
20. future

Practice Exercise No. 53

1. He (she) will walk toward the narrow streets.
2. They were standing in front of the temples.
3. You were swimming out of the ocean.
4. They will fight on the water.
5. She was pleasing to the women.
6. They ought to have a free country.
7. The girls will swim.
8. He liked his neighbors.
9. You will save your uncles.
10. They will praise the queen.
11. Where ought you to be?
12. You were calling the boy.
13. He will be unfriendly to the messenger.
14. It is not near to the province.
15. We shall not fear your swords.
16. Your slaves are helping.
17. The man will remain there.
18. We were preparing a deep ditch.
19. The master will tell a story.
20. We shall plow the field.

Practice Exercise No. 54

1. walk (s.)
2. love (pl.)
3. swim (pl.)
4. fight (s.)
5. praise (pl.)
6. sail (pl.)
7. give (pl.)
8. dwell (s.)
9. fear (pl.)
10. see (s.)
11. stand (pl.)
12. have (pl.)
13. hold (s.)
14. rule (s.)
15. hold (pl.)
16. conquer (pl.)
17. stand (s.)
18. help (pl.)
19. warn (pl.)
20. stay (s.)

Practice Exercise No. 55

1. a farmer
2. sailors
3. Britain
4. a friend
5. a girl
6. our allies
7. a boy
8. enemies
9. a friend
10. boys

Practice Exercise No. 56

1. friends
2. wars
3. goddesses
4. god
5. master
6. mistress
7. son
8. glory
9. messengers
10. my slave
11. good man
12. good language
13. many friends
14. good farmer
15. our friend

Practice Exercise No. 57

1. The sick boy, your son, will stay in the town.
2. You ought to have allies in the battle, friend.
3. Arouse your men, Roman people, against war.
4. Warn the inhabitants of Gaul, messengers.
5. I shall call the Sabines, our neighbors, to the games.

6. See the temples, girls, beautiful buildings.
7. Rome, a town in Italy, will be famous.
8. Remember Gaul, my son.
9. Shall we have a big forum, friends?
10. I shall wait for my uncles, the messengers.

Practice Exercise No. 58

1. simple question
2. simple question
3. simple question
4. answer yes
5. answer no
6. answer yes
7. answer no
8. simple question
9. simple question
10. simple question

Practice Exercise No. 59

1. debebam
2. locabas
3. incitabat
4. properabant
5. parabatis
6. tenebamus
7. servabas
8. tenebam
9. manebamus
10. monebat

Practice Exercise No. 60

1. videbo
2. stabunt
3. timebis
4. regnabit
5. necabitis
6. habebimus
7. aedificabo
8. superabis
9. curabimus
10. nuntiabunt

Practice Exercise No. 61

1. serva, servate
2. mone, monete
3. incita, incitate
4. mane, manete
5. naviga, navigate
6. para, parate
7. tene, tenete
8. propera, properate
9. neca, necate
10. pugna, pugnate

Practice Exercise No. 62

1. popule, populi
2. memoria, memoriae
3. legate, legati
4. amice, amici
5. femina, feminae
6. bellum, bella
7. avuncule, avunculi
8. vir, viri
9. puer, pueri
10. puella, puellae
11. fili, filii
12. agricola, agricolae

Practice Exercise No. 63

1. you will be feared
2. I was praising
3. I am being cared for
4. they are praised
5. they will be related, told
6. I shall stand
7. he, she, it was being armed
8. you are plowing
9. he, she, it will be seized
10. you will stand
11. he was killing
12. they will be built
13. I shall overcome; conquer; surpass
14. he will sail
15. I was living in
16. I was being pointed out
17. they were walking
18. he, she, it will be given
19. you are being helped; aided
20. I shall be called

Practice Exercise No. 64

1. exspectabar
2. tenentur
3. monebitur
4. videbatur
5. amabitur
6. habetur
7. videbamini
8. portabitur
9. movebimini
10. parantur
11. laudabuntur
12. locamini
13. properabuntur
14. timemur
15. incitor
16. monebaris
17. servaris
18. debebatur
19. videntur
20. monebantur

Practice Exercise No. 65

1. with the lieutenant	6. by a messenger	11. with horses	16. with wisdom
2. with a sword	7. with uncles	12. by arrows	17. by the people
3. by the boys	8. by wars	13. by an archer	18. with enemies
4. with ditches	9. by the masters	14. by a goddess	19. with water
5. by friends	10. with a comrade	15. with a slave	20. by a man

Practice Exercise No. 66

1. Money will be given to the man and the girl because the boy is ill.
2. I was remembered when I was moving to the neighboring town.
3. They seem to grieve, but a gift will be brought.
4. On account of the dangers the men were afraid of the letters.
5. Fight well for Britain, your native country.
6. Many people were walking toward the temples of the gods.
7. Where (when) will the game be given by your friend?
8. We were living in the cottage where you see the girls.
9. The man will not be attacked by a sword, will he?
10. The people were preparing to move camp, weren't they?

Practice Exercise No. 67

1. of the long peace	8. by happy men	15. on their heads
2. for the soldier	9. suitable part	16. against dictators
3. famous soldiers	10. in an ancient city	17. with the men
4. Roman peace	11. of our sea	18. without your soldiers
5. your heads	12. strong soldiers	19. about pleasing peace
6. to, for their dictators	13. good men	20. friendly man
7. your head	14. long peace	

Practice Exercise No. 68

1. of	3. the, a	5. in, on	7. with	9. the
2. of	4. the, a	6. the	8. of	10. about

Practice Exercise No. 69

1. **paces**, the peaces	11. **militum**, of the soldiers
2. **militibus**, from, with, by, in the soldiers	12. **partium**, of the parts
3. **capitibus**, to, for the heads	13. **homines**, the men
4. **partes**, parts	14. **pacum**, of peaces
5. **hostibus**, to, for the enemy	15. **dictatores**, the dictators
6. **urbium**, of the cities	16. **pontibus**, to, for the bridges
7. **caedes**, slaughters	17. **marium**, of the seas
8. **pontes**, bridges	18. **pontium**, of the bridges
9. **homines**, men	19. **hostes**, the enemy
10. **capita**, heads	20. **urbibus**, from, with, by, in the cities

Practice Exercise No. 70

1. Cincinnatus was being called from his field and was giving aid.
2. Men rule on earth, but the gods rule heaven and earth.

3. Rewards will be given to a great man by the Roman people.
4. The Latin language will always be preserved.
5. He will not plow tomorrow, but he will soon save our country.
6. He was swimming toward the river bank because the bridge was not standing.
7. Fight well, Horatius, for your country with your sword.
8. The soldiers, my sons, will be armed with swords.
9. Because of the dangers you ought to save your water.
10. The sailor loves the sea, but the farmer loves his fields.

Practice Exercise No. 71

1. gods and goddesses
2. the god and the goddess
3. we have and we give
4. he had and he gave
5. a man and women
6. of the men and of the women
7. toward the sun and moon
8. toward the sun and moon
9. from the sea and land
10. from the land and sea

Practice Exercise No. 72

1. in the middle of the roads
2. in many towns
3. in a great war
4. on the tops of the buildings
5. in a good part
6. on (in) wide oceans
7. in many lands
8. in the middle of the sky
9. on the top of the sea
10. in the middle of the ocean

Practice Exercise No. 73

1. toward the sea
2. from the cities
3. with their fathers
4. in front of the forum
5. behind the temple
6. concerning the box
7. without a plan (advice)
8. across the ocean
9. through the seas
10. because of wings
11. for your queen
12. against the people
13. among the enemy
14. by (away from) the men
15. away from the towns
16. in front of the camp
17. through the dangers
18. toward the master
19. across the field
20. concerning peace

Practice Exercise No. 74

1. he, she, it will be; there will be
2. he, she, it will be frightened
3. he, she, it was flying
4. he, she, it will swim
5. they are grieving
6. we are being carried
7. he, she, it was being held
8. we shall be loved; liked
9. I shall move
10. they were being praised
11. he, she, it was fighting
12. you will place
13. I shall be called
14. we were being warned
15. they will work
16. they are being stirred up; aroused
17. he, she, it will owe; ought
18. they are preparing
19. they were being cared for
20. you will be freed

Practice Exercise No. 75

1. The man, my uncle
2. Good friends
3. Good son
4. Of the nations, Italy and Germany
5. Because of the money, the reward
6. Of the women, queens
7. Famous man
8. The boy, a slave
9. To, for the girls, my daughters
10. Our father

Practice Exercise No. 76

1. vocare, to call
2. debere, to owe
3. ambulare, to walk
4. stare, to stand
5. esse, to be
6. monere, to warn
7. timere, to fear
8. narrare, to tell
9. curare, to take care of
10. dolere, to grieve
11. nuntiare, to announce
12. volare, to fly
13. terrere, to frighten
14. adorare, to worship
15. movere, to move
16. parare, to prepare
17. servare, to preserve, save
18. laudare, to praise
19. dare, to give
20. videre, to see

Practice Exercise No. 77

1. paravi, I have prepared
2. incitavi, I have aroused
3. aravi, I have plowed
4. debui, I have owed
5. liberavi, I have freed
6. locavi, I have placed
7. terrui, I have frightened
8. aedificavi, I have built
9. habitavi, I have lived in
10. monui, I have warned
11. properavi, I have hurried
12. habui, I have had, held
13. dedi, I have given
14. tenui, I have held, kept
15. servavi, I have preserved, saved
16. monstravi, I have shown, pointed out
17. timui, I have feared
18. natavi, I have swum
19. movi, I have moved
20. mansi, I have remained, stayed

Practice Exercise No. 78

1. amatus, having been loved
2. habitus, having been had
3. liberatus, having been freed
4. necatus, having been killed
5. monitus, having been warned
6. exspectatus, having been waited for
7. narratus, having been told
8. territus, having been frightened
9. occupatus, having been seized
10. portatus, having been carried
11. datus, having been given
12. monitus, having been warned
13. servatus, having been saved
14. iutus, having been helped
15. visus, having been seen; seemed
16. adoratus, having been worshipped
17. motus, having been moved
18. spectatus, having been seen
19. obtentus, having been obtained
20. locatus, having been placed, put

Practice Exercise No. 79

1. Both your mother and your father were giving advice about courage.
2. In the middle of the town there were many buildings.
3. The report about my nation will be carried by the messengers.
4. The girl and the boy are swimming under the water.
5. We ought to walk around the city and see many things.
6. You remember many bad things, don't you?
7. The sun seemed to be on the top of the water.
8. The nations of Europe will not always fight.
9. Sailors sail on seas and oceans.
10. Roman soldiers have great courage.

Practice Exercise No. 80

1. dolere	5. obtinere	9. laudare	13. habere	17. occupare
2. terrere	6. dare	10. manere	14. videre	18. stare
3. movere	7. spectare	11. debere	15. necare	19. iuvare
4. vocare	8. volare	12. timere	16. parare	20. monere

Practice Exercise No. 81

1. spectavi	3. moneo	5. motus	7. servatus	9. habito
2. curare	4. dedi	6. paravi	8. territus	10. laudare

Practice Exercise No. 82

1. of the animals and men
2. by the father
3. by the mothers
4. the sea and star
5. fathers and mothers
6. of speed and size
7. by Mercury
8. by the soldiers
9. by Pluto
10. war and peace

Practice Exercise No. 83

1. he, she, it was being praised
2. they will grieve
3. we were being warned
4. they are being killed
5. you are being called
6. we shall obtain, secure
7. you are being seen; you seem
8. you were helping
9. I shall have, hold
10. you will be moved
11. they are being occupied, seized
12. they were being feared
13. he, she, it will be prepared
14. you will give
15. you are being saved
16. we were being prepared
17. it will be owed
18. you were being cared for
19. we were being watched, looked at
20. they will frighten, terrify

Practice Exercise No. 84

1. ambulavi	3. monui	5. portavi	7. vocavi	9. dedi
2. laudavi	4. debui	6. servavi	8. movi	10. rogavi

Practice Exercise No. 85

1. he, she, it has asked
2. they have watched
3. we have warned, advised
4. I have helped, aided
5. you have been
6. you have killed
7. you have told, related
8. I have lived in, dwelt
9. I have seen
10. they have feared
11. you have grieved
12. you have had, held
13. we have owed, ought
14. they have worked
15. you have overcome, conquered
16. he, she, it has pointed out, shown
17. they have told, related
18. you have occupied, seized
19. we have prepared
20. he, she, it has flown

Practice Exercise No. 86

1. I had walked
2. they had adored
3. he, she, it had plowed
4. they had moved
5. we had remained, stayed
6. you had seen
7. you had prepared
8. you had given
9. you had held, kept
10. I had stood
11. he, she, it had prepared
12. they had placed
13. you had stirred up, aroused
14. you had cared for
15. I had swum
16. we had grieved
17. he, she, it had asked
18. they had watched, looked at
19. he, she, it had seen
20. you had called

Practice Exercise No. 87

1. you will have loved
2. he, she, it will have cared for
3. I shall have praised
4. we shall have placed
5. they will have had
6. he, she, it will have frightened
7. he, she, it will have moved
8. they will have given
9. you will have stood
10. he, she, it will have held
11. we shall have called
12. I shall have saved
13. he, she, it will have carried
14. they will have prepared
15. you will have announced
16. we shall have told, related
17. you will have had
18. he, she, it will have owed
19. they will have worshipped
20. you will have walked

Practice Exercise No. 88

1. they have been
2. he, she has walked
3. he has been carried
4. they have been loved
5. you have been cared for
6. they have been praised
7. I have been warned
8. we have owed, ought to have
9. you have stood
10. it has been related, told
11. we have been called
12. I have swum
13. you have been saved
14. it has been announced
15. they have been moved
16. you have feared
17. he has been prepared
18. they have been placed
19. they have praised
20. you have moved

Practice Exercise No. 89

1. they had given
2. he, she, it had moved
3. he had been frightened
4. you had remained, stayed
5. you had held
6. he, she, it had fought
7. I had been praised
8. they had been cared for
9. you had been loved
10. you had been aroused, incited
11. they had been prepared
12. you had occupied, seized
13. you had been freed
14. he had been killed
15. we had been saved
16. he had warned, advised
17. you had had
18. you had held, kept
19. we had been helped
20. they had worshipped

Practice Exercise No. 90

1. I shall have warned, advised
2. he, she, it will have been
3. it will have been carried
4. they will have been warned
5. they will have had
6. you will have frightened
7. we shall have moved
8. you will have been seen
9. he, she, it will have feared
10. she will have been moved
11. we shall have given
12. they will have stood
13. we shall have been
14. you will have been killed

15. we shall have been praised
16. you will have been armed
17. they will have been cared for
18. it will have been placed
19. they will have been; there will have been
20. she will have been saved

Practice Exercise No. 91

1. it had been had
2. I shall have seen
3. they will have been attacked
4. you will have been praised
5. you had been carried
6. it will have been owed
7. they had owed
8. you have waited for
9. you have seen
10. it has been pointed out, shown
11. they have been warned, advised
12. we have been asked
13. they have looked at, watched
14. we have been moved
15. we had prepared
16. he has been warned, advised
17. he, she, it had stood
18. they had been given
19. they have told, related
20. I shall have held, kept

Practice Exercise No. 92

1. for many years
2. in the next year
3. for many hours
4. in the next hour
5. for seven hours
6. in the middle of the year
7. in six hours
8. for long years
9. in an hour
10. for twelve hours

Practice Exercise No. 93

1. to the cities
2. from the towns
3. from Rome
4. to Rome
5. into the camp
6. in front of the forum
7. in back of the garden
8. in the field
9. into the fields
10. down from the hills
11. out of the cottage
12. in the country
13. at home
14. away from the river
15. under the seas
16. under the walls
17. into the ditch
18. away from the temple
19. out of the roads
20. about, down from the sun

Practice Exercise No. 94

1. I shall see
2. he, she, it had fought
3. you were standing
4. we shall work
5. he, she, it had been; there had been
6. they will obtain
7. we were swimming
8. he, she, it will be; there will be
9. we see
10. it has been looked at
11. he, she, it will be moved
12. they had been built
13. you have been
14. we were being attacked
15. they have remained, stayed

Practice Exercise No. 95

1. Next year we shall move to Rome.
2. For six hours they remained in the city.
3. They had been attacked half way up the hill.
4. I stayed in Italy for many hours.
5. He (she) will be there for an hour.
6. They will work for many years, won't they?
7. He walked toward the town for many long hours.
8. He has not been freed by the king.
9. Are they in the garden with the boys?
10. I moved seven miles from the city.

Practice Exercise No. 96

1. they are sending
2. I have been shown, taught
3. we are being sought
4. he, she, it ought; owes
5. you had been warned
6. they will have been prepared
7. he, she, it has led
8. you have freed
9. I was worshipping
10. he, she, it will have sent
11. he, she, it will order
12. we were being watched, looked at
13. you are showing
14. they will ask
15. you were leading
16. he, she, it will send
17. I have saved, preserved
18. you had feared
19. you had sought
20. they have remained, stayed

Practice Exercise No. 97

1. on account of the injury
2. from the battles
3. for six hours
4. on the road, march, journey
5. out of the territory
6. toward Gaul
7. away from the hill
8. in the letter
9. by the men; away from the men
10. into the river bank

Practice Exercise No. 98

1. I seek them.
2. of these, those books
3. his, her garden
4. I gave these, those things to them.
5. He was fighting.
6. You have seen him.
7. in these, those places
8. to, for his (her) father
9. They are being sent by him.
10. You sent them.
11. this, that hour; in this, that hour
12. her, his, their own signals
13. out of these, those cities
14. this, that woman
15. We are being led by them.
16. their apples
17. his, her, their own kings
18. with them
19. this, that road, journey
20. this, that cause

Practice Exercise No. 99

1. ducitur
2. ductus sum
3. ducebam
4. duxerunt
5. ducar
6. missus es
7. mittebant
8. mittetis
9. misisti
10. missus erat
11. petiti sunt
12. petiverimus
13. petetur
14. petit
15. petebas
16. currentur
17. cursus est
18. currit
19. currebantur
20. cucurrerat

Practice Exercise No. 100

1. in, on the feet
2. away from the hill
3. toward the rivers
4. out of the fields
5. into the fire
6. in, on the walls
7. about the body
8. in the country
9. from Rome
10. to Rome
11. at home
12. out of the night

Practice Exercise No. 101

1. he, she, it had been; there had been
2. we have ruled
3. he has been asked
4. you will have carried
5. they have given
6. they have placed

7. they have been given
8. you have sent
9. it will have been sought
10. it had been increased
11. we have moved
12. we have been
13. they had been aroused

14. you had hurried
15. they will have been; there will have been
16. I have been asked
17. he, she, it stood
18. you have called
19. we shall have been praised
20. he had had

Practice Exercise No. 102

1. in the next year
2. for seven hours
3. in the next hours
4. late in the year
5. for six years
6. on this, that night
7. for these, those nights
8. for these, those years
9. in this, that year
10. in this, that hour

Practice Exercise No. 103

1. his, hers, its
2. them
3. they
4. to, for him, her, it; they
5. it
6. them
7. she; they; them; from, with, by, in her
8. their
9. to, for, from, with, by, in them
10. him
11. they
12. from, with, by, in him, it

Practice Exercise No. 104

1. this, that love
2. of this, that boldness
3. these, those names
4. these, those causes
5. to, for, from, with, by, in these, those territories
6. of these, those journeys
7. these, those apples
8. to, for this, that woman
9. this, that body
10. of this, that place
11. to, for this, that king
12. this, that night
13. these, those laws
14. from, with, by, in this, that mountain
15. of this, that signal

Practice Exercise No. 105

1. because of the delay
2. because of my care
3. because of the dangers
4. because of fear
5. because of death
6. because of diligence
7. because of speed
8. because of boldness
9. because of the delays
10. because of the time

Practice Exercise No. 106

1. with zeal, eagerness
2. with great care
3. with great diligence, care
4. with great fear
5. with speed
6. with much zeal, eagerness
7. with great zeal, eagerness
8. with delay
9. with great speed
10. with great delay

Practice Exercise No. 107

1. posui
2. superare
3. dedi
4. capere
5. servatus
6. facio
7. verti
8. terrui
9. duco
10. paratus

Practice Exercise No. 108

1. he, she, it has ordered
2. you have led
3. they have shown
4. I was asking
5. we have made, done
6. he, she, it is being shown
7. you are being sent; will be sent
8. you are being taken, seized
9. he, she, it will look at, watch
10. we shall increase
11. they will seek
12. they were flying
13. you were obtaining, getting
14. he, she, it was being turned
15. he, she, it had terrified
16. you had sought
17. they had taken, seized
18. they will have been moved
19. we had been led
20. he, she, it was taking, seizing

Practice Exercise No. 109

1. because of the hour
2. because of the weapon
3. in front of the camp
4. from fear
5. down from the tree; about the tree
6. by the king; away from the king
7. out of the trees
8. into this, that place
9. with the father
10. with care
11. in, on the water
12. under the ocean
13. around the walls
14. against him
15. between, among the towns
16. through the field
17. in back of the camp
18. without them
19. across the sea
20. about, concerning the men

Practice Exercise No. 110

1. this wall
2. that city
3. in that place
4. these leaders
5. to, for those soldiers
6. to, for that lieutenant
7. these commanders
8. those plans
9. of that ocean
10. of these men
11. in that garden
12. that goddess
13. of that foot soldier
14. about this master
15. out of that tree
16. this hindrance
17. to, for these fathers
18. these ships
19. that book
20. to that girl
21. these weapons
22. of these parts
23. about that peace
24. of those sands
25. in these years
26. for that hour
27. that sign, standard
28. of this horse
29. toward these women
30. those messengers

Practice Exercise No. 111

1. his, her, its
2. he
3. to, for him, her, it; they
4. them
5. to, for, from, with, by, in them
6. of them, their
7. it; from, with, by, in him, it
8. to, for him, her, it
9. she; from, with, by, in her; them; they
10. they
11. she; them; they
12. her
13. them
14. him
15. them

Practice Exercise No. 112

1. the goddess herself, the very goddess
2. out of the temples themselves, out of the very temples
3. the same city
4. the men themselves, the very men
5. by the same youth
6. the same name, the very name
7. of the same nation
8. with the same horsemen
9. the same roads, ways
10. to, for, from, with, by, in the same men
11. out of the field itself, out of the very field
12. in the years themselves, in the very years
13. the boys themselves, the very boys
14. of the lieutenant himself, of the very lieutenant
15. the same hour; in the same hour
16. the law itself, the very law
17. the mountain itself, the very mountain
18. the girls themselves, the very girls
19. the same journey, road, way
20. by the women themselves, by the very women
21. at the same time
22. of the same generals
23. the same towns
24. in the cities themselves, in the very cities
25. of the same people
26. the same men
27. out of the same places
28. in the same years
29. on the very night, in the night itself
30. peace itself, the very peace

Practice Exercise No. 113

1. to, for him (himself), her (herself), it (itself); they (themselves)
2. of (the same) him, her, it
3. (the same) it
4. she (herself); they (themselves); them (themselves)
5. them (themselves)
6. (the same) she; they; them; from, with, by, in her
7. (the same) him
8. of (the same) them
9. out of (the same) them
10. of him (himself), her (herself), it (itself)

Practice Exercise No. 114

1. they were able to lead
2. you can stay
3. he, she was not able to worship
4. he, she, it will be able to free
5. they can care for
6. we were not able to kill

7. I had been able to order
8. you can show, point out
9. we were able to ask
10. I was not able to increase
11. we shall be able to help
12. you will be able to fight
13. they have not been able to call
14. I can not work
15. you have been able to stay

Practice Exercise No. 115

1. in one year
2. no care
3. of which gift
4. to, for any ship
5. for all the years
6. with the father alone
7. of no deaths
8. to neither nation
9. in the other road
10. with, by another name
11. to which river
12. of any hill
13. to, for one book
14. for no reasons
15. by neither man

Practice Exercise No. 116

1. they had feared
2. you have been
3. they will send
4. he, she, it took
5. he, she, it will fear
6. they were looking at
7. they will be held
8. I shall be sent
9. they have been praised
10. it had been done, made
11. you were sailing
12. they were being given
13. he, she, it carries on, bears
14. they had been; there had been
15. they have had

Practice Exercise No. 117

1. one is a boy, the other is not
2. at no time
3. of any war
4. toward which camp
5. the women themselves alone
6. of neither youth
7. other cities
8. one part
9. about neither girl
10. another road, journey, way

Practice Exercise No. 118

1. in a short hour
2. of a bold slave
3. swift horse
4. in, on a swift river
5. by bold men
6. for all times; all times
7. by a keen lieutenant
8. short life
9. at all hours
10. in a swift ship
11. bold work
12. in a short time
13. active troops
14. of a swift horse
15. active women
16. swift death, quick death
17. short journeys, roads
18. to a bold man
19. for a short year
20. in every, each place

Practice Exercise No. 119

1. of the golden sun
2. out of neither place
3. on the top of the mountain
4. of an easy journey
5. any hours
6. grave punishments
7. of the nearest nations
8. bold citizen
9. strong body
10. of swift rivers
11. Latin books
12. other men
13. your ship
14. of many fathers
15. of each king

Practice Exercise No. 120

1. Who are you?
2. To whom did he give those things?
3. Whom shall I see?
4. whose eyes?
5. What things does he know?
6. With whom does he (she) walk?

7. By whom has he been captured?
8. Who is shouting?
9. Who is fighting?
10. whose weapons?
11. What do you have?
12. Whom has he killed?
13. To whom shall I give it?
14. What has been asked?
15. To whom have you sent the gift?
16. Whom do you like?
17. Who is fleeing?
18. What is easy?
19. Whose is it?
20. with whom?
21. Whom will he send?
22. What is he doing?
23. Who are struggling?
24. By whom has it been carried on?
25. Who is calling?

Practice Exercise No. 121

1. pugnare	5. laudare	9. cognoscere	13. habere	17. augere
2. mittere	6. rogare	10. necare	14. movere	18. servare
3. regere	7. scribere	11. capere	15. parare	19. vincere
4. dare	8. videre	12. timere	16. ducere	20. terrere

Practice Exercise No. 122

1. demonstrari	5. verti	9. doceri	13. accipi	17. iuvari
2. duci	6. armari	10. occupari	14. timeri	18. teneri
3. moveri	7. amari	11. mitti	15. vocari	19. cognosci
4. iuberi	8. faci	12. geri	16. interfici	20. simulari

Practice Exercise No. 123

1. they take, seize
2. it had been learned
3. they have been conquered
4. they will turn
5. we were killing
6. they have done, made
7. you had taken, seized
8. he, she, it was fleeing
9. he, she, it will be put
10. they will have carried on, waged
11. he, she, it writes
12. you throw
13. they will hurry
14. they have been put
15. it has been carried on, waged

Practice Exercise No. 124

1. because of death
2. because of injury
3. with great diligence
4. because of the general
5. because of food
6. because of the fleets
7. with a small punishment, fine
8. with great zeal, eagerness
9. because of the hindrance
10. because of the sand

Practice Exercise No. 125

1. him	5. he	9. he	13. whose
2. his, hers, its	6. their	10. their	14. to, for whom
3. them	7. the same things; she	11. whom	15. with whom
4. that	8. his, hers, its	12. what	

Practice Exercise No. 126

1. he, she was able to shout
2. they were able to take
3. you can do, make
4. we can put, place
5. you have been able to conquer
6. he, she will be able to hurry
7. they have been able to write
8. we were able to recognize, learn
9. you are able to turn
10. they are able to carry on, wage

Practice Exercise No. 127

1. of one work
2. of all the citizens
3. another hindrance
4. new weapons
5. in a short time
6. to, for the whole stone
7. of no fear
8. any injury
9. bold horsemen, knights
10. swift punishment

Practice Exercise No. 128

1. **pulchre**, beautifully
2. **longe**, far, distant
3. **magnopere**, greatly
4. **nove**, recently, newly
5. **acriter**, keenly
6. **graviter**, seriously
7. **breviter**, briefly
8. **alte**, high, on high
9. **grate**, with pleasure
10. **audacter**, boldly
11. **misere**, wretchedly
12. **proxime**, next, most recently
13. **fortiter**, bravely
14. **celeriter**, swiftly
15. **libere**, freely

Practice Exercise No. 129

1. you carry, do carry
2. I have, hold
3. they lead, are leading
4. he throws, is throwing
5. you have heard
6. he has been freed
7. they had been seen; had seemed
8. they have been heard
9. you have been received, accepted
10. I had been heard
11. they were hearing
12. he will have been prepared
13. he, she, it will hear
14. they have sought
15. they hear, do hear
16. you were being helped
17. we were being heard
18. we were turning
19. they will be taken, seized
20. you will be heard
21. you are being heard
22. he, she, it has done, made
23. they will ask
24. we have heard
25. they had been heard

Practice Exercise No. 130

1. they are fighting bravely
2. we saw very recently
3. he, she, it carried on with difficulty
4. they will be widely accepted
5. we are being taught well
6. he, she walks far
7. they stand well
8. he easily recognized
9. he, she liked greatly
10. not keenly enough

Practice Exercise No. 131

1. The place will be defended easily.
2. At first nothing was able to be prepared.
3. Because of fear you did not fight bravely.

4. Which door do you like?
5. The land by nature has been defended with difficulty.
6. Not only the king but also the queen heard it.
7. About whom has he (she) written boldly?
8. In that year we were preparing many things.
9. Eurydice lived unhappily under the earth.
10. He led them far from this place.

Practice Exercise No. 132

1. 1. who are making the journey with their forces
  2. The men, who are making the journey with their forces, are brave.
2. 1. which he built
  2. The tower, which he built, was keeping the barbarians from the town.
3. 1. with whom I was walking
  2. The woman, with whom I was walking, is my mother.
4. 1. whose name we can not see
  2. The ship, whose name we can not see, is sailing toward Italy.
5. 1. to whom I gave the letter
  2. The boy, to whom I gave the letter, will come quickly.
6. 1. which you will have
  2. The fear, which you will have, soon will not be remembered.
7. 1. to which they were fleeing
  2. The river, to which they were fleeing, was deep and wide.
8. 1. about which he wrote
  2. The place, about which he wrote, is far from the city.
9. 1. which he had
  2. Everything, which he had, now is mine.
10. 1. whose boys you see
  2. The men, whose boys you see, are friends.

Practice Exercise No. 133

1. in what places?
2. which man?
3. what town?
4. what booty?
5. which men?
6. with what speed?
7. in what year?
8. of what name?
9. at what hour?
10. at what time?
11. with what soldiers?
12. of what citizens?
13. what baggage?, what hindrances?
14. of what size?
15. with what plan?

Practice Exercise No. 134

1. they make, do
2. he, she, it will order
3. you have found, learned
4. he, she, it will arrive
5. to be had
6. he, she, it was running
7. he, she, it had been
8. he, she, it took, seized
9. they have looked at
10. it was happening
11. you hear
12. you have arrived
13. he, she, it was fighting, hurrying
14. they had given
15. to be seen; to seem
16. they have prohibited
17. they will be; there will be
18. I shall be seen; I shall seem
19. to be asked
20. I shall have

Practice Exercise No. 135

1. he, she, it has not been able
2. of that place
3. your sons
4. others come; some come
5. he, she wishes to come
6. brave people
7. because of the storm
8. with great zeal
9. he, she remained at home
10. of this (that) nation
11. in the next year
12. my friend
13. all men
14. he, she fears nothing
15. not only your mother

Practice Exercise No. 136

1. for many paces
2. your group; your hand
3. long attack
4. because of his arrival
5. each wing
6. of our armies
7. on your wing
8. out of the army
9. into the house
10. for six miles
11. against the armies
12. because of your arrival
13. the attack (attacks) of the enemy
14. group (groups) of soldiers
15. by the army

Practice Exercise No. 137

1. their battle lines
2. late in the day
3. on the next day
4. because of these things
5. of any hope
6. the whole thing
7. for one day
8. of what things
9. our battle lines
10. what things
11. in what battle line
12. of each day
13. because of this (that) thing
14. in these battle lines
15. much hope

Practice Exercise No. 138

1. he, she has walked
2. we are seen; we seem
3. they were; there were
4. he, she, it had done, made
5. he, she was fleeing
6. he, she, it finds
7. it had been given
8. he, she, it can, is able
9. it has been drawn up
10. to be seen; to seem
11. they have been left behind
12. they will fight
13. he, she, it has drawn up
14. he, she makes a journey
15. they will be heard

Practice Exercise No. 139

1. All things seem to be easy.
2. After six days neither soldier had any hope.
3. The captives whom you led back came out of their army.
4. Who hindered the strong attack greatly?
5. In one hour the men will come home.
6. For what reason was he drawing up his battle line on the hill?
7. Among these things which we have is a small supply of water.
8. The soldiers in that wing are turning their horses toward the field.
9. Neither the wing nor the battle line saw hope.
10. Who among these peoples hold the royal power?

Practice Exercise No. 140

1. you
2. we; us
3. by you
4. their; of them
5. she; they; them; from, with her
6. to, for her, him, it; they
7. you; from, with, by, in you
8. I
9. him
10. to, for me

11. with us
12. you
13. to, for you; from, with you
14. them
15. that; it
16. to him, her, it
17. his, her, its
18. with you
19. their; of them
20. toward you

21. to you
22. your; of you
23. our; of us
24. about me
25. to, for them; from, with, by them
26. about them
27. she; from, with, by her; they; them
28. with her
29. their; of them
30. them

Practice Exercise No. 141

1. to, for himself, herself, itself; to, for themselves
2. yourself; from, with, by, in yourself
3. by myself
4. yourselves
5. himself, herself, itself; themselves; from, with, by, in himself, herself, itself, themselves
6. to, for yourselves; from, with, by, in yourselves
7. to, for myself
8. to, for ourselves; from, with, by, in ourselves
9. myself; from, with, by, in myself
10. ourselves

Practice Exercise No. 142

1. The man himself knows us.
2. I sent help to you.
3. We found you in this place.
4. Will you come with me?
5. You give books to us.
6. You do not hear him.
7. They were fleeing toward us.
8. He sent these things to me.
9. He (She) will not be able to walk home with you.
10. This is our native country.
11. You will tell this (that) to them.
12. We shall lead her home.
13. They were seeking peace from them.
14. I was being terrified by you and your sword.
15. We had saved ourselves at that time.
16. You can help us, can't you?
17. He saw their city.
18. We ourselves shall order them to come.
19. You will point out these things to us.
20. His spirit did not frighten me long.

Practice Exercise No. 143

1. **late**, widely
2. **acriter**, keenly
3. **difficile**, with difficulty
4. **misere**, wretchedly
5. **longe**, far
6. **magnopere**, greatly
7. **laete**, happily
8. **libere**, freely
9. **parum**, too little, not enough
10. **anguste**, narrowly

Practice Exercise No. 144

1. I shall come
2. he, she knew
3. he has been heard
4. we were arriving

5. they will be hindered
6. they find, discover
7. you were being heard
8. it had been known

9. they have wished
10. you will be heard

Practice Exercise No. 145

1. whose
2. whom
3. who, which, that
4. who
5. with whom

6. we; us; ourselves
7. to, for me, myself
8. me; myself; from, with, by, in me, myself
9. of you
10. to, for you, yourself

11. with you, yourself
12. his, her, its
13. their, of them
14. him
15. her

Practice Exercise No. 146

1. to, for the army
2. the thing; things
3. of the horn, wing
4. the battle line
5. hope
6. of the hands, bands
7. on, from, with, by the day
8. to, for, from, with, by, in the attacks

9. the arrival
10. home; the house
11. to, for, from, with, by, in the things
12. horns, wings
13. of the armies
14. to, for the hand, group
15. to, for hope

Practice Exercise No. 147

1. fifteen
2. nine
3. twenty
4. five
5. sixteen

6. ten
7. three
8. seventeen
9. four
10. eleven

11. one hundred
12. fourteen
13. eight
14. eighteen
15. two

16. thirteen
17. seven
18. one
19. eighteen
20. one thousand

21. twelve
22. six

Practice Exercise No. 148

1. fourth
2. eighth

3. tenth
4. third

5. seventh
6. second

7. fifth
8. ninth

9. first
10. sixth

Practice Exercise No. 149

1. a thousand ships
2. three men
3. of thousands of soldiers
4. for fourteen days
5. of one man
6. twenty miles
7. a hundred boys

8. for five years
9. six of the soldiers
10. in seven hours
11. in a hundred years
12. eight of the boys
13. for two days
14. of ten laws; ten of the laws

15. three places
16. two of the provinces
17. in twelve days
18. of six animals
19. eighteen of the kings
20. in three years

Practice Exercise No. 150

1. to, for, of the tenth girl
2. on the eighth day
3. in the sixth hour; the sixth hour
4. the seventh ship
5. in the fifth summer
6. for the third day
7. in the tenth winter
8. the seventh attack
9. to, for, of the ninth hour; ninth hours
10. in the first year

Practice Exercise No. 151

1. a difficult way, road
2. a wretched home
3. of the free men
4. keen fears
5. similar armies
6. a long day, for a long day
7. on a high mountain
8. swift rivers
9. wide streets
10. of pretty girls

Practice Exercise No. 152

1. narrower streets
2. a taller boy
3. of happier girls
4. a friendlier people
5. a longer road, way
6. in more pleasing places
7. of more famous sisters
8. a longer winter, for a longer winter
9. wider rivers
10. bolder man

Practice Exercise No. 153

1. of a very sweet spring
2. out of very pretty gardens
3. a very narrow temple
4. because of very wretched memories
5. very famous oracles
6. a very happy citizen
7. out of a very wide field
8. with very pretty mothers
9. on a very new ship
10. very short names

Practice Exercise No. 154

1. This is a very wretched place.
2. The bravest men arrived at the island.
3. The very keen horses were among the first.
4. What is an easier way to Greece?
5. The people of Italy are very free.
6. This is the narrower part of the water.
7. These things are also very similar.
8. We saw a very deep and rather wide river.
9. Our men chose a shorter way to the city.
10. You can see a high building from this place.

Practice Exercise No. 155

1. These towers are higher than those.
2. You are taller than your father.
3. Those roads are not easier than others.
4. You are more like your father than your mother.
5. Men are much stronger than women.
6. His house in the country is newer than that in the city.
7. The boy is happier than his sister.
8. The barbarians are much bolder than their neighbors.
9. He will be friendlier to you than to me.
10. Is the hand quicker than the eye?

Practice Exercise No. 156

1. they will be; there will be
2. it has been shown
3. he, she, it decided
4. he, she, it will be prepared
5. they were leading
6. he has been left behind
7. he, she, it will be sent
8. you are being carried
9. we were seeing
10. he, she has walked

Practice Exercise No. 157

1. more things
2. better
3. of the worst
4. of a bigger
5. of smaller
6. of very many
7. to, for, from, with, by, in more
8. the next
9. more suitable; of more suitable
10. most suitable

Practice Exercise No. 158

1. in very many cities
2. out of smaller springs
3. the greatest courage
4. best voice
5. down from higher walls
6. more water
7. more suitable time
8. of the worst thing; to, for the worst thing
9. toward a better part
10. with a bigger army
11. on a longer day
12. very many states
13. worse end
14. best years
15. smallest sister
16. of very many difficulties
17. better way
18. of the worst summer
19. very many gifts
20. of a smaller ship

Practice Exercise No. 159

1. wide
2. widely
3. wider
4. more widely
5. very wide
6. very widely
7. free
8. freely
9. freer
10. very free
11. more freely
12. very freely
13. pretty
14. more pretty
15. very pretty
16. prettily
17. more prettily
18. very prettily
19. swift
20. swiftly
21. swifter
22. more swiftly
23. very swift
24. very swiftly
25. keen
26. keenly
27. keener
28. more keenly
29. keenest
30. most keenly

Practice Exercise No. 160

1. They were being attacked most severely.
2. He fights more bravely.
3. They have been burned quickly.
4. They will speak much more briefly.
5. He will be warned very boldly.
6. They drew up the battle line with difficulty.
7. He waged war more keenly.
8. They walk proudly.
9. He gave more pleasingly.
10. He is praised very highly.
11. They have been sent more widely.
12. He gave very freely.
13. He sails very far.
14. He moves more wretchedly.
15. They were seen recently.
16. They move more beautifully.
17. He will fear very keenly.
18. They have been taken boldly.
19. He was speaking very briefly.
20. They fight bravely.

Practice Exercise No. 161

1. well	5. little	9. more	13. less	17. longest
2. greatly	6. long	10. more	14. more often	18. most often
3. badly	7. often	11. better	15. most	19. best
4. much	8. longer	12. worse	16. most	20. worst
				21. least

Practice Exercise No. 162

1. They arrive more often.
2. He fought as long as possible.
3. He has been aroused more.
4. He was being hindered more.
5. You have been loved best.
6. It has been heard most often.
7. He walks with less difficulty.
8. They are very powerful among us.
9. He flies more swiftly.
10. He will stay much longer.

Practice Exercise No. 163

1. one of the sisters
2. three rivers
3. two years; for two years
4. a thousand years
5. two wives
6. a hundred words
7. of one voice
8. twenty springs, fountains
9. the fourth hour; in the fourth hour
10. on the fifth day
11. in the second year
12. the seventh word
13. the first oracle
14. in the fourth harbor, port
15. out of the sixth gate, door

Practice Exercise No. 164

1. the longer winter; for the longer winter
2. the very pretty summer
3. of the longest years
4. the sweeter word
5. a very similar burden
6. of an immortal voice
7. easier way, journey
8. clearer lights
9. of a very keen difficulty
10. of stronger husbands

Practice Exercise No. 165

1. sweet, sweeter, sweetest
2. keen, keener, keenest
3. long, longer, longest
4. similar, more similar, most similar
5. high, higher, highest
6. free, freer, freest
7. swift, swifter, swiftest
8. wide, wider, widest
9. clear, clearer, clearest
10. bold, bolder, boldest

Practice Exercise No. 166

1. big, bigger, biggest
2. small, smaller, smallest
3. good, better, best
4. bad, worse, worst
5. much, more, most
6. many, more, very many
7. suitable, more suitable, most suitable

Practice Exercise No. 167

1. he was walking farther
2. he has been oppressed miserably
3. he sleeps little
4. it will burn for a very long time

5. they have been more keenly aroused   8. they are very powerful
6. they were touching more   9. it, he, she will be more powerful
7. they have surrendered more easily   10. they will be forced less easily

Practice Exercise No. 168

1. to warn
2. to have increased
3. to be thrown
4. to be about to place
5. to have fled
6. to hinder
7. to have swum
8. to be about to frighten
9. to have remained
10. to be about to hear
11. to have written
12. to be about to fight
13. to be about to praise
14. to be aroused
15. to have been sought
16. to send
17. to be touched
18. to have been attacked
19. to be known
20. to be about to carry on
21. to be received
22. to have been conquered
23. to be said
24. to be about to walk
25. to have feared

Practice Exercise No. 169

1. **petere**, to seek
2. **cepisse**, to have taken
3. **habere**, to have
4. **rexisse**, to have ruled
5. **portare**, to carry
6. **vocavisse**, to have called
7. **facere**, to do, make
8. **dedisse**, to have given
9. **instruere**, to draw up
10. **vertere**, to turn

Practice Exercise No. 170

1. **narrari**, to be told
2. **defensum esse**, to have been defended
3. **videri**, to be seen; to seem
4. **iuvari**, to be helped
5. **pugnatum esse**, to have been fought
6. **motum esse**, to have been moved
7. **vocari**, to be called
8. **inveniri**, to be found
9. **necatum esse**, to have been killed
10. **relinqui**, to be left

Practice Exercise No. 171

1. **futurum esse**, to be about to be
2. **iussurum esse**, to be about to order
3. **facturum esse**, to be about to make
4. **defensurum esse**, to be about to defend
5. **oppugnaturum esse**, to be about to attack
6. **properaturum esse**, to be about to hurry
7. **capturum esse**, to be about to take
8. **inventurum esse**, to be about to find
9. **daturum esse**, to be about to give
10. **positurum esse**, to be about to place

Practice Exercise No. 172

1. Those soldiers said the men would carry aid.
2. Do you think your work has been done?
3. We were hoping the enemy would come as quickly as possible.
4. The girls seem to be happy.
5. This king wished to rule well.
6. He will not want to be called.
7. To defend our town is best.
8. To have had hope was better than to have retreated.
9. He announced that the speed could be increased.
10. He ordered us to find a better place.

Practice Exercise No. 173

1. calling
2. having been moved
3. about to send
4. receiving
5. about to come
6. having been watched
7. arriving
8. about to take
9. placing, putting
10. having been announced
11. having been warned
12. fearing
13. about to say
14. having been aroused
15. seeing

Practice Exercise No. 174

1. the ships, sailing
2. the leader, about to order
3. they, having been attacked
4. the men, about to arrive
5. seeking peace
6. the dog, running
7. the cities, having been captured
8. the temples, having been built
9. the harbors, having been found
10. the rivers, running

Practice Exercise No. 175

1. The people of the cities, which had been captured, were as brave as possible.
2. The men, who were about to arrive, were making the trip as quickly as possible.
3. The king, who is now ruling your country, seems to be timid.
4. The woman will give aid, when (if) she sees your difficulty.
5. The storm will not be very fierce, if it does not increase.
6. The father had great joy, because he was about to see his sons.
7. They were running as fast as possible, because they fear our men.
8. The men, who (because they) had been defeated, were especially frightened.
9. When she arrived in the town, she told her story.
10. They, who are defending the gate, were not friends.

Practice Exercise No. 176

1. bravely
2. as quickly as possible
3. least, not at all
4. for a very long time
5. more keenly
6. with difficulty
7. very easily
8. better
9. badly
10. greatly
11. more often
12. very unhappily

Practice Exercise No. 177

1. When the oracle had been heard, many people decided to come to our land.
2. When the signal had been given, they made an attack onto the field.
3. The men, although their weapons were not many, nevertheless fought bravely.
4. Because many soldiers had been killed, they sought peace.
5. The men, because the booty is large, will be received at home with great joy.
6. When this thing has been done, the boys will come home.
7. If he is the leader, we shall do it without difficulty.
8. When these things had been reported to me, I wanted to make the trip from the city.
9. If these have been killed, the people will be ruled better.
10. When the day had been set, they prepared everything as quickly as possible.
11. Because the door was open, he was able to come into the cottage.
12. He had no hope, because the city had been captured.
13. When these things had been done, the king was more powerful.
14. If the rest have been seen, we shall run toward the forest.

Latin Made Simple

15. When his father is the leader, they do everything boldly.
16. When peace has been made, he will sail away from the island.
17. If many are timid, they will not be able to find the rivers.
18. Because the time is now short, no help will arrive.
19. Because the place is suitable, you wish to stay here longer.
20. Because help was given, there was great joy.

Practice Exercise No. 178

1. to be
2. to have been
3. to be about to find out
4. to be found out
5. to have been thought
6. to have thought
7. to carry back, report
8. to be about to carry back, report
9. to have hoped
10. to be going to hope
11. to be led
12. to have led
13. to have been had
14. to have
15. to wish, want
16. to be wished, wanted
17. to have been able
18. to be able
19. to have fought
20. to have been fought
21. to be warned
22. to have warned
23. to have said
24. to be said
25. to be feared
26. to have feared
27. to have been made, done
28. to be about to make, do
29. to be seen; to seem
30. to be going to see, seem

Practice Exercise No. 179

1. leading
2. about to lead
3. having, holding
4. having been had
5. having been thought
6. about to think
7. finding out
8. having been found out
9. carrying back, reporting
10. about to carry back, report
11. hoping
12. having been hoped
13. about to move
14. moving
15. coming
16. about to come
17. fearing
18. having been frightened
19. about to place, put
20. putting, placing
21. sending
22. having been sent
23. about to see
24. seeing
25. about to say
26. saying
27. warning
28. having been warned
29. having been placed, put
30. placing, putting

Practice Exercise No. 180

1. they having been seen
2. he, it having been captured
3. these having been said
4. the war having been made
5. the men fearing
6. the girl walking
7. the leaders being afraid
8. the number being small
9. sleep coming
10. the prison being big
11. the city having been captured
12. the remaining speaking
13. the word having been heard
14. hope having been found
15. the kinds being many